Beginning New Testament Study

Bruce Chilton

Beginning New Testament Study

First published in Great Britain 1986
SPCK
Holy Trinity Church
Marylebone Road
London NW1 4DU

Third impression 1992

British Library Cataloguing in Publication Data

Chilton, Bruce D.
Beginning New Testament Study.
1. Bible. N.T.—Criticism, interpretation, etc.
I. Title
225.6 BS2361.2

ISBN 0-281-04210-1

Typeset by Latimer Trend & Company Ltd
Crescent Avenue, Plymouth
Printed in Great Britain by
The Longdunn Press Ltd, Bristol

Contents

Preface   vii

Some Significant Dates in the Formation and
Interpretation of the New Testament   ix

Map   xii

Introduction: Reading the New Testament   1

1   Fact and Fiction in the Gospels   21

2   Paul, the Radical Apostle   51

3   The Church Awaiting the Lord   75

4   Which Translation? And How to Use It   95

5   The Worlds of the New Testament:
   Judaism and Hellenism   120

6   The New Testament and Our World:
   The Task of Interpretation   149

7   Paths of Faith: The New Testament and Theology   172

Index of Subjects   193

for Mary Sharrock

Preface

Where *do* you begin studying the New Testament? Probably, one thinks about it whenever it is heard or read; one wonders, 'What exactly is it saying, and is it true?' Some of us fervently believe the New Testament is true, in whatever it says. But from your own particular point of view, you begin studying in a serious way when you relate the texts of the New Testament to your own questions and convictions about it, and assess whether the opinion you started with is valid. If you are about to undertake that task, this volume is intended for you.

Some of you will know more of the content of the New Testament, and some less, as you start reading. That necessarily means that part of what I have to say will seem too obvious, or too demanding, to different groups of people. Please take the trouble to have a copy of the New Testament open in front of you as you read; this book should then be more rewarding, no matter what level you begin from. The list of dates and the map at the start of the volume might also help to clarify matters. If you are reading this book in the context of a course in a church, school, college, seminary, or university, you may have recourse to a teacher who can sort out any difficulties you might have. The advice for further reading at the close of each chapter is particularly intended to help teachers prepare their lessons and guide their groups. There is also an index of subjects covered so that no teacher need feel bound to the order of the book.

My friends in Sheffield have contributed enormously to my understanding of how the New Testament might be taught. Just to teach them, preach to them and speak with them has been most fulfilling. I hope they will see this volume as a token of my esteem, and Mary Sharrock as a representative of them all, in churches, the town, and the University.

vii

The book has benefited greatly from the comments on the manuscript I received from Morna Hooker, Lady Margaret's Professor at Cambridge University, and Lorraine King, Head of Religious Education at the Snaith School in Humberside. I have in some way incorporated almost all of their suggestions into the final product, but hope they do not mind that I continue to say 'she' before 'he', and 'her' before 'him'. The order is not just a matter of fashion; women have formed a majority of my students over the years.

Pentecost 1985   BRUCE D. CHILTON

Some Significant Dates

In the Formation and Interpretation
of the New Testament

587 BC   The capture of Jerusalem, the destruction of the Temple, and the deportation of many Jews to Babylonia. Chapters 56–66 of Isaiah were written in the wake of these events, perhaps around 530 BC. Over a century later, Ezra was a principal figure in the return of some Jews to Jerusalem.

323 BC   The death of Alexander the great, whose tutor, Aristotle, died the year before. Diogenes died near the same time.

270 BC   The death of Epicurus.

c. 265 BC   The death of Zeno.

c. 250 BC   The beginning of the process which produced the Septuagint.

167 BC   The desecration of the Temple by the Seleucid ruler, Antiochus IV 'Epiphanes'. The book of Ecclesiasticus was written just before this event, and Daniel was written shortly thereafter. Material in 1 Enoch began to be compiled; Wisdom was perhaps written in the following century.

63 BC   Pompey's entry into Jerusalem, and the commencement of Roman dominance in the area.

4 BC   The death of Herod the great.

---

c. AD 30   The crucifixion of Jesus.

c. AD 50   The death of Philo of Alexandria.

Some Significant Dates

AD 51–2	Tenure of the Roman governor Gallio in Corinth.
c. AD 53	The letter to the Galatians.
c. AD 55–6	The Corinthian correspondence.
c. AD 57	The letter to the Romans.
AD 60–2	Tenure of the Roman governor Festus in Caesarea, in succession to Felix.
AD 65	The death of Seneca.
AD 68	The death of Nero.
AD 70	The ruin of the Temple as the result of a fire set by the troops of Titus. Near this time, the scrolls found in 1947 at Qumran were stored.
c. AD 71	The Gospel according to Mark.
c. AD 78	*The Jewish War* of Josephus.
c. AD 80	The Gospel according to Matthew.
c. AD 85	The exclusion of many Christians from meetings in Jewish synagogues.
c. AD 90	The Gospel according to Luke, and Acts; 1 Peter.
c. AD 100	The Gospel according to John; the Pastoral Epistles; the Revelation; 4 Ezra.
c. AD 120	*The Annals* of Tacitus.
AD 132–5	The second great revolt of Jews in the holy land against Rome.
c. AD 135	The death of Papias.
c. AD 150	The Shepherd of Hermas.
c. AD 159	The death of Marcion.
c. AD 165	The death of Justin.

Some Significant Dates

c. AD 160   The Gospel according to Thomas.

c. AD 170   The death of Valentinus; the formation of the canon of the New Testament, as reflected in the Muratorian fragment.

AD 180   The death of Marcus Aurelius.

c. AD 200   The final compilation of the Mishnah.

AD 217   *The Life of Appolonius of Tyana*, by Philostratus.

c. AD 253   The death of Origen.

AD 325   The formulation of a creed at a council in Nicea, which (as supplemented by the creed of 381, agreed at Constantinople) became an agreed statement of Christian faith.

AD 337   The death of Constantine.

AD 339   The death of Eusebius. During the course of the fourth century, works discovered in 1946 near Nag Hammadi were collected.

AD 373   The death of Athanasius, whose festal letter of 367 marks an important moment in the acceptance of the canon of the New Testament.

AD 420   The death of Jerome.

AD 430   The death of Augustine.

c. AD 500   The final compilation of Talmud.

1274   The death of Thomas Aquinas.

c. 1350–1600   The Renaissance.

1517   The posting of Luther's 'Ninety-five Theses', which is taken to initiate the Reformation, and the reaction of the Counter-reformation.

1536   The death of Erasmus.

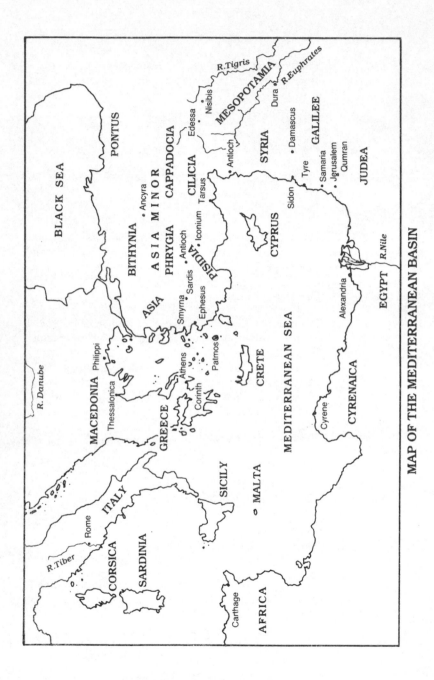

MAP OF THE MEDITERRANEAN BASIN

Introduction
Reading the New Testament

It is almost impossible to open the New Testament without having the feeling one already knows its contents. The book is a classic within Western civilization, with the result that the story of Jesus, Paul's missionary activity, the faith of the early Church, and even the vivid imagery of the Revelation all seem well known. They are commonly referred to directly in speech, written word, film, video and song. Even when they are not the topic at issue, they are sometimes alluded to; a cinematic character might be called a 'Christ-figure', for example, or a prediction of nuclear holocaust might be called 'apocalyptic' (a word taken from 'Apocalypse', the alternative name of the Revelation). The style of the Authorized or King James Version is now obscure to some modern readers, but that does not stop us speaking of the 'widow's mite' (a long outdated currency) when we wish to refer to a poor person giving as much as possible (see Mark 12.41–4). The New Testament, in other words, has passed into the common stock of conventional wisdom and proverb.

Unfortunately, it sometimes suffers in the transition. Even people without biblical learning believe they can cite the Bible; 'money is the root of all evil', they might confidently quote, although they have never read that saying in the New Testament. What the Authorized Version actually has is, '*The love of* money is the root of all evil' (1 Timothy 6.10). When a work is treated as a classic, whether it is the *Odyssey* of Homer, or the New Testament, or Shakespeare, that does not mean it has been correctly understood. It rather means that the work is used by people as part of their language, in order to speak of the events of their own day. We can say a gift with strings attached is a Trojan horse, or that a wayward child is a prodigal son, or that an indecisive politician is a Hamlet, without having the original

1

sources of those figures in mind. Once a work is classic, its them:s, images and wording become a part of ordinary speech, and can acquire a life of their own.

The fact that the New Testament has influenced our language demonstrates the power of its expression, and much can be learned by seeing the ways in which that power has been used over the course of time. To some extent, the force of a classic can be appreciated by observing how various writers, poets and artists use it to express their vision of the human situation. In a powerful book entitled *The Last Temptation of Christ*, the Greek novelist Nikos Kazantzakis evokes a searing picture of Jesus as a man driven by an all-consuming, almost violent experience of God. We can appreciate that he catches something of what must stand behind a career such as Jesus', even though we might equally enjoy and assent to the picture of Jesus as an attractive teacher of home truths, which is given by the musical 'Godspell' (by John-Michael Tabelak and Stephen Schwartz). But the New Testament need not be named openly for its themes to be taken up. Fyodor Dostoyevsky, for example, deliberately attempted in his novels to create a Christ-like character. He himself admitted he was only partially successful, but most readers can see in the Myshkin of *The Idiot* some of that suffering simplicity which is part of the compelling allure of Jesus as the Gospels portray him. Indeed, writers such as Dostoyevsky may help us to see the Gospels in a new light, even though they write fiction and do not deal at all directly with Jesus.

The difficulty with reading any classic work is that readers are tempted not to concentrate on the text in front of them, and instead to think in terms of what their culture has taught them to expect from the classic. Someone influenced by 'Godspell' might feel quite at home with the gentle sayings of Jesus, but find it hard to cope with his stern demand for repentance; equally, someone operating with Kazantzakis' picture of Jesus would indeed encounter much in the Gospels that could be explained in terms of mystical experience, but also some very direct statements about God's action in the ordinary world. The eternally suffering Christ of Dostoyevsky can only be found from time to time in the Gospels, and there is also a very different Christ, who is capable of enjoyment, anger and active organization. If we wish to study the New Testament, and not what we have been told is in the New Testament, we need to have a different approach. We need to be willing, difficult though the task is, to correct our idea of what we expect to find in the text with what we actually find there.

What is called for, in other words, is critical reading. In our ordinary speech, 'criticism' is often taken to refer to finding fault. But the term derives from a Greek word (*krinō*) which refers to judgement, and 'critical reading' means reading in such a way that we use our judgement to arrive at the meaning of the text. In practice, reading of this kind requires both imagination and discipline. By means of our imagination, we get beyond our conventional idea of what the text should say; we think of other things it might mean, and how it might have sounded to those long ago, in different historical circumstances, who were the intended audience of the text. But critical reading also demands that we discipline our imagination; once an idea comes to us, we test it against the text. We ask ourselves: is the work really open to our proposed interpretation? Was such a view ever held by the writer concerned, or by the people of the writer's time? Taken by themselves, neither imagination nor discipline are of much use to critical reading. The first alone will merely produce a series of more or less bright ideas, the second merely a dry restatement of what we expected the text to say in the first place. But the reader who uses both is on the way to freeing herself or himself from second-hand ideas of the text; one's mind is open to a new reality, the discovery of meaning as the text conveys it.

'Discovery' may seem an odd word to use in talking about the study of the New Testament. Scholars have been at the New Testament for nearly two thousand years, and it is commonly said that all its possible meanings must by now be exhausted. But those who actually work in the field would never agree. They are all too aware that basic questions in understanding the New Testament remain to be settled. Do the Gospels report reliably on the historical Jesus, or are they more like free compositions which express the faith of early Christians? Was Paul determined to establish a new religion, or did he remain faithful to Judaism? When early Christians spoke of the end of the world as something they expected in the near future, were they speaking literally?

Such questions, among others, lie behind much of the seemingly technical discussion which is presented in books and articles. The principal reason for which we continue to grapple with these issues is that they are *not* the same old questions which have been asked from the beginning. They arise out of the attempt to read the New Testament as a collection of historical documents, and that is a relatively recent approach.

Prior to the eighteenth century, the meaning of the New Testament was normally believed to accord with the teaching of the Church. Scholars such as Thomas Aquinas and Martin Luther did indeed make historical comments from time to time, but to them and their contemporaries, the belief of the Church seemed basically identical with the meaning of the New Testament. The idea that the two might not be the same was largely the result of the lively, sometimes violent controversies associated with the Reformation. The Reformation and the Counter-reformation began as attempts to insist on the unity of the Church and the New Testament, with Protestants demanding that the Church order itself on the biblical pattern, and Catholics maintaining that only the Church could interpret the Bible in the first place. But both sides aroused such interest in the Bible and its study that people began to find that biblical religion was really quite different from their own. The Gospels do not present a Jesus who speaks constantly of his own divinity; Paul is not merely concerned with the salvation of individual souls, but with the redemption of Israel; the later documents of the New Testament preach, not life after death, but the end of the world.

Of course, such basic features of the New Testament were recognized before the modern period, but scholars tended to explain them away by treating them as symbolic expressions of what the Church said more straightforwardly. If Jesus did not speak of himself, it was because of his humility as God's son; Paul's concern for Israel is really for the new Israel, the Church; language about the end of the world is a vivid way of referring to the death of individuals. But the Reformation definitively broke this marriage between the Bible and religious dogma, at least in the West. Increasingly, people appealed for the New Testament to be interpreted in its own terms, not in terms of later doctrine. There is, however, no such thing as a document which stands all

4

by itself in a vacuum. It is composed at a given period of time, with the circumstances of that time in mind, in order to inform, or entertain, or persuade. Just this awareness increasingly grew in New Testament scholarship from the sixteenth century, and by the eighteenth century it dominated discussion.

For roughly two hundred years, then, critical reading of the New Testament has been guided by the desire to achieve a historical understanding of the documents in their own time and setting. Much scholarly work before our period might be called 'critical', because some interpreters were well aware that the Bible's language was not that of the Church. But because they believed that the New Testament's language was finally to be understood in terms of the Church's teaching, their work on the whole could not be described as 'historically critical'. The historically critical approach to reading the New Testament seems fairly recent, especially when one bears in mind the amount of work involved in it. To understand the New Testament in its own time requires Jewish and Greek literature of the period to be taken into account, since they reflect how people of the time thought; of course, the most influential events of the period also need to be appreciated.

New finds in this area are not unusual. The most famous textual discovery since the Second World War has been that of the scrolls found near the Dead Sea. They have been immensely useful in developing an understanding of Jewish religion in the time of the New Testament. No less significant was the chance find of an entire library of sources in Egypt, near a place called Nag Hammadi. Some of these documents reflect Christian Gnosticism, which was an attempt to portray Jesus as the revealer of divine knowledge (for which the Greek word is *gnōsis*, hence: 'Gnosticism'), but a knowledge which contradicts the old Jewish view of God. These Gnostic works may be of use in understanding the environment in which the later documents of the New Testament were written. But it should not be imagined that discoveries in the field are limited to unexpected finds in the desert. Since the sixteenth century, the Bible in Aramaic (the language of Jesus, which is distinct from Hebrew) has been available in printed form, but the task of translating the whole of it into English was only begun in 1981 (although parts of it have been translated). Once the translation has been completed, scholars will need to study the ways in which the Aramaic Bible (known as the 'Targum', which is the Aramaic word for 'translation') may have influenced the language and thought of those who produced the New Testament.

In the critical reading of the New Testament, however, discoveries are not only made by professional scholars. Everyone who reads the New Testament critically, using imagination and discipline in the ways described, embarks on a voyage of discovery. The reader sails past the second-hand ideas of the text which she or he has been taught to expect, and finds a new territory to explore – the text as it presents itself to the reader's mind. Even if one forms an impression of the text which is rather like what someone else has suggested previously, it is *for the first time* the impression of the reader concerned. And every reader is unique. The imaginative range and skills of discipline which she or he brings to critical reading are the product of the talents, the experience, the effort and the temperament of that person. In critical reading we not only realize what the text means; we also realize at least some of our own ability to appreciate a fresh point of view. We are given the opportunity better to understand both texts and ourselves.

It will be all too obvious to some of those who read this book that nothing has so far been said of the specifically religious value of the New Testament. What place does faith have in critical reading? The importance which faith might have in the mind of the individual reader must be acknowledged; one's religious orientation – of whatever kind – is part of the unique background one brings to the text. There is no way of bracketing it out of one's mind; it is simply present, or not, along with other formative influences. But the fact that one has certain religious convictions is no proof that the text one reads expresses the same convictions. For example, a modern Christian might believe firmly that Jesus was the Christ, or the Messiah (the equivalent Hebrew term), who was promised in the Scriptures of Israel, and that it is a duty to proclaim him as such. But when, in the first three Gospels, Peter openly states Jesus is the Christ, Jesus responds by telling the disciples *not* to speak in these terms (Matthew 16.20; Mark 8.30; Luke 9.21). This passage obviously

6

does not indicate Jesus denied being the Messiah, but no critical reader would claim that it amounts to a command to preach Jesus' Messiahship. Indeed, the passage proceeds to show that Jesus' conception of himself did not accord completely with what Peter was thinking (Matthew 16.21–3; Mark 8.31–3; Luke 9.22). The contention of Peter is corrected: Jesus identifies himself as 'the son of man' who must, according to God's will, suffer, die, and be vindicated. The text, in other words, invites the reader to suppress any triumphal overtones the term 'Christ' may have, in order to discover Jesus' identity in divinely vindicated suffering and death. The meaning of the text can only be discovered when the reader is willing to revise her or his initial expectation, that Jesus in the passage will embrace the term 'Christ'. And no Christian who takes this story seriously will ever again use the word 'Messiah' as if it implied that Jesus was simply a victorious saviour.

Critical reading is not an alternative to something called 'religious reading', for the simple reason that religious faith is not a matter of reading off a page. Faith which is biblically based involves relating God as known in the believer's experience to God as known in the Bible. Those who believe God is supremely revealed in Christ commonly use the New Testament as a standard, which enables them to discover what their faith implies. To return to the example given above, a critical reading comes to the conclusion that, in the passage, Jesus is presented less as a victorious Messiah than as the son of man who is to suffer and be vindicated. Those who use the New Testament to inform their faith might additionally come to the conclusion that the text expresses the heart of who Jesus really is here and now. For them, human suffering will no longer appear a proof that God does not exist; rather, suffering will be seen as the way to God's vindication, which is the path already opened by God's son. But the significance of the text for faith is found by reflecting upon what is read, not by the act of reading itself. Reading will often lead to such acts of reflection, and books described as 'devotional' often move back and forth between reading and reflection quite freely, but there is an important distinction between the two. 'Reading' can be undertaken by anyone who is willing to use imagination and discipline in encountering a text. Theological 'reflection' requires that the results of reading are considered within the context of firmly held beliefs.

During its long history, the study of the New Testament has been open to the charge that it undermines faith. In the sixteenth century, the first critical editions of the New Testament in Greek appeared. From the point of view of the orthodoxy of the time, the Greek manuscripts omitted something crucial. They had no reference to the Trinity at 1 John 5.8, where the Latin version spoke of 'the father, the word, and the spirit' in heaven. Erasmus of Rotterdam, who is credited as the editor of the first Greek New Testament to be published, decided that the words should be omitted. After all, none of the Greek manuscripts he consulted included them, and he was editing the *Greek* New Testament, not the Latin translation. But his decision seemed to put the New Testament at odds with a central dogma of the Church, and he succumbed to the pressure to include the words in a later edition. In fact, his initial instinct has long been accepted as a matter of consensus, and the words are taken to be an addition which none of the most accurate manuscripts contain. But while the particulars of that old debate are no longer seriously discussed, the principle behind it remains a live issue. Should the New Testament be approached as offering proof of the doctrines of the Church?

To some extent, the history of the Church in the West has been the story of attempts to answer that question. The New Testament has been claimed as 'proving' Catholic teaching, Protestant teaching, and much else besides. Historical criticism provided a means of understanding the documents in the context of their own time and setting, so that people from differing religious backgrounds could join in discussion about the Bible without being obliged to enter into dogmatic controversy. But the gain involved in freeing study of the New Testament from dogmatic considerations necessarily includes a loss. It is now impossible for any group in the Church to claim authoritatively that its doctrine is the only one which accords with the New Testament. Any such claim can be tested by individuals in their critical reading of the texts, who know very well that historical conditions have changed radically over the past two thousand years, so that continuity with the New Testament is scarcely a matter of course. Today, any reader might, on reflection, decide that the New Testament is consistent with her or his faith, but there is also the risk that a revision of one's beliefs will be necessary. Indeed, the open attitude of critical reading invites revision; the meaning which is discovered might well be other than what was expected. And a new meaning might itself be reflected on, to see whether any theological issue is in play. In our time, for good or ill, the Church cannot determine from the outset what a reader, or even a believer, will find in the New Testament.

The situation of theology in the twentieth century is one of ferment. Part of the reason for the varied activities of Christian theologians is that they are challenged on two fronts. There is the challenge of understanding what the New Testament says, and there is the challenge of coming to a satisfactory view of God which is consistent with the New Testament. But it only confuses the issue to imagine that these two fronts are identical. The New Testament must be permitted to speak on its own terms, apart from the preoccupations of our time, if it is to be understood at all, and modern theology must develop its own language if it is to mean anything to our contemporaries. Precisely because the study of the New Testament is not itself a wing of dogmatic theology, it can be taught in good faith in secular universities, without reference to the beliefs of students or teachers.

The study of the New Testament is, however, equally at home in a properly theological context. The meaning of the documents is obviously of importance for those who wish to reflect on the God of whom the Bible speaks. In such a context, discussion will naturally – and perhaps inevitably – move from what texts mean to how they might apply to faith. Even here, however, it is vital for students and teachers to be aware that texts must be read critically before they can be reflected on theologically. Theology must begin with what religious texts actually say, not with what we might wish them to say. The goal of critical reading, in any context, involves exegesis. 'Exegesis' (from the Greek term *exēgeomai*, 'to lead out' from a text) refers to a reading which starts with the document under consideration and brings out the meaning which is expressed by the words themselves in context. It is the opposite of 'eisegesis', which occurs when readers uncritically impute their own ideas to the text they read. Whenever readers begin with a set understanding of what the Bible means, whether it is Protestant or Catholic, conservative or liberal, pious or humanist, or for that matter idealist or Marxist, it is all the more crucial that the meaning of the text be arrived at by exegesis; the alternative is that the text will be used as a pretext to express the reader's pet ideas.

In recent years, discussion of biblical interpretation has given currency to the word 'presupposition', which refers to the consciousness, the understanding of life, which a reader brings to a text. Sometimes it is argued that a believing Christian has presuppositions so different from an atheist's, for example, that a Christian reading of the New Testament must always be distinctive; Christians and atheists must simply agree to differ. But the entire purpose of critical reading is to discover the meaning of texts, not to generalize the view of the world we may have had before we started reading. Indeed, the sense of the word 'presupposition' has been cheapened in much popular debate. It derives from German philosophical discussion, in which 'presupposition', or 'pre-understanding' (*Vorverständnis*), designates the entire complex of assumptions and ways of seeing things which a person uses to understand the world. Such a pre-understanding indeed determines *how* a reader approaches a text, but it by no means determines *what* she or he finds in a text. If the text should prove challenging, the reader might enlarge, revise, or even thoroughly revamp her or his mental equipment. Just because this is the case, people are able to change their minds in profound ways. In other words, 'pre-understanding' or 'presupposition' refers to the manner in which we approach texts, not to fixed ideas of the precise content to be found in them. When a person uses the language of 'presupposition' to defend fixed interpretations, be they fundamentalist, materialist, symbolic, or whatever, she or he is in effect saying that the text does not matter. For such a reader, only the 'interpretation' counts; the text is not permitted to speak unless it agrees with the desired 'pre-understanding'.

Of course, any so-called 'interpretation' which is not open to a critical discussion of what texts say is no interpretation at all. Those enamoured of such 'interpretations' may quote a few passages from documents (often out of context) in order to 'prove' their position, but in the end they are more concerned with their party line than with anything else. Two frequently cited cases may be given as examples. Some fundamentalists are fond of quoting the first words of 2 Timothy 3.16, 'Every writing is inspired of God'; they claim that the author supports the contention that the Holy Spirit dictated the words used in the New Testament. What they ignore is that Timothy is told in vv. 14, 15 to remain true to 'the sacred texts you have known from your infancy'. Because the person addressed is an early Christian believer, the only writings available in his childhood were Jewish Scriptures, not the New Testament. Moreover, the remainder of v. 16 itself makes it quite clear that the term 'inspired' is not used to speak of verbal dictation by the spirit, but to insist that the Scriptures are useful for the purposes of teaching. In very different circles, the claim is sometimes made that the resurrection of Jesus in the New Testament is purely symbolic. One Gospel (Mark's) presents no account of the resurrection in the manuscripts usually followed, and the other Gospels give quite different stories of what happened. If the New Testament does not give a clear, consistent version of events, the argument runs, it must be speaking of a mere hope expressed in vivid imagery. Again, the case looks convincing only when a great deal of material is ignored. Mark in fact does have Jesus refer in advance to his resurrection (8.31; 9.31; 10.33, 34), and 16.6 makes it quite plain that the promise is regarded as fulfilled. And although there are substantial differences among the Gospels in the treatment of the resurrection, the accounts are not merely embellishments of a single abstract theme. Rather, the differences are so substantial as to demonstrate the accounts contain *independent* stories, and many of them refer in detail to what Jesus said and did with his disciples after his death.

Even the briefest consideration of 2 Timothy 3.16 and the resurrection accounts suggests that the first does not claim verbal inspiration for itself, and that the second group of passages are not to be explained as purely symbolic fantasy. To continue to insist on such notions reflects the preoccupations of those who make them, not the meaning of the texts involved. They belong to the realm of propaganda, not critical reading, and have no proper place in exegesis. Of course, one cannot prove from the texts cited that the New Testament is *not* inspired verbally, or that the resurrection accounts have *no* symbolic elements; the point is that we must resist the idea that texts 'prove' our cherished theories if we wish to grasp what they say. After that is understood, considered and reflective interpretation can take place, on the basis of the text.

The canon of the New Testament

The reader of the New Testament, then, begins by preparing her or his mind for a fresh encounter with the text. But the text is not merely a haphazard collection of documents, although there is a great deal of variety to be found among them. By no means does the New Testament contain all of the documents used in the early Church. It is the outcome of principles of selection which were at work in the early Christian centuries. The question of how individual books in the New Testament were written will concern us later in this volume. At the moment, the issue is: how did these documents come to be included in the New Testament? Put another way, the question is, what exactly is the New Testament?

The Bible of the early Church, from the time of Jesus until much later, was first and foremost the Jewish Scriptures, which we now call the Old Testament. The books which were to be included in the Old Testament were a matter of general agreement. The book of Jesus ben Sira, also known as Ecclesiasticus, already refers (in the second century BC) to the law, the prophets, and other books (see the prologue). Its division of the Bible, or Torah ('law' in Hebrew, with the sense more of divine guidance than of legal prescription), corresponds to the threefold division which became conventional among the rabbis. The first five books (the Pentateuch) were known as the 'Law' proper; 'Prophets' designated both the classical prophetic writings and what we call the historical works (such as the books of Kings, for example); 'Writings' referred to the remainder. Luke 24.44 similarly refers to the law of Moses, the prophets and the psalms. But there was considerable discussion among rabbis throughout the period of the New Testament and later concerning exactly which books did or did not qualify for reading in synagogue. The

Song of Songs, for example, caused some doubt, to some extent owing to its explicitly sexual imagery. Nonetheless, the Jewish historian Josephus shows that by the first century AD the contents of the Bible were a matter of broad agreement (see *Against Apion* 1.37–43).

There were, however, other writings which were greatly revered, but which did not come to be included within the Hebrew Bible. Some of them were included in the Greek translation of the Old Testament known as the Septuagint (because it was held to be the work of seventy-two translators working in Alexandria). One of these is the book of Jesus ben Sira, which has already been mentioned; another is the Wisdom of Solomon. At the time of the Reformation, these works were treated differently from the rest of the Old Testament, because the Hebrew Bible did not include them. They were called the Apocrypha (a term used long before by Jerome), 'hidden', 'secret', or 'obscure' works of uncertain origin. The designation is still commonly used, although it seems clear that Hebrew originals of at least some of these works once did exist; a Hebrew fragment of Jesus ben Sira was actually discovered at Qumran. But it is important to bear in mind that early Christians did not think of these Scriptures as 'apocryphal'; the book of Jesus ben Sira (11.18, 19), for example, finds an echo in the New Testament (Luke 12.16–21).

In addition to the Apocrypha, other works were read by many Jews, even though they also were not included in the Hebrew Bible (or the Septuagint). Among the best known of them is the Book of Enoch (or 1 Enoch, to distinguish it from other works in Enoch's name), parts of which were again found at Qumran. Books of this sort are known as the Pseudepigrapha, because many of them were falsely ascribed to ancient authorities (such as Enoch himself, Ezra and Baruch; see chapter three). Again, however, it would be rash to suppose that early Christians would have been entirely happy with our modern category; 1 Enoch 1.9 is cited in the brief letter of Jude (14, 15). The general picture that emerges is that Christians were content to read the Jewish Scriptures, the 'Old Testament', as it was normally recognized, and that therefore there was some variation in the books that were accepted.

The drastic step which Christians took (from the point of view of Judaism) was to read other works as well in the context of their worship. From the time of the mission of Paul as remembered in Acts (see 13.13–42), Christians had been given the opportunity to speak in Jewish synagogues after the Bible had been read. They took their chance to relate the Scriptures to Jesus, the object of their new faith. But once Christians were excluded and withdrew from worship in synagogues (gradually, towards the end of the first century AD), they developed their own practices. Justin, called Martyr (that is, 'witness'), a Christian writer of the second century, refers to the memoirs of the apostles *or* writings of the prophets being read in churches (*Apology* 67.3). Such 'memoirs', which we would recognize as Gospels of the New Testament, already had a long history by the time of Justin. The apostles had been sent by Jesus himself to spread his message, and their remembrance of Jesus and their understanding of him were recollected by their disciples and treasured in the early Church. By the second century, the apostolic memoirs were read in churches as a matter of course alongside or instead of Scripture; effectively, they *were* Scripture.

The writings of Christians from the second century, such as Justin, amply attest the esteem in which various documents of the New Testament were held. Indeed, there is even reference within the New Testament itself (2 Peter 3.15, 16) to the reading of Paul's letters. But only gradually did there emerge a standard, or 'canon' (from the Greek term *kanōn*, 'measure'), of which documents were to be used in public worship. The canon of the New Testament was formed less because there was a positive desire for a published list than because the fluid situation of early Christianity permitted certain groups to deviate unacceptably from normal practice.

Mention has already been made of Gnosticism; one of the prominent figures in the movement was Marcion, who came from Asia Minor to Rome and there founded his own community during the middle of the second century. He opposed the God of Jesus to the God of the Jews, and repudiated the use of the Old Testament. But because the Jewish Scriptures feature so prominently within the documents of the New Testament, the majority of them was also rejected by Marcion. His collection of acceptable works included only Luke's Gospel and ten letters of Paul, and even here, Marcion expunged what he considered to be Jewish additions to the text. Another immigrant to Rome (this time from Egypt), named Valentinus, was also a Gnostic. Valentinus was not the organizer Marcion was, but his teaching was highly influential. He represents the wing of Gnosticism which was concerned with the existence of the present, evil world: how could it derive from God, who is truly good? Valentinus argued that the Father is transcendent, quite apart from and other than what we can see around us. The world came into existence after a series of quasi-divine beings were generated from the Father; the last of these was Wisdom. Wisdom desired to find her way back to the Father, but her ignorance led to spirit being imprisoned in matter. Such, according to Valentinus, is the predicament of spiritual people, who are trapped in the false world of matter, and only knowledge of the Father (in Greek, *gnōsis*) can save them. Schemes of this kind seem abstract and complicated today, but they enjoyed a tremendous appeal in the second century. For all their complexity, they offered a theological account of the very human feeling of being trapped in an evil world, far from a remote spiritual home. The followers of Valentinus produced a considerable literature to explain their position, including what is probably the first commentary on John's Gospel, and some of the material in the Nag Hammadi library.

The early Church tolerated a great deal of variety, but teachers such as Marcion and Valentinus appeared, in effect, to hijack the emerging Christian Bible for their own purposes. The ideal of the apostolic memoir degenerated in their hands into specialized and sectarian tractates which relied as much on their authors' inspiration as on the established tradition of the Jewish Scriptures and the Church. An early response to Marcionite and Valentinian teaching is contained in what is known as the Muratorian list, after its discoverer (Lodovico Antonio Muratori). The dating of the document is still under discussion, but it addresses the conditions of the second century in Rome, and expressly repudiates Marcion and Valentinus. Before doing so, however, the list names most of the works of what we now know as the New Testament, and makes some comments on the derivation of the documents from the apostles and their followers.

The list, however, has some remarkable inclusions and omissions, and its fragmentary condition fully explains neither. Although possibly in error, the Wisdom of Solomon is listed, a fact which may suggest that the debate about the canon fundamentally concerned Scripture in the mind of the anonymous writer, not the New Testament as a separate work. After the Revelation of John, he mentions a Revelation of Peter, but points out that it is not permitted to be read throughout the Church. In other words, a principle of universal acceptance (catholicity) is set alongside a principle of apostolicity (the authorship of an apostle or one of his followers). A popular document called the Shepherd of Hermas, which features a series of angelic visions of various figures who instruct the author, especially one called his 'Shepherd', is not to be read publicly, according to the writer, although it may be read privately. He knew very well it was written recently in Rome, and was neither prophetic (as the Jewish Scriptures) nor apostolic (as the Christian Scriptures). There is no apparent mention of 1 Peter or 2 Peter (unless the work called the Revelation of Peter has something to do with one or both of them), and none at all of Hebrews, James or 3 John (unless the last was in some way included in the two letters of John which are mentioned).

The Muratorian list therefore reflects a canon which is provisional, and discussion concerning whether certain books should be included stretched over centuries. Hebrews and the Revelation were especially objects of contention, largely because their apostolic origin was seriously questioned. But in AD 367, Athanasius, bishop of the prominent Alexandrian church, wrote a festal letter which designates as the canon of the New Testament the twenty-seven books known today. The matter was not definitively settled by Athanasius, but his position was gradually accepted, both in the Greek-speaking east and the Latin-speaking west of the Christian world. It is notable that the formulation of the canon in the fourth century lagged somewhat behind the formulation of creeds; the fluidity of an earlier period was still tolerated to some extent. Nonetheless, the twin principles of apostolicity and catholicity were commonly agreed; it was in applying these principles that disputes arose.

The canon which emerged amounted to a refusal of some

works, and an insistence that others should be recognized. The Shepherd of Hermas, as we have seen, was rejected despite its popularity. Other works were also excluded, even though apostolic authorship was claimed for them. The most famous among them today is the Gospel according to Thomas, which was probably composed in the form in which we know it during the second century. The 'Judas Thomas' of whom the Gospel speaks is probably to be identified with Judas, the brother of Jesus (see Mark 6.3), who was considered Jesus' twin in Syrian tradition, because 'Thomas' means 'twin' in Aramaic. Despite this claim to the authority of an intimate of Jesus, the Gospel was never accepted in the Church, and the same fate was suffered by the many writings under the names of apostles which were produced in the second century. Their rejection resulted not only from doubts about their actual authorship, although such doubts were often involved, but also from their lack of general acceptance. On the other hand, Hebrews was endorsed in the East, even though no less an authority than Origen had written, 'Who knows who wrote the epistle? God knows!' (see the *Church History* of Eusebius, 6.25.11–14). The wide use of the letter, and its general consistency with Paul's thought, were enough to assure its eventual inclusion in the canon.

The terms 'Apocrypha' and 'Pseudepigrapha' have been applied to early Christian documents outside the New Testament. The usage is perhaps unfortunate, since these terms are applied very differently in respect of the Old Testament. The adjective 'non-canonical' might be recommended as being more descriptive, and less prejudicial. In any case, it must be borne in mind that the canonical writings were by no means the only ones read by early Christians. The religious atmosphere of Christianity in Rome, for example, is better reflected in the Shepherd of Hermas than it is, say, in Matthew's Gospel. And although the Gospel according to Thomas seems to rely on the canonical Gospels for many of the sayings of Jesus it presents, some appear quite independent and may be authentic. The probably late attribution to Jesus' 'twin' should not be taken to foreclose the question of the historical value of the document for understanding Jesus' teaching; the source directly reflects a type of Christianity which maintained close contact with the tradition of Jesus' sayings, even as it moved in the direction of Gnosticism. Those who are interested in the history of the Christian movement, then, must be prepared to look outside the New Testament for relevant information. 'Canon' is essentially not a historical category; that a work is canonical does not necessarily make it the best source for understanding every aspect of early Christianity, although on the whole the New Testament is more primitive than 'the New Testament Apocrypha and Pseudepigrapha'.

If the canon is not a historical category, then from the point of view of critical reading, what is it? It is the collection of those works which the Church understood as basic to its faith, after long and considered discussion. There has been a perennial debate between Protestants and Catholics whether the canon created the Church or vice versa. Both positions are only partly true; it would be more accurate to say that the various documents of the New Testament shaped the faith of the Church and that the Church's understanding of its apostolic and catholic faith then determined the precise canon of the New Testament. For this reason, the canon as a whole reflects the faith of the Church. It sets the literary boundaries within which public worship and discussion should take place, and also the horizons towards which such activities may be stretched.

The critical reader cannot, of course, be required to assent to that version of faith which the canon reflects; indeed, one may not know what she or he is being asked to believe until reading commences. But any reading of the New Testament would be *un*critical which did not recognize that the canon by its very nature is a testament of the Christian faith. It reflects what people believed, and to some extent why they believed it; according to the Church, both ancient and modern, those beliefs amount to a coherent and compelling view of God. Whether or not one wishes to accept the faith of the Church, the fact remains that its canon is first and foremost an anthology of its beliefs and practices. Study of the New Testament as such is therefore the study of those documents which express early Christian faith in Jesus. And a proper, critical goal of study is to understand the contents and grounds of that faith in its various expressions.

The present volume can offer nothing like a full account of what early Christians believed and why they came to believe. But key issues which have been raised repeatedly in critical discussion will be dealt with; they all concern the faith of the New Testament directly. Our first chapter concerns Jesus as the Gospels present him: is he portrayed as he actually was, or is he more a figure of religious poetry? Obviously, one's answer to that question will greatly influence one's assessment of Christian faith and the New Testament overall. The second chapter concerns Paul, and how he should be seen in his time. Was he a representative preacher, or a radical reformer who changed the shape of Christian faith for all time? The third chapter will address itself to the expectation of early Christians, particularly as expressed in its Church-directed writings (that is, those addressed primarily to questions of order and belief in established Christian communities as a whole). How could they believe that Jesus would return to earth in the near future to judge the world and bring human history to a close? What was meant by this belief?

The three topics will be addressed in such a way as to initiate the reader into the major documents of the New Testament: the Gospels, the Pauline letters and the Church-directed writings. The purpose will not be to settle the issues raised, but to show the reader how the text might be approached so that answers can be discovered. In the interests of the reader's own work, the topic treated in the fourth chapter involves the various translations of the New Testament which are generally available, and how they might be used. The fifth chapter concerns the religious environments in which the documents of the New Testament were written, and therefore the meaning they were seen to have. The worlds of Judaism and Hellenism are in some ways different; to what extent are our texts intended for Jews and Jewish sympathizers, or for citizens of the Graeco-Roman Empire as a whole? What adjustments need we make as we imagine first one background and then the other? A shift in cultural background is also at issue in the sixth chapter, but now the shift is from the world of the New Testament to our world. Although critical reading involves the use of historical imagination and discipline, there is a sense in which any document has a meaning of its own in the present, which is its value as literature. More literary approaches to the New Testament will therefore be discussed. Lastly, the seventh chapter raises the theological issue: how may the canon be used to shape and express an understanding of God? Although critical reading by no means requires faith, faith is often the reason for which the Bible is read, or the outcome of reading. The use of the New Testament in theology is therefore a legitimate, but not a necessary, concern of the beginner.

FOR FURTHER READING

The present Introduction is merely intended to initiate the reader into the art of reading the text. Further reflections, and a more systematic discussion of approaches to the New Testament, are available in J. H. Hayes and C. R. Holladay, *Biblical Exegesis: A Beginner's Handbook* (Atlanta: Knox, 1982). *Introduction to the New Testament* is the title borne by volumes which discuss questions such as the authorship and date of the documents in a comprehensive fashion. Those of R. F. Collins (London: SCM Press, 1983 and Garden City: Doubleday, 1983) and W. G. Kümmel (London: SCM Press, 1975 and Nashville: Abingdon, 1975) may be recommended. They have useful sections on the canon, but a more lucid treatment may be found within C. F. D. Moule, *The Birth of the New Testament* (London: Black, 1981). For a fuller, but still thoroughly readable account, see R. M. Grant, *The Formation of the New Testament* (London: Hutchinson, 1965 and New York: Harper & Row, 1965).

1

Fact and Fiction in the Gospels

The New Testament begins with Jesus. That may seem an obviously true statement, but it is worth pausing to consider how importantly true it is. Jesus is the origin of the faith which is expressed in our documents; none of them can be fully understood except as statements of belief in him. But Jesus is also the beginning of the New Testament in another sense. His preaching and ministry started the religious movement which gave rise to the canon as we know it. The documents attest both the faith *of* Jesus, the beliefs he taught and lived and died for, and faith *in* Jesus, the beliefs early Christians no less dramatically maintained. The distinction between the faith of Jesus and the faith in Jesus is nowhere more crucial to realize than in the study of the four Gospels.

'These things are written so you can believe Jesus is the Messiah, the son of God, and so by believing you can have life in his name' (John 20.31). That precise statement of purpose is made only in the Gospel according to John, but all of the Gospels relate the story of Jesus and his teaching in the interests of belief. Since that is the case, readers are commonly brought to one of two extreme conclusions. One tendency is to assume that when the Gospels speak of Jesus, they do so with complete – or almost complete – historical accuracy. If they did not, the assumption runs, the faith which they encourage would not be valid. The weakness of this position is that it is not based on critical reading; it operates by forcing the Gospels into the mould of historically based faith. They may or may not fit that mould, but wishing will not make the Gospels more or less historical. Equally uncritical, however, is the mere assumption that the Gospels are 'myths'. The term 'myth' was given currency in the study of the New Testament during the nineteenth century (and since) by David

21

Friedrich Strauss. When he used the word, he alleged that, in the Gospels, Christian beliefs about Jesus were projected back in time, and made to look like part of his life story. Such a contention presupposes that we know Christian faith was so creative as to invent Jesus' teaching and ministry; we are far from knowing any such thing.

For reasons already discussed in the Introduction, there is no way of deciding in a purely theoretical way which (if either) of these positions is more correct. But we can approach our texts with a preliminary question in mind: as we read, are we in the realm of fact or of fiction? Most readers are likely to think that, in documents which speak of past happenings, 'fact' is superior to 'fiction'. Whether or not that is so, there is no proof that the Gospels were composed from such a point of view. 'Fact', in this chapter, will be used to speak of elements in the Gospels which primarily reflect what Jesus actually said and did (at least, as far as we can know). 'Fiction' will be used with its first sense in *The Oxford English Dictionary*, 'The action of fashioning or imitating.' The term will refer to those elements in the Gospels which were shaped by the early Church in view of their belief in Jesus (again, as far as we can know).

In the usage of these terms here, there is no assumption of superiority, one way or the other. 'Fact' merely refers to what is in the world of experience, to what Jesus was heard to teach and seen to do. 'Fiction' refers as straightforwardly to the world of belief, to material composed by Christians in their expression of belief in Jesus. ('Poetry' might also be used in reference to such material, and some of the prejudicial overtones of 'fiction' in current English would then be avoided. On the other hand, 'poetry' conveys a sense of formal structure in ordinary English which is no part of what is being described here.) The distinction between fact and fiction lies at the heart of the controversy between those who regard the Gospels as historical and those who regard them as mythical. But 'history' and 'myth' are variously defined by different scholars, and some technical discussion would be required before those categories could be used. To avoid that necessity, the more ordinary language of 'fact' and 'fiction' has been chosen in chapter one.

For a document to be considered factual in its account of past events, it must have some demonstrable connection with those events. If Jesus had actually written something, as Paul did, that writing would be taken as presenting the best possible evidence about him. But if – as in the case of some of the 'apocryphal Gospels' of the second century – a document gives a long discourse in Jesus' name which bears little relation to his teaching as it can be known in earlier sources, it is rightly considered fictional. The Gospels fall between those two stools, which is what makes them difficult to categorize. On the one hand they present material in Jesus' name, but on the other hand they attest the faith of the early Church. For us to understand the extent to which the Gospels are factual, we need to know how closely they relate to the historical Jesus in the claims they make about him. How did the Gospels come into being?

The authorship of the Gospels

We would be a long way along the road towards answering our question if we had a clear notion of who wrote the canonical Gospels. The names 'Matthew', 'Mark', 'Luke' and 'John' are, of course, traditionally attached to them in titles which were added over the course of time. But none of the documents actually names its author, and the association of the Gospels with the four people known as Evangelists is not evidenced before the second century.

'Matthew' is counted among Jesus' élite circle of twelve followers (Matthew 10.3; Mark 3.18; Luke 6.15), and the Gospel according to Matthew says he is a collector of taxes (Matthew 9.9; 10.3). But Mark (2.14) and Luke (5.27) name only Levi as a tax-gathering disciple, and they do not name him as one of the twelve. It is not obvious from this data who precisely 'Matthew' was, nor even that the person so named in the Gospels was in any sense the author of the first Gospel; the actual claim that he wrote the work is nowhere made in the document itself.

'Mark' is an even more mysterious figure. A certain John Mark is named in Acts (12.25; 13.5, 13; 15.37–40) as an early associate of Paul and Barnabas, and perhaps the mention of a 'Mark' in 1 Peter 5.13 relates to the same person, who was also associated

23

with Peter (see Acts 12.12). In any case, 'Mark' is nowhere said to be an immediate follower of Jesus, nor is he openly mentioned in the Gospel according to Mark.

Not much more can be said of 'Luke'; a person so named appears as a companion of Paul (Colossians 4.14; Philemon 24; 2 Timothy 4.11), and Acts, which was produced together with the Gospel according to Luke (see Acts 1.1, 2 and Luke 1.1–4), does frequently break into the usage 'we' while describing the travels of Paul and those with him. But the Gospel, once again, does not name 'Luke'; much less does it identify the man named 'Luke' elsewhere in the New Testament as its author.

The Gospel according to John speaks most openly of its authorship, but its testimony is frustratingly elusive. An anonymous group of people calling themselves 'we' in 21.24 say that they know the witness of a certain disciple, whom Jesus loved (see 21.20), is true. Their statement amounts to the most direct claim that a Gospel was composed by an immediate disciple of Jesus which can be found in the New Testament. From the second century, this beloved disciple, who is mentioned frequently in the Gospel, has been identified as John, the son of Zebedee, a prominent member of the twelve named in Matthew, Mark, and Luke. The identification may be correct, but the fact remains that, taken on its own terms, the Gospel is the work of an anonymous disciple. The name 'John' itself was common, and the beloved disciple need not have been a member of the twelve named in the first three Gospels; Jesus was followed by many people, of whom the twelve were a select few.

Almost from the moment the New Testament was widely read, Christians and others have discussed the authorship of the Gospels, and for good reason. The documents themselves say so little in this regard that it must be considered an open question; the four names were associated with the four Gospels from an early period, but without further information. (Books which give further information have derived the material from the speculation and legends of later Christians.) Even if we take the attributions to 'Matthew', 'Mark', 'Luke' and 'John' at face value, there is no justification for the claim that all the Gospels were written down by Jesus' immediate followers. The early Church cherished the Gospels as the memoirs of the apostles and their followers. An 'apostle' (the form derives from the Greek verb *apostellō*, 'to send') is someone 'sent' or 'commissioned' by Jesus. In the early Christian understanding, the commission might have come after Jesus had been raised from the dead, so that 'apostles' must be distinguished from 'disciples', all of whom followed Jesus during his ministry. Those who handed on the apostolic witness might include those in the circle of Paul and Barnabas, who were apostles (see Acts 14.14 and Galatians 1.1, 19) even though they had not been in the company of Jesus. 'Mark' and 'Luke' may belong to this category. 'Matthew' and 'John' are names which probably do reflect the authority of actual disciples of Jesus, whether or not they are counted among the twelve. But John 21.24, which was cited in the last paragraph, clearly indicates that sole authorship is not claimed for the 'beloved disciple', and the precise contribution of 'Matthew' to the Gospel which bears that name is not known. Speculation as to who wrote the Gospels will no doubt continue, and it is of historical interest; nonetheless, there is simply not enough hard evidence to be certain about their authorship. The acceptance of the Gospels by the early Church, and to a limited extent the names they carry, suggest that they derived from the testimony of apostles, disciples and their followers. But the names are loosely attached to the Gospels (in titles, rather than in clear statements within the documents themselves), and any information about the people so named is thin; effectively, the documents come to us as anonymous writings from the circle of apostles and disciples.

While the names attached to the Gospels take us little further in the quest to understand how the documents came into being, they do provide us with a degree of insight into how they were viewed in the early Church. They were cherished as apostolic, even though they appear anonymously apostolic; they came through the line of Jesus' disciples and the apostles, and through followers within both those groups. The Gospel which most fully attests the sources on which it is based, that according to Luke, refers to material handed on by those who were 'eyewitnesses and ministers of the word' (Luke 1.2). Who those people were, and how they delivered their testimony, are questions which are not answered, but the Gospel clearly identifies itself as a document based on early Christian preaching. Judging from the statement in Luke, the general similarity between Luke and the rest of the Gospels, and the acceptance of all four in the Church as apostolic and catholic (that is, widely accepted), one may come to the initial finding that our documents were produced within the Christian community. To move beyond this initial finding, we must consider the information of the texts themselves in respect of how they were produced. Matthew, Mark, Luke and John provide the only secure evidence available of how they came to be; the texts themselves are the appropriate starting point, not speculation regarding the individuals who stand behind the texts. As is now customary, the documents will here be referred to by their traditional names, without prejudice to the question of who actually wrote them.

The formation of the Gospels

Fortunately, the Gospels do provide indications of how Jesus' teaching was passed on to his followers, and how they, in turn, passed on what they knew. The disciples feature prominently in the New Testament as those who heard Jesus and, in many cases, travelled with him. The term 'disciple' refers to someone who learns from constant study and personal familiarity with a teacher; in Jewish circles, such followers were called *talmidim* ('learners'), and such teachers were called rabbis. The fact that Jesus is frequently addressed as 'rabbi' in the Gospels, while his followers are taken as disciples, suggests that rabbinic methods of learning might help us to understand the way Jesus' teaching was originally passed on. A rabbi's student was expected first of all to know his master's position by heart, in a precise way. Memorization was far more valued in antiquity than it is today, partially because the cost of materials for writing was high. More importantly, the actual words used by teachers were held in high esteem, and to have a vivid recollection of them was considered a great mark of respect. Beginning *talmidim* were expected to memorize extensive amounts of the material they were taught, which was then taken as the basis for discussion. It was held in the Talmud (a title which means 'learning' and refers to the classic collection of rabbinic opinion) that, before any man could claim to be a scholar, he should have learned the Torah, commentaries on Torah and the opinions of respected teachers (see Kiddushin 49b). Even a *talmid*, a learner, the passage continues, should be competent in the full range of his studies. The obvious strains such a system placed on students were balanced by the patience required of teachers: one rabbi is said to have been ready to repeat his material four hundred times, if that was necessary before the lesson sank in (see Erubin 54b in the Talmud)!

The bulk of rabbinic literature was only produced after the New Testament was written, so that the formal standards which Talmud lays down cannot be applied directly to Jesus and his followers. Nonetheless, there are indications in the Gospels that Jesus treated them as a rabbi would his disciples. He gives them instructions for prayer (see Matthew 6.7–15; Luke 11.1–13), which he apparently expected them to retain, and his teaching is peppered with commands to 'hear' and 'understand' what he is saying (see the variously worded injunction, 'He who has ears to hear, let him hear', Matthew 13.9, 43; Mark 4.9; Luke 8.8; 14.53, and the more direct, 'hear and understand', Matthew 15.10; Mark 7.14). Jesus is addressed as 'rabbi' in the Gospels (see Matthew 26.25, 49; Mark 9.5; 10.51; 11.21; 14.45; John 1.38, 49; 3.2; 4.31; 6.25; 9.2; 11.8; 20.16), and it seems clear that his own disciples and his sympathetic hearers generally – however else they thought of him – considered him as such. From the outset, therefore, a certain care would have been taken in the handing on of his teaching, even if his followers were not formally up to the exacting standards of later *talmidim*.

Within the wide range of rabbinic literature, the teaching of past masters certainly has pride of place, but there is also some interest in stories about such teachers. In antiquity, to learn from someone involved living near him and observing his habits; his composure and attitudes and ways of dealing with difficult situations were considered part of his teaching. Further, a certain biographical context is sometimes necessary to bring out the significance of someone's teaching.

A famous story concerning two contemporaries of Jesus conveys very different attitudes to would-be converts (see Shabbath 31a, again in the Talmud). A man approached a rabbi named Shammai, and asked to be taught Torah while he (that is, the inquirer) stood on one foot. Shammai was so insulted by the suggestion that the study of Torah should be cheapened into an instant affair that he shoved the man away with a measuring rod. The Gentile, or non-Jew, then went to Hillel, Shammai's well-known competitor, and made the same request. Hillel said, 'What is hateful to you, do not do to your neighbour: that is the whole Torah, while the rest is commentary thereon. Go and learn it.' In the story, Hillel is no less aware than Shammai that the 'commentary' is going to require more time to master than the interval in which one can normally stand on one foot; but the story illustrates a profound difference of attitude between the two men, and makes Hillel's statement the expression of his own particular attitude. A story told in order to illustrate the point of teaching is called *haggadah*.

Sometimes *haggadoth* (the plural of the same noun) are quite plausible stories, as in the present case. Even in the example, however, not a great deal hangs on the alleged incident actually having taken place. The attitudes of Hillel and Shammai would still be illustrated, even if there was never such a stubborn Gentile convert who approached Hillel after Shammai rebuffed him so severely. Moreover, sometimes *haggadoth* seem to belong to the world of fiction, as – for example – when Moses (who had been dead for centuries) is portrayed as discussing with God the merits of Aqiba, a rabbi of the second century AD (see Menaḥoth 29b in the Talmud). Since no one could claim to have heard such a conversation, it seems clear that the value of the *haggadah* resided more in what it illustrated than in the details of its content. In this case, the story is fictional both in the basic sense that it is made up, and in the modern sense that it has no claim to be taken literally, as reporting an actual occurrence.

The disciples of Jesus did not differ greatly from their contemporaries in recalling and interpreting the teaching of their rabbi, and in telling illustrative stories about him. But, as compared to the rest of rabbinic literature, the Gospels' unique focus on Jesus is unusual and startling. Nothing like the Gospels has been found among Jewish sources. Generally, rabbinic documents contain the sayings of many teachers, arranged more or less topically, with occasional *haggadoth*. The Gospels, of course, maintain a consistent focus on Jesus alone and their interest in the story line of his ministry is at least as great as their interest in his teaching. To the extent the Gospels represent the traditions handed on by Jesus' first followers, their very type of presentation suggests that a unique literature grew out of the response to a unique teacher.

There is, however, no indication that the first followers of Jesus instantly produced and handed on material about Jesus in the shape of Gospels such as we would recognize today. On the contrary, the material handed on by the disciples, which is known as their 'tradition', seems to have evolved gradually. The Gospels themselves relate that Jesus entrusted a select group of his disciples to share in his own ministry of preaching God's kingdom and healing the sick (see Matthew 10.1–15; Luke 10.1–12). Clearly, a disciple sent in his rabbi's place would need fully to understand the teaching he was expected to hand on, and to act as he was expected to. The two passages cited amount to a commissioning of those sent, and it is assumed they are fit to explain the authority of the one who sent them. Any differences between Matthew and Luke would therefore reflect somewhat distinctive views of what the disciples' commission amounts to.

Even this basic scene of authorization is presented in different ways by Matthew and Luke, although the similarities between them are also substantial. In Matthew, Jesus sends twelve named disciples to cast out demons and heal (10.1–4). He commands them to restrict their activity to those of Israel (vv. 5, 6) as they proclaim that the kingdom of God has come near (v. 7), and act to demonstrate that proclamation (v. 8). They are not to take provisions with them, but to live from the generosity of those they preach to (vv. 9, 10). Finally, advice is given on how to act in face of either acceptance or rejection (vv. 11–15). Luke's scene looks different from the beginning, in that Jesus sends seventy-two disciples (10.1) *after* he has sent the twelve (9.1–6). He gives them advice about travelling lightly and coping with the reaction to them (10.2–7), but the wording is different from Matthew's, and this instruction occurs before the command to heal and preach the kingdom (v. 9). Again, the actual words used differ as compared to Matthew, as is true of the final injunction on how to handle rejection (vv. 10–12).

At the moment, we need not pose such questions as whether Jesus actually sent twelve or seventy-two disciples, or whether he sent both groups at different times. The point is rather that in Matthew's Gospel we have one scene of commissioning, and in Luke's Gospel another. The Matthean passage limits those commissioned to twelve, the number of the tribes of Israel, and their mission is restricted to Israel (10.5, 6). A wider circle is envisaged in Luke, and the number seventy-two corresponds to the number of Gentile nations in Jewish reckoning. (It may be remembered from the Introduction that seventy-two translators were held to have rendered the Old Testament into Greek.) The Matthean disciples are explicitly directed to Israel, while Luke's seem to be on the verge of the sort of wider activity which Christian missionaries, as described in Acts, were later to engage in. For the moment, it is true, the disciples go only where Jesus will later visit (10.1), but their number alludes to the global mission of which their activity is the beginning.

The authorization of disciples to preach the kingdom and heal therefore comes to us in the Gospels as two differing but similar traditions. What they have in common is the activity which those sent are to perform. Mark also has Jesus send twelve followers (6.7–13) in order to preach (see v. 12 and 3.14), but the actual terms of the kingdom preaching are not set down. Mark emphasizes the authority of the twelve over demons (6.7, 13), but in this case the text should not be regarded as significantly different from what we have in Matthew and Luke; since in antiquity demons were thought to cause disease, their removal was often considered the basis of healing (compare Mark 6.13 with Matthew 10.1 and Luke 9.1). John contains no such scene of commissioning. Important though the disciples' terms of reference were, the commissioning scene was not included in all the Gospels, and the Gospels which do have such a passage have clear differences among them.

The picture of the formation of the Gospels which emerges from this evidence is one of evolution. At the point of origin, we find various disciples recollecting their commission; they and their followers passed their tradition on in somewhat different terms. As the various stories were told, interpreted and told again, each acquired a distinctive profile. At the end of the evolutionary process, the stories were incorporated into the Gospels in distinctive ways. In the case of John, the commissioning stories were either unknown or overlooked at the time the Gospel was written. Mark has a brief, somewhat general, scene, Matthew a more precise commission of the twelve, and Luke a double commission of twelve and seventy-two followers. Each story, or combination of stories, makes a contribution of its own by highlighting certain aspects of Jesus' appointment of disciples. The development of the individual traditions would have been determined within the particular circles in which they were spoken of; among those traditions which happen to have been known at the time a given Gospel was written, some would have been selected for inclusion.

Those who handed on traditions about Jesus are known as 'tradents'; of them we know only that they were among Jesus' disciples, and his disciples' followers. But it is possible to infer the sorts of settings in which they handed on their material. A story such as the commissioning scenes in Matthew and Luke would appropriately have been recounted as Jesus' followers came to new areas to preach and heal, whether in Palestine or the Mediterranean world generally. Under such circumstances, one would have to explain on whose behalf one taught and acted, and what was intended to be conveyed by one's teaching and actions. It would also be appropriate to give a sample of Jesus' own kingdom preaching and stories of his healings; the Gospels contain much material of that kind. Because the process of inferring the settings in which traditions were handed on begins with a consideration of the shape of those traditions, it has become known as 'form criticism'.

Form critics have distinguished many settings as the situations in which traditions about Jesus were developed. The Lord's Prayer would have – and still has – obvious interest within the worship life of many Christian communities. Within a more instructional setting, Jesus' many ethical sayings were collected at an early stage to provide Christians with advice on how to conduct themselves in a manner consistent with his message. The traditions of the Gospels were not merely shaped, however, to evangelize those unfamiliar with Jesus and offer elementary instruction. Teachers themselves also require guidance, and much of the material in the Gospels addresses the concerns of discipleship, of passing Jesus' message on, often under difficult

31

circumstances. Some of Jesus' sayings appear in the Gospels as discourses which explain his teaching on the kingdom, repentance, and other crucial matters. Then, too, there are stories, particularly of miracles, which seem designed to celebrate Jesus' authority in a way which might enrich Christians at any stage in their development.

Although it is possible to describe the forms of traditions, and sometimes to infer the settings in which they were related, the way in which traditions were handed on remains something of a mystery. At the earliest stage, they were probably transmitted orally, by word of mouth from teacher to disciples, and on to successive groups of followers. Form critics once tended to describe each passage, even if only a single saying or a brief story, as an independent 'unit' which was at first handed on without reference to other material. But it is difficult to imagine anyone citing a single saying or story completely apart from a context; unless a tradition is linked to a narrative or a discourse, its point is likely to be lost. Moreover, rabbinic literature suggests that Jewish learning inclined people to memorize streams of material, not isolated units.

One such stream of tradition is the passion narrative. Jesus' execution by means reserved for dangerous criminals in the Roman Empire was something his disciples needed to explain. In what way was such a death consistent with God's providence? The story of Jesus' 'passion' (a word derived from the Latin term for 'suffering') answers that question on several levels. First and foremost, Jesus' own awareness of his relationship to God is shown as bringing him to accept a shameful death: conflict with religious authorities, the disastrous result of that, and his vindication by God were all part of his adherence to the truth he was entrusted with. The passion narrative also weaves the Old Testament into its description of events, so that the sense that there was a divine compulsion involved in the proceedings is vividly conveyed. No less vivid, however, are the portraits of intrigue by religious and secular authorities, the initially responsible parties in the crucifixion.

Relatively speaking, the passion narrative evidences less variety among the Gospels than other traditions about Jesus, largely because the sequence of material follows an order which the events as they were remembered set down. In this tradition, more evidently than in others, the narrative line of the material is just as important as the sayings and stories related. But here as well, principles of development and selection were at work; each Gospel presents a passion narrative which is closely related to, but distinct from, what we find in the others. The relationship among them is nonetheless so close that one is tempted to suppose the tradition was written down before the Gospels were written. Even at an early stage, those whose principal mode of communication was oral may have made use of written notes, and as Jesus' movement grew in Palestine and beyond, the financial and human resources necessary for writing more extensively became available. The precise point at which written tradition predominated is not known; even Papias, a second century Christian, said he preferred the 'living voice' of tradition to written texts (see Eusebius, *Church History* 3.39.4). The writing of our Gospels clearly represents a watershed, however, in that they assured the ultimate predominance of the written word. Such written material as may have existed before that time would have constituted a check on oral development, but would not have stopped it altogether.

The last stage in the production of the written Gospels was that at which traditions about Jesus, whether written or oral, were selected, brought into the context of continuous narratives, and consigned to the actual wording which is now available. Those who were responsible for writing the Gospels were somewhat in the position of editors, who have to choose from the material to hand and select the final order and format in which that material will be published. The study of how the Gospels were finally put together is known as 'redaction criticism', because 'redaction' refers to the editorial process of revision. Obviously, the best way to understand the work of any editor (or 'redactor') is to study the material submitted to her or him, and compare that with the final product. In the case of the Gospels, however, we no longer have direct access to the traditions which circulated before the writing of the documents.

The Lord's Prayer

In certain instances, the tradition incorporated in two or more Gospels seems to have been reasonably well fixed, and it is possible to infer that differences between one Gospel and another are the result of redactional changes. In the Gospel according to Luke, for example, Jesus is said to teach his disciples to pray immediately after he had finished a prayer of his own 'in a certain place' (Luke 11.1). An unnamed disciple approaches and asks, 'Master, teach us to pray, just as John taught his disciples' (11.1b, c). Such a scenic context, as will be seen below, is quite typical of Luke. Jesus responds by teaching the Lord's Prayer (11.2–4); the wording differs from Matthew's version and the whole is much shorter, but such deviations primarily reflect differences in the traditions available to Matthew and Luke, not redactional changes. But the setting of the prayer in Matthew seems another matter. Here, Jesus offers the unsolicited advice not to 'bandy words about as the Gentiles, because they think they will be listened to for their wordiness' (Matthew 6.7), and then gives the Matthean version of the Lord's Prayer (6.9–13). The presentation of the prayer belongs to a long sequence of teaching in Matthew customarily known as 'the Sermon on the Mount', in view of how it begins (see 5.1). Prayer is the topic of the sequence from 6.5, and the traditions contained in the Sermon were probably collected to address such topics and developed over the course of time before the Gospel was written. But the decision to organize these traditions into a long discourse (of three chapters!) is an editorial one. As it stands, the Sermon is the first full, pace-setting presentation of Jesus' message in Matthew, and is part of the overall format of the Gospel, in which sayings of Jesus are strung into discourses and sandwiched between narrative sections.

Jesus may obviously have taught his recommended prayer on more than one occasion, and perhaps in slightly different words. But we know only one version from Luke, and one from Matthew, while Mark and John relate nothing at all on the matter. And the Lucan and Matthean presentations influence the ways in which the reader sees the prayer. The Lucan Jesus offers words which come out of his own prayer life, in response to his disciple's

34

specific request to teach in the style of John the Baptist. It is scarcely a coincidence that, in Luke particularly, Jesus is portrayed as praying privately (see 3.21; 5.16; 6.12; 9.18, 28, 29; 22.41, 44) and his life and ministry are related with John the Baptist's (compare the stories about them in chapters one and two, and 3.1–18 with 4.14–30). By the same token, 'Gentile' is a word which only appears in Matthew among the Gospels: its only other appearances are at 5.47, also within the Sermon, and at 18.17, where Jesus says an unrepentant brother, who does not heed the Church, is to be treated as a Gentile and a tax-gatherer. The later saying is also in a longer discourse (18.1–35) which is unique to Matthew. As in 'the Sermon on the Mount', Jesus is portrayed as offering timeless guidance for the 'Church' (a term which, again, only appears in Matthew among the Gospels), not only advice to his contemporaries. In the context of Matthew's carefully constructed discourses, the Lord's Prayer becomes the authoritative foundation of worship in the community established by Jesus.

The settings of the Lord's Prayer provided in Luke and Matthew are more complementary than contradictory, but they are clearly distinctive. Their redactional nature is suggested by comparing the texts, but also by observing that the settings are typically Lucan and Matthean from the point of view of language, format, and theme. Redaction critics do not rely only upon the existence of discernible traditions which the redactors have reworked. They also consider whether the language of a passage is typical of a redactor in its wording and grammar, whether the format of the passage accords with the normal manner of presentation, and whether it expresses motifs which the redactor was fond of. In this way, it is possible to make fine distinctions between what the redactor has composed, and what was known to him from his tradition.

The judgement that a passage, or part of a passage, is redactional does not imply that it is invented, or totally unrelated to traditional material. The redactors stood at the end of a traditional process of which they themselves were a part: the fact that they helped to shift the medium of communication from the spoken to the written word by no means implies they suddenly introduced a completely new degree of creativity into the process.

They wrote for communities in which what Papias called the living voice of tradition could still be heard, and they were in no position flagrantly to contradict what was known about Jesus, even had they wished to. Matthew and Luke offer plausible accounts of the setting of the Lord's Prayer, even though, by selection, emphasis, choice of words, and format, they present the traditional material from the points of view which are peculiar to them.

The parable of the sower

The first three Gospels present Jesus' parable of the sower (Matthew 13.1–9; Mark 4.1–9; Luke 8.4–8) and its interpretation (Matthew 13.18–23; Mark 4.13–20; Luke 8.11–15). Together, this material illustrates the stability and development of traditions about Jesus, and their appropriation by redactors. The setting of the parable evidences the sort of deviation among the Gospels which is plain in the case of the Lord's Prayer. Matthew (13.1–3) and Mark (4.1–3) similarly portray Jesus as teaching from a boat to a crowd gathered on the shore, and speak of his reference to several parables. The language chosen by each redactor is, however, distinctive. Luke merely has a great crowd from different towns coming together, and refers only to one parable (8.4). In this chapter, Luke presents less teaching material than do Mark and Matthew; Matthew presents the greatest quantity of parables among the three, in a characteristically long and authoritative discourse which contains some parables unique to the first Gospel (13.3–52).

The wording of the parable itself is remarkably stable among the three Gospels; indeed, there is less deviation in this case than in that of the Lord's Prayer. Jesus speaks of a farmer who scatters seed broadcast, following the practice of ancient Palestine. As described, the ground may seem quite unsuitable for sowing, but that is because at that time seed was plowed into the soil *after* sowing. Jesus calls attention to the perils of the technique, which were probably all too evident to his hearers. Some seed, on or near an exposed path, is eaten by birds; some grows in rocky soil which cannot support growth in the blazing sun; some is choked off by weeds. In the end, however, the farmer's efforts pay off; the fruitful seed yields thirty times, sixty times, or even a hundred times the initial amount.

Even within this parable of Jesus, however, there are small changes of wording among the Gospels which may manifest the characteristic style of the redactors. Mark's Jesus begins, 'Hear! Behold, the sower went out to sow . . .' (4.3). The maladroit combination of 'hear' and 'behold' is not a normal feature of Jesus' teaching, but there is a greater emphasis on correct hearing in Mark (see 4.33, and the uniquely worded 4.24), which perhaps explains why 'hear' is tacked on to the start of Jesus' discourse. On the other hand, Mark 4.6 presents a simple sentence structure ('And when the sun rose, it was scorched'), while Matthew 13.6 makes use of the sort of construction with a participle ('The sun *having risen*, they were scorched') which was preferable as Greek style. Luke 8.6, however, presents the smoothest phrasing ('and as it grew, it withered, because it had no moisture'). Such stylistic improvements make the parable more understandable or vivid, without altering its meaning.

All three Gospels present the parable as part of Jesus' preaching of God's kingdom (Matthew 13.10, 11; Mark 4.10, 11; Luke 8.9, 10). 'The kingdom of God' was a phrase used in the time of Jesus by Jews generally to refer to God's powerful revelation of himself, his intervention on behalf of his people. It was the heart of Jesus' message and the primary content of his preaching (see Matthew 4.17; Mark 1.15; Luke 4.43). The kingdom was for him a *final* intervention by God in human affairs which was at last to right all wrongs and introduce true mercy, justice and peace under God's kingship; as such, he called his followers to pray that its future coming might be speedy (Matthew 6.10; Luke 11.2). Clearly, the kingdom was essentially supernatural in Jesus' thinking, since it depended wholly on God's own disclosure of himself; Jesus could describe it as involving the fellowship of the living and the dead in a banquet of celebration (Matthew 8.11, 12; Luke 13.28, 29). But the origin of the kingdom outside human experience and control did not mean, in Jesus' thinking, that the kingdom had nothing to do with people's lives. On the contrary, he preached that the kingdom confronts people with the crucial moment of decision, when they will repent or not (see Matthew

4.17; Mark 1.15). Particularly, his own ministry – as he saw it – brought to expression the pressing reality of the kingdom (see Matthew 12.28; Luke 11.20; 17.20, 21).

Because Jesus' language of the kingdom refers essentially to the activity of God himself, as king on behalf of his people, it has both a future and a present emphasis. The future is the time when God will be known fully as king, and when those who have decided for God will enjoy his fellowship in an unqualified way. But this future is not completely unconnected to the present: God's ruling activity at the very moment is already an aspect of his kingdom. By accepting or rejecting God's rule in the present, one is determining one's relationship to it in the future. To use the metaphor of the present parable, God already rules, but in a germinal way: he is a sower who scatters seed. Each seed, the sower's every movement, carries the potential of harvest, but the condition of the soil also determines success or failure. By a proportion of three out of four, Jesus describes the soil as mostly unsuitable for growth. But when the soil is suitable, success is extravagant, with rewards miraculously in excess of the initial effort. In the parable, Jesus urges his hearers to become the right kind of soil, to respond to the hints of God's rule in the present which are the seeds of its future glory. Any other response brings only barrenness, useless growth, the marks of wasted opportunity.

The interpretation of the parable within the context of Jesus' preaching of the kingdom unfolds his meaning quite plainly, although the kingdom of God is not referred to in so many words. The Gospels clearly suggest that the kingdom is the implicit reference of the parable (again, see Matthew 13.10, 11; Mark 4.10, 11; Luke 8.9, 10), but there is an alternative interpretation developed within Matthew (13.18–23), Mark (4.13–20), and Luke (8.11–15). Comparison of the three versions will show that there are more variations of wording here than in the parable itself, but they agree on the substance of the interpretation. All focus on the issue of how the 'word' of preaching is heard. Satan might remove it, as the birds of the parable carry away seed. The word might be accepted with an apparent enthusiasm, which proves how rootless it is in the face of persecution. Again, some might accept the word, only to have its growth choked off by their fretting and striving over worldly cares. Finally, some at least both hear the word, and hear it in such a way that they bear fruit.

The interpretation of the parable as found in the Gospels involves a shift of focus from the kingdom of God to 'the word', understood as the message of preaching. In fact, this shift of focus is accompanied by a change of scene in all three accounts: Jesus is no longer speaking to a crowd in general (see Matthew 13.10; Mark 4.10; Luke 8.9), but to his disciples. There is evidence that, as they handed on material intended for them, the disciples introduced their own experience of Christian mission into the interpretation. First of all, 'the word' is commonly found as a designation for preaching among Christian writings (see Luke 1.2; Acts 8.4; 16.6; 17.11; Galatians 6.6; Colossians 4.3), but not in the sayings of Jesus. Then, too, the fate of the word as described in the interpretation – its acceptance with joy (see 1 Thessalonians 1.6), its cause of persecution (see 2 Timothy 2.8, 9), its growth and fruitfulness (see Colossians 1.5, 6), and its vulnerability to worldly cares on the part of those who accept it (see 1 Peter 5.7) – accords much more with the language of early Christian preaching than with the sayings of Jesus himself. Above all, the interpretation misses the future emphasis which was regularly part of Jesus' kingdom preaching, and which is stressed especially in his parables of growth. Indeed, the kingdom is notable in the interpretation only for its absence.

The basic similarity of the interpretation in the first three Gospels suggests it is not essentially redactional, but traditional: the editors seem to have handed it on among the materials known to them. There are certain deviations among them which may, however, reflect redactional alteration. For example, the positive reception of the word is described with the verbs 'hearing' and 'understanding' in Matthew (13.23), 'hearing' and 'accepting' in Mark (4.20), and 'hearing' and 'holding fast' in Luke (8.15). Obviously, such differences should not be pressed to the point they seem contradictory, but each manifests its own nuance. Matthew's wording emphasizes intellectual understanding, Mark's focuses more on genuine assent in hearing, and Luke's calls for faithful endurance, each in language which is characteristic of or unique to the Gospel in question.

The Synoptic problem

The strong similarity of the three accounts of the parable and its interpretation brings an obvious question to mind: was one of the Gospels the traditional, *written* source used by the others? Scholars during this century have concentrated on the possibility that Mark is just such a source. It has been the most likely candidate for treatment of this kind because in many ways it seems the common term among the first three Gospels. Almost the whole of Mark – some 95 per cent – is contained in what Matthew and Luke together report. Even more significantly, the order and wording of this material is often common to all three Gospels; when either Matthew or Luke departs from the common order and wording, it is frequently on its own, with the other agreeing with Mark. Deviation from Mark's wording can often be explained as an attempt at stylistic improvement (see the discussion above of Mark 4.6, and the corresponding passages in Matthew and Luke). The substantial similarity of the first three Gospels is so great that one can print them side by side in parallel columns and follow them passage by passage to the end, without totally ruining the order of each. They can be 'seen together', or are 'synoptic' (a term derived from the Greek equivalent of 'seen together').

Matthew and Luke contain much material in addition to that found also in Mark. They present a common tradition of some 200 verses, primarily sayings of Jesus (such as the Lord's Prayer). This tradition, whether it was written or oral, is known as 'Q', from the first letter in '*Quelle*', the German word for 'source'. Moreover, some one third of Matthew and some one half of Luke are unique to those Gospels (see, for example, their very different stories of Jesus' birth). The special material of Matthew is known as 'M', while that of Luke is known as 'L'. On the supposition that Mark was the first Gospel to be written, and was used independently by those who composed Matthew and Luke, Matthew has been explained as a redaction of Mark, 'Q', and 'M', while Luke has been explained as a redaction of Mark, 'Q', and 'L'.

Recent discussion has, however, challenged the security of the hypothesis of four sources behind the Synoptic Gospels (Mark,

'Q', 'M' and 'L'). Some scholars argue for the gradual expansion of the Synoptic material, running from Mark, to Matthew, and then to Luke. Others hold that the first Gospel was Matthew, and that Luke supplemented it, while Mark abbreviated them both. So far, none of these theories has managed to displace the theory of four sources as the consensus. But the relationship among the Gospels is a matter for continuing discussion, and it would be unwise to treat any theory as an established fact. At some points the alternative theories work quite well, and they do not require hypothetical sources (such as 'Q', 'M' and 'L') to be imagined.

The most nagging difficulty which confronts the assumption that Mark was a source of Matthew and Luke is that, in some cases, study of the triple tradition shared by all three Gospels shows that Matthew and Luke agree *against* Mark. Such instances are not easy to explain on the supposition that Mark was precisely the written source incorporated within Matthew and Luke. There has been a certain tendency in recent years to return to a view held in the nineteenth century, particularly in Germany: perhaps the tradition behind all three Gospels, whether written or oral, was rather like, but not identical with, the text of Mark as we know it. Particularly, the assumption that the material we know as the 'triple tradition', 'Q', 'M' and 'L' was actually written down before the redaction of the Gospel is today not as confidently expressed as it once was. As a result of growing familiarity among scholars with techniques of Jewish teaching, the possibility that what were once called 'sources' might have been streams of oral tradition has received renewed consideration.

In the material so far considered, the Synoptic Gospels manifest both continuity with the teaching of Jesus, and also development of his teaching. The essential content of his announcement of the kingdom seems to have been well maintained as it was passed from tradents to redactors. But the terms of reference of later Christian experience seem to have strongly influenced the interpretation of the parable of the sower. It is clearly traditional, that is, not the product of redactional change alone, but neither does it inform us directly of Jesus' position. Although there is a historical element in it, which reflects the attitude of Jesus' followers, this interpretative material does not rest on the sort of hard facts about Jesus which are evident elsewhere in the Gospels. In this sense, the attribution of the interpretation to Jesus himself (see Matthew 13.11; Mark 4.11; Luke 8.10) seems fictional. Jesus may, of course, have said some such thing to his disciples privately; but the wording appears more theirs than his. The various settings of Jesus' sayings within their narrative contexts suggest there was a degree of freedom exercised in the final redaction of the Gospels, as well as in the tradition.

Within the Synoptic Gospels, then, facts and fictions about Jesus are woven together. Indeed, they are woven together in a way which makes them difficult to disentangle. But, within the limits of the evidence available, it is often possible to distinguish between what reflects the particular orientation of Jesus, and what reflects traditional or redactional developments of Jesus' position. The considerations we have already gone through belong to the stock and trade of scholars in their attempt to separate stages in the development of traditions about Jesus. His distinctive preaching of the kingdom, and its implications, are taken as a touchstone: what does not easily suit that is viewed with some suspicion. Alternative developments in the traditions about him can be traced by comparing the Gospels with one another, and more particularly by being aware of the attribution to Jesus of language which was dear to later tradents or redactors.

John's Gospel

The Gospel according to John must be dealt with in a somewhat different way, because it has a shape all its own. Not only does much of its material differ from the Synoptics, but its format of presentation is different. The scene of Jesus' occupation of the Temple, for example, comes at the end of his ministry in the Synoptics, but at the beginning in John (see 2.13–22). Moreover, Jesus is made to speak in extensive, rhetorical sermons in John, while his discourses in the Synoptics consist of short, pungent sayings. Indeed, the word 'discourse' can only be applied in a loose way to what Jesus says in the Synoptics, since they lack the overall structure of his statements in John.

One of the Johannine sermons is set in Jerusalem, at the time of the visit to Jesus of a Jewish leader named Nicodemus, just after the occupation of the Temple (3.1–21). Nicodemus comes in good faith (see v. 2), but Jesus immediately confronts him with something of a riddle. 'Unless', he says, 'one is born from above, he is not able to see the kingdom of God' (v. 3). The Greek word used (*anōthen*) can mean 'again' or 'anew' as well as 'from above'. (The play on words is also possible in English; 'take it from the top' normally refers to starting again in a musical score, but the expression could be used directionally.) The difference in meaning is what leads Nicodemus astray in v. 4: 'How can a man be born, being old? He can hardly enter his mother's womb a second time and be born!' But the play on words operates only in Greek; in Aramaic, the language of Jesus, the reference would have been more straightforward. Together with the traditional kingdom usage in v. 3, there seems to be a more developed turn of phrase, which assumes that Greek is the normal language of communication.

Within the same passage, there is a similar mix of material in v. 5. Here again, Jesus speaks of the kingdom, but also calls for birth 'from water and spirit'. Nicodemus is in no position to know what that might mean, but the phrase accords with the later understanding of baptism in the Church (see Titus 3.5; 1 Peter 1.3, 23). Indeed, John elsewhere (7.39) maintains that the Spirit was only effective and knowable after Jesus' crucifixion and resurrection; apparently, Jesus' language has been supplemented in v. 5 with the perspective of disciples long after the event (see also 2.22). John's presentation can be particularly challenging, because there were no quotation marks in the original Greek manuscripts. The rather philosophical comment in v. 6 ('What is born from the flesh is flesh, and what is born from the spirit is spirit') might be intended as Jesus' own words, or as a further elucidation of the meaning of Christian baptism. Whatever the intention, the effect of John's presentation of traditions about Jesus is to weave fact and fiction together even more closely than they are in the Synoptics. Although Jesus' teaching is scenically directed to Nicodemus, it functions as a sermon for the Christian readers of John.

The dates of the Gospels

The length of time during which the various streams of the traditions in the Gospels developed, interacted with one another, and were finally redacted, is not known precisely. Presumably, the periods varied from stream to stream, although *approximate* dates can be assigned to each Gospel. The assignment of dates must be tentative, along with any discussion of places of writing, because conclusions are based purely on inference from the texts, not on first hand information. Scholars locate Gospels in the sort of way historians of art place unsigned paintings within schools, cities and periods; it is a matter of observing style, and catching any telltale incidentals in which scenes are set. Just as style of presentation can suggest the essential orientation of a document, its references to incidental details may reflect contemporary events or circumstances.

The prominence given to prophecies involving the destruction of the Temple in the Synoptics has generated the consensus that they were written rather near the time of its actual destruction by the Romans in AD 70. Mark has no allusion to the destruction having taken place, so that the Gospel may be placed shortly before AD 70. But the discourse in Mark 13 seems to be a collection of sayings ordered around the themes of the Temple and cosmic tribulation. Some scholars would argue that the collectors were motivated by their recent experience of the Temple's destruction, which they took to mean the son of man (Jesus) would soon come to judge the world. The number of Latin loan words in the Gospel gives some support to the traditional opinion that Mark was composed in Rome. The uniquely Marcan statement that Simon the Cyrenean, who carried Jesus' cross, was the father of Alexander and Rufus (see 15.21 and 'Rufus', although not necessarily the same person, in Romans 16.13), may be a further hint in this direction.

The Gospels according to Matthew and Luke may allude to knowledge of the Temple's actual destruction; on other grounds, as well, they appear later than Mark. (Of course, on the hypothesis that Mark was their source, they must be later.) Matthew 22.7 seems to many scholars to reflect awareness of the firing of Jerusalem under Titus: 'The king was angry, and sent his troops to destroy those killers and burn their city.' Although this is a statement in a parable, it refers to the sort of detail which would perhaps not be mentioned unless it touched a nerve in the memory. The Gospel was written in Greek, but it has a particular interest in and conflict with partisans of Judaism (see chapter 23). Because Christians seem to have been excluded from worship in synagogues around AD 85, and no mention is made of this in Matthew, a date around AD 80 is often accepted. Syria is frequently mentioned as the likely place of redaction. Luke 19.43, 44 seems an even more precise allusion to the Roman siege and its result than appears in Matthew, and the publication of the Gospel with Acts shows an awareness that Christian preaching has moved on since Jesus. Indeed, the closing scene of Acts presents Paul as a figure quite distinct from, and rejected by, Judaism, yet acceptable to the Roman authorities. That is the picture of Christian mission which is promoted by the Lucan redaction, probably around AD 90. Luke–Acts has both a cosmopolitan outlook, and access to Semitic traditions about Jesus (see the birth stories) and the early Church. As a result, Antioch is sometimes taken to be the place of redaction.

Ephesus was traditionally considered the place where John's Gospel was written down. Open conflict with the leaders of synagogues was for Christians a feature of Ephesian life (see Acts 19.23–41; Revelation 1.9–11), and the Gospel presents excommunication as such a natural response by Jews to Christians that it is projected back into the time of Jesus (see John 9.22; 12.42)! The settled acceptance of life outside Judaism, and the reference to the synagogue as a clearly separate institution suggest that the Gospel was composed near the end of the first century. The close weave of early traditions with later interpretations, as if material about Jesus had constantly to be explained, would seem to point to the same conclusion.

Although the dates commonly assigned to the Gospels must not be regarded as certainties, they do allow for a full generation of handing on and interpreting material between the death of Jesus (around AD 30) and the final redaction of the Gospels. Such a time span would allow for the sorts of development we have already encountered. It would also explain how the Gospels can be at some variance, even when basic events in Jesus' ministry are at issue.

The death of Jesus in the Gospels

The scene of Jesus' death provides an example of significant variation among the Gospels. John here presents the most sober and circumspect narrative (19.28–30). Jesus says he is thirsty in order to fulfil Scripture, and in fact he is given vinegar, somewhat as is said in Psalm 69.21. Having taken the vinegar, Jesus says, 'It is finished', inclines his head, and dies. The starkly necessary, one might almost say routine, character of John's account accords with the unique feature in this Gospel that Jesus is said to die on the day of preparation (see John 19.14), near the time lambs were sacrificed for Passover. In Mark (15.33–7), the scene is more supernatural, in that darkness descends from the sixth hour (that is, twelve noon; compare what happens in John 19.14 at the same time, although the day is Passover itself in the Synoptics). But Jesus here recites a mournful verse from Psalms,'My God, my God, why have you forsaken me?' (22.1), and is mistaken by those who watch the end. Their attempt to revive him momentarily with vinegar fails, and Jesus dies with a wordless cry. He is a far more pathetic, unappreciated figure than he is in John.

The pathos of the Marcan scene is represented also in Matthew, although in slightly different words (see 27.45–50). But this pathos is only a foil to the earthquake, which Matthew alone mentions, after Jesus' death (see 27.51–3). The pathetic elements serve to underline Jesus' supernatural vindication. A different tack is taken in Luke (23.44–6). Here, the darkness from the sixth hour is ascribed to a failure of the sun itself (as distinct from cloud, for example), which heightens the supernatural atmosphere of the scene (v. 45). Moreover, the tearing of the curtain in the Temple, which is mentioned after Jesus' death in Matthew and Mark, is mentioned beforehand in Luke. These elements give added emphasis to the actual moment of death, which is uniquely portrayed in Luke. Jesus simply cries, 'Father, into your hands I commend my spirit,' and dies. The supernatural setting is only there to emphasize the sublime nobility of Jesus.

The Gospels' scenes of Jesus' death have been used by Christians for centuries, and they are strangely moving. From age to age, sustenance has been found in them, as God's own son is portrayed as crucified in vividly human terms (Mark), as suffering nobly (Luke), as dramatically vindicated (Matthew), and as a necessary sacrifice (John). There is no doubt of the basic facts with which the different versions began, because Jesus' shameful death is well attested, in Christian, Jewish and Roman sources. But it is entirely obvious that the stories are not precise chronicles; rather, they are *haggadoth*, illustrative scenes which help believers to appreciate the significance of Jesus' death. Their force and vigour is only demeaned when they are read as merely dry records of past events. Much more, they express insights into what it meant and means to be God's son. They suggest what Jesus went through, how he went through it, and where believers might find strength to bear their own crosses. Because the Gospels are less than history in one sense, they are more than history in another sense.

Conclusion

Facts and fictions are both to be found in the Gospels, but neither can be found unadulterated. Because traditions about Jesus represent to some extent a continuous line of development, starting with the rabbi himself and his impact on his followers, they are durable vehicles of factual information about Jesus. Once allowance is made for how tradents and redactors may have shaped the material, it possesses an irreducibly factual element. Even at their point of origin in the ministry of Jesus, however, traditions were designed less to convey facts than to offer insights about God. For this reason, facts in the Gospels can only be discovered by inference. Obviously, Jesus prayed for and preached the kingdom, and died on the cross; but the Gospels do not simply relate such items as straight history. Rather, Jesus' message is handled in such a way that it is more easily appreciated as his disciples understood it, and the cross also becomes the focus of discipleship.

Sometimes, the interpretative work of tradents and redactors seems extreme. Their divergences from one another make us uncertain of the exact terms in which Jesus taught his favourite prayer, and the circumstances under which he taught it; similarly, the exact setting of the parable of the sower is uncertain, and the interpretation ascribed to Jesus seems secondary; even Jesus' death, for all the power of the various scenes, seems to occur behind a gauze of interpretation which keeps us from the event itself. Such uncertainties, and the observable flexibility of traditions about Jesus, require the recognition of a fictional element in the Gospels. But just as 'fact' must be defined afresh in the categorization of materials in the Gospels, so 'fiction' will not do if it is applied in its usual sense. The traditions about Jesus were flexible, as well as durable: the lines of development from him evidence stretching, pulling, compressing, and other forces, all in order to interpret and illustrate his significance for faith. But pure invention does not seem to have been the order of the day. The Gospels are as far from being novels as they are from being learned histories: their fictional elements are only encountered within a development whose ultimate basis was actual event and teaching.

The distinction between fact and fiction is an inevitable aspect of a modern, critical reading of the Gospels. There is in our minds a meaningful difference between reporting actual events and recounting stories and sayings in order to convey a claim of faith. But the Gospels do both at the same time. Jesus' preaching of the kingdom, his forceful announcement of God's intervention on behalf of his people, was the starting point of a new tradition. That tradition was appropriated by his disciples, and also interpreted by them in order to account for what God had done in their own lives. Above all, the traditions about Jesus were more and more shaped, as time went on and his disciples reflected on their experience, by the belief that God himself was active in what Jesus said, did and suffered. The redaction of the Gospels represents the culmination of handing on, interpreting and shaping traditions of Jesus, and the unique character of the Gospels as literature attests the freshness of their message. Their guiding conviction is that the man who announced God's kingdom himself spoke and acted on God's behalf. That vigorous faith explains the care and the creativity which were involved in the composition of the Gospels.

The challenge of the Gospels lies primarily in their nuanced presentation of Jesus' sayings and doings. The reader is confronted with historically accurate traditions, but also with substantially innovative material which tradents and redactors contributed in the interests of interpretation and illustration. She or he is confronted with this multi-layered product as four complete, integrated texts, and often without much warning of when fact leaves off and fiction begins. Indeed, it seems early Christians did not draw the line between the two as clearly as is generally done today. But it is often possible, by means of the sort of study introduced in this chapter, to distinguish among redactional elements and streams of tradition, and to assess their likely relation to Jesus himself. The student must unavoidably make such judgements, if the text is to be appreciated in its depth through time. Any other reading produces a flat understanding of the Gospels, in which Jesus' ministry appears as having length in duration, and breadth in its impact on others, but no depth in its development through tradition and redaction. If the reader fails to understand the third dimension of the Gospels, she or he will take a flat reading as being entirely fact or entirely fiction. The alternative is to take account of how the Gospels were formed, and to recognize in them richly variegated portraits of a living faith. What permitted those portraits to be produced is that their raw materials were both durable in their connection with Jesus, and flexible in their development by his followers.

FOR FURTHER READING

A useful introductory essay concerning how traditions about Jesus were passed on by his disciples and followers has been written by B. Gerhardsson, *The Origins of the Gospel Traditions* (London: SCM Press, 1979 and Philadelphia: Fortress Press, 1979). An influential older study, which takes account of (then) recent developments in form criticism, is V. Taylor's *The Formation of the Gospel Tradition* (London: Macmillan, 1945). But the classic form critical study is that of R. Bultmann, *The History of the Synoptic Tradition* (Oxford: Blackwell, 1972), although it makes for more demanding reading. A more thematic approach is adopted by T. W. Manson in *The Teaching of Jesus. Studies of its Form and Content* (Cambridge: University Press, 1955). A lucid account of redaction critical approaches to the Gospels is provided in G. N.

Stanton, *The Gospels and Jesus*: The Oxford Bible Series (Oxford: University Press, 1986).

Discussion of Jesus' kingdom preaching, and its study, may be found in a collection of articles in B. D. Chilton, *The Kingdom of God in the Teaching of Jesus*: Issues in Religion and Theology (London: SPCK, 1984 and Philadelphia: Fortress Press, 1984). Manson's book includes much useful material on the parables, but the pace-setting book in the field was J. Jeremias, *The Parables of Jesus* (London: SCM Press, 1972 and New York: Scribner, 1972); further considerations, based on newer approaches, may be found in N. Perrin, *Jesus and the Language of the Kingdom. Symbol and Metaphor in New Testament Interpretation* (London: SCM Press, 1976 and Philadelphia: Fortress Press, 1976).

The present state of investigation into the relationship among the Synoptic Gospels is well represented in G. M. Styler, 'The Priority of Mark' in Moule's *Birth* (see the advised reading in the Introduction), 285–316. A fuller, frequently argumentative, account is contained in W. R. Farmer, *The Synoptic Problem. A Critical Analysis* (Dillsboro: Western North Carolina Press, 1976). A useful introduction to the passion narrative is offered by H. Hendrickx, *The Passion Narrative of the Synoptic Gospels* (London: Geoffrey Chapman, 1984).

Among the many commentaries that may be recommended for consultation are: E. Schweizer, *The Good News according to Matthew* (London: SPCK, 1976 and Atlanta: Knox, 1975); H. Anderson, *The Gospel of Mark*: New Century Bible (London: Oliphants, 1976); E. E. Ellis, *The Gospel of Luke*: New Century Bible (London: Oliphants, 1974); C. K. Barrett, *The Gospel according to St. John* (London: SPCK, 1978 and Philadelphia: Westminster, 1978).

2

Paul, the Radical Apostle

Paul is the most influential writer in the New Testament. His letters are matched in volume only by Luke–Acts, and Acts devotes more attention to Paul than to any other person. While the Gospels (and Acts) represent the gradual evolution of traditions, in which redactors played a limited part, the authentically Pauline letters are vigorous expressions of one man's faith. They are crisp, generally clear, and frequently original. Even within the documents of the New Testament, Paul's brand of Christianity aroused discussion (see James 2.14–26) and perplexity (see 2 Peter 3.15, 16). Paul gives the fullest account of what baptism means, of the ethical life which is to flow from baptism, of believers' relationship to Israel and its law, and of their hope for resurrection. He takes his stand on his claim to have encountered the risen Jesus, and preaches a gospel which he says came by direct revelation from God. His imprint on Christian theology is evident by the usage today of concepts he coined; to consider the Church as the 'body' of Christ and to see 'righteousness' as by faith alone are part of the Pauline inheritance. Jesus may be said to lie at the heart of Christianity, but Paul captured its mind.

Paul was no 'ivory tower' theologian. He worked out his vocation to preach the gospel around the Mediterranean basin by constant travel, enduring hardship, persecution from enemies, and conflict with other preachers (see 2 Corinthians 11.22–33). No consideration of his own well-being, no desire to enjoy the status his ceaseless activity afforded him, seems ever to have dampened his vital drive to preach the gospel where it had not been heard before. He is a religious event in his own right.

As in the case of Jesus, Paul's importance as a religious figure led to a considerable development of stories about him, and of accounts of his teaching. The book of Acts provides good

51

examples of material of this kind. We first meet Paul under his Jewish name (Saul), in the story of Stephen's death (Acts 7.58; 8.1). In his own letters, Paul admits that he 'persecuted' the Church, perhaps in Judaea (see 1 Corinthians 15.9; Galatians 1.13, 22, 23; Philippians 3.6). What he means by persecution is not specified, but his use of the term elsewhere does not suggest it refers to murder (see Romans 12.14; 1 Corinthians 4.12; 2 Corinthians 4.9; Galatians 4.29). The further statement in Galatians 1.13 that he 'destroyed' or 'laid waste' the Church indeed indicates the violence of his early feeling against faith in Jesus, but it falls short of a confession that he was involved in the killing of Stephen, or in any such activity in Jerusalem.

Stories of this sort in Acts, when they cannot be substantiated with reference to Paul's own letters, should be considered *haggadoth*, narratives that illustrate Paul's attitudes. There may or may not be a kernel of historical truth in them, but the old problem of fact and fiction – such as we have seen in the Gospels – is with us again, because we have no fool-proof rule for deciding what in Acts is historical, and what is not. Indeed, the presentation of these stories in Acts may suggest they are not even offered to the reader as straight reports.

Luke's account in chapter nine of Paul's commissioning to be an apostle is probably the best known in the New Testament. Paul is said to be on the way to Damascus to bring Christians back to Jerusalem (9.1, 2). (There is a problem in imagining that Roman authorities would have permitted their boundaries to be crossed in the interests of religious persecution, but that is a side issue.) On the way, Paul is blinded by a light and addressed by a voice (vv. 3–6). His companions are clearly said to have heard the voice, but to have seen no one (v. 7); they take the blind Paul to Damascus (vv. 8, 9), where he meets Ananias, is healed and baptized (vv. 10–19).

This account seems clear and straightforward, but so does the statement in chapter twenty-two, which Luke ascribes to Paul himself (22.6–16). The outline of events is broadly similar, although the words attributed to the divine voice and Ananias differ from what we read in chapter nine, and Paul's companions are said to see the light, but to hear nothing (22.9). It would have been quite easy for a redactor to clean up the discrepancy; why was this signal difference left to stand? Whether the editorial reason has to do with design or inadvertence, what emerges is that this detail of the story (or stories) is not treated as a crucial feature. The impact of the narration seems to have been seen as more important than its particulars.

Paul himself says remarkably little of his call to be an apostle, and almost nothing of the circumstances in which he received it. For him, it was simply the moment at which God revealed his son 'to' him, or 'in' him (Galatians 1.16, where the Greek text may be rendered either way). The vital assertion in Paul's argument was that Jesus' sonship was a revealed truth he was commissioned to preach, not a matter of human learning. He goes on to insist that he did not 'consult with flesh and blood' immediately afterwards (v. 16c). That clear denial of any human mediation does not easily square with the story of Ananias in Acts. Possibly, Paul here glosses over the conditions of his call; indeed, he does not even mention being baptized. His argument in Galatians is so directed to the revelatory basis of his apostolate that the particulars of his experience are not on his mind. But, even allowing for Paul's argumentative bias, the stories in Acts take on a legendary appearance as compared to the apostle's own words. However valuable they may be in illustrating the impact of Paul's experience, their emphases are different from those Paul himself stressed, and their specific assertions of fact look shaky.

Historically speaking, Paul's own letters are unquestionably more valuable as sources for his ministry than Acts, or any other derivative document. Acts does not even mention the fact about Paul which is most obvious to any reader of the New Testament: that he wrote letters! Readers' knowledge of his letter-writing is perhaps taken for granted, but, even if it is, Acts would only be recommending itself as a supplementary narrative of Paul's ministry, not as an account sufficient in itself. If – as seems less likely – Acts is written in ignorance of Paul's letters, its historical value to the student of Paul is even more tenuous. In either case, Paul's theology as depicted in Acts is in some tension with the thought developed in his own letters. When Paul is made to speak in Acts (see 13.16–41, by way of example), he refers to God's election of Israel, their inheritance of the promised land, and the subsequent rule of judges, Saul and David (13.16–22). The mention of David occasions his preaching of Jesus, who came from David's 'seed' (v. 23). In this sketch of the promise made to Israel, Abraham does not appear specifically. The reverse is the case in Paul's letters, where Abraham appears frequently as the very centre of the promise to Israel (see Romans 4; Galatians 3.6–18), and any other figure – Moses included, through whom the Torah was given – is considered subordinate (see Galatians 3.19–29). The portrayal of Paul's teaching in Acts is not necessarily useless as history. After all, in Acts 13 Paul is speaking in a synagogue to those who have not received the message about Jesus (see 13.14, 15), while his letters are directed to Christians. Moreover, there is a Pauline ring about the statement that Jesus came from the seed of David (13.23, see Romans 1.3), and more particularly in the assertion that through Jesus one can be justified in a way which is not possible by means of the law of Moses (13.38, 39, see Romans 3.21, 22; Galatians 2.16). Even in the account offered by Acts of Paul's conversion, he is said to preach Jesus as God's son as a result of his experience (9.20); that claim accords with Paul's own reference to the content of his call (Galatians 1.16). But these sporadic agreements between the Paul of Acts and Paul's own letters do not establish that the Lucan sermons are anything like a stenographic record of what was originally said. The emphasis in Paul's sermon in Acts 13 on the experience of Israel before Jesus is somewhat similar to the structure of Stephen's sermon in Acts 7. The contents of the two discourses are certainly distinctive from one another, but their presentation may reflect the general line Christian missionaries took with Jewish audiences during the time Acts was compiled. More crucially, the Paul of Acts gives us nothing like the detailed explanations of his position which are available in his letters.

Books continue to be published which treat Acts as the principal source of our knowledge about Paul, and attempt to fit Paul's letters into that framework. On historical grounds, however, the primacy of his letters can scarcely be denied. The tendency of Acts is to weave Paul's ministry into the entire tapestry of early Christian mission, which is the principal topic of the entire work. By its omission to mention Paul's letters and their crucial explanations, its inclusion of variously developed *haggadic* legends about Paul, and its shaping of Paul's ministry to accord with a generally Christian pattern, Acts rules itself out as a source which can stand above or alongside the letters. It tells us as much about what the Church made of Paul as about the man himself; and because there is only one edition of this material, unlike the case of traditions in the Gospels, one can distinguish stages of development only in an extremely tentative fashion. Treated as a derivative source, Acts can illuminate both the faith of post-Pauline Christians and some of the incidental material the letters mention allusively (or not at all). But it can only be used with caution as a source for understanding Paul's life and ministry. To understand his theology, which is his principal contribution to the New Testament, his letters are the only sound point of departure.

The emergence of Paul's faith

Fortunately, Paul does give a clear account of his early apostolate in his letter to the Galatians. The document is sometimes considered to be written around AD 53, shortly after Paul visited Corinth and was brought before the proconsul Gallio. Gallio's tenure is placed between AD 51 and 52 on the basis of Roman records, and Acts 18.12–16, where Paul is denounced before Gallio, would seem to reflect a historical occurrence; Paul's letters to Corinth certainly reflect a background of conflict and difficulty. The opening of Paul's letter to the churches of Galatia, a region in Asia Minor, announces his astonishment that the readers have deserted his proclamation 'so quickly' in favour of 'another gospel' (1.6). Evidently, his return from Greece to Asia Minor was greeted by the news of some defection by the Galatians. His anger is sufficient for him to abandon the habit evident in other letters of offering thanks for his readers' faith before addressing the subject on his mind: the topic to hand is so pressing that he becomes quite abrupt.

Against the background of possible betrayal by his readers, Paul insists that his gospel was not derived from human teaching, but came 'through a revelation of Jesus Christ' (1.11, 12). Prior to his call, he persecuted the Church because he was an advanced adherent of Judaism who was zealous for the traditions of his fathers (1.13, 14). He was, as he says elsewhere (Philippians 3.5), a Pharisee, one who cared for the developing tradition of Jewish law. Today, the term 'Pharisee' is used to imply senseless or trivial legalism. But Judaism was emerging in the time of Paul as a religion of fidelity to the guidance of Torah, both as written in Scripture and as discussed by means of oral tradition. The traditions of which Paul speaks in Galatians 1.14 were the means by which Jews were able to apply Scripture, the promise of God himself, to the conditions of their own lives. The Pharisaic focus on explaining and applying Torah gave expression to a vibrant religious impulse, which ultimately dominated Jewish theology. Paul does not here even hint that he was dissatisfied with his Pharisaic religious life prior to his call; on the contrary, he was an enthusiastic opponent of those who did not accept it. His acceptance of Jesus as God's son came about as a prophetic call in Paul's understanding, not as the end product of a psychological process. The revelation came to him in such a way that he felt his new ministry of preaching was the very purpose for which God had dedicated him in his mother's womb (Galatians 1.15, see the use of similar language in Jeremiah 1.5).

Paul goes out of his way in Galatians to insist that, even after his conversion, human teaching was not the basis of the gospel he preached. He saw no one immediately after his call (1.16c), not even the apostles in Jerusalem (1.17a), but preached in Arabia before returning to Damascus in Syria (1.17b). Only then, after three years, did he go to Jerusalem to make Peter's acquaintance (1.18a, 'Cephas' in the text being the Aramaic equivalent of 'Peter', or 'rock'). In the event, he stayed only fifteen days, and saw none of the other apostles with the single exception of James, the brother of Jesus (1.18b, 19). The seriousness of Paul's declaration here is solemnly attested by the words which follow: 'In what I write you, I say before God, I do not lie' (1.20). In this compressed, argumentative account of his call and early ministry, Paul can hardly have maintained more emphatically that his gospel was a revelation, not acquired teaching. 'Gospel' for him was something quite unlike the traditions he was schooled in as a Pharisee.

Paul's apostolic commissioning was the bedrock of his gospel in his own mind, and at the same time the basis on which others should accept his gospel. But the subject matter of Paul's teaching was obviously not limited to his personal experience of revelation. He attacks the Galatians as being foolish in 3.1 because they deserted the preacher who displayed Jesus Christ crucified before their very eyes. The content of the message is not spelled out here, but it does not need to be: the Galatians have, after all, heard it before. But for Paul's preaching to be so vivid that what was heard was accepted in faith (see 3.2), some detail about Jesus' crucifixion, and some account of the reasons for it, must have been given. Indeed, Paul's reference to his proclamation of Jesus' passion lends support to the view, already discussed in chapter one, that a passion narrative was a primitive feature of early Christian preaching.

Paul's acceptance of the man who was crucified as God's son was a matter of revelation in his experience and understanding, but how did he come to know there was a Jesus who might be accepted in this way? It is one thing to say that one's evaluation of Jesus is grounded in revelation, but quite another to claim that all one's information about Jesus comes directly from God. Paul would have had some knowledge of the movement centred on Jesus from the people he persecuted; his case would not be the only instance of persecutors coming to share the faith of their victims. Moreover, as one trained in the oral tradition of Judaism, Paul would naturally come to know his opponents' position fairly well, particularly if public dispute with Christians was a feature of his activity as a Pharisee. What happened in Damascus, which is where he seems to place his call (see Galatians 1.17), is that Paul came to see Jesus, the target of his persecuting zeal, as God's own son (1.16). 'Son' here implies, not any particular story about Jesus' birth, but Paul's realization of Jesus' relationship to God. Jesus made God known in Paul's experience in the way a son embodies his father's character. Because Jesus was understood to reveal God himself, he occupied the very centre of Paul's intellectual and emotional attention. He became the aim of Paul's dedicated service of God, rather than the object of his contempt. From the experience of his call to serve this son of God, it followed that Paul had to preach him, even among the Gentiles (again, see 1.16); he could no longer accept an exclusive restriction to Jewish custom, because God had revealed himself to Paul in a person, not a law or an interpretation.

Paul's knowledge of Jesus was not gleaned only during the period in which he persecuted Christians. Although he emphasizes his independence from the apostles in Jerusalem within Galatians, he admits to spending fifteen days with Peter (1.18). As it has become conventional to point out, their conversation was presumably not limited to the weather. When a disciple who had known Jesus as well as Peter did met the ardent new apostle who had been trained in traditional techniques of learning, a considerable amount of recollected material about Jesus must have come Paul's way. His acquaintance with James is not detailed by Paul (Galatians 1.19), but Jesus' own brother was doubtless a potential mine of information, as well.

Paul's letters to Corinth suggest the range of his mastery of traditions about Jesus. Two books in the New Testament, called 'To the Corinthians' in their oldest titles, represent a series of communications Paul wrote to the Christians of Corinth in Greece, probably during AD 55–6. His purpose in writing was not expressly to hand on his traditions, any more than in his other letters. But in the course of dealing with disputes which had arisen in Corinth, Paul reveals a close familiarity with earlier traditions. Pride of place among them is enjoyed by the primitive statement about Jesus' death and resurrection (1 Corinthians 15.3–7). Paul says quite precisely that he 'handed on' at the first what he himself had 'received' (15.3); both of these verbs reflect the language of Jewish traditional learning, in which accurate recollection and faithful transmission were held to be essential. He then states the tradition itself: Jesus died for our sins, was buried, and rose again in fulfilment of scriptural promises (15.3, 4). His appearance to Peter, the twelve, more than five hundred people, James, and 'all the apostles' is also attested (vv. 5–7). Lastly, Paul refers to his own experience of the living Jesus as the final element in the traditional list. The diversity of those named as witnesses of Jesus' appearances after his death helps to explain why the Gospels offer differing collections of stories about the resurrection. In any case, 1 Corinthians presents the earliest written account of the resurrection in the New Testament, in that the Gospels were still in their formative stages when Paul wrote it.

Paul uses the language of traditional learning to introduce his account of the last supper, as well (1 Corinthians 11.23–5). Notably, he claims he received this tradition 'from the Lord', which apparently refers to Jesus. This reference suggests that Paul appreciated the continuity of his preaching with what Jesus taught: an authoritative chain of tradition bound them together. Of course, the ultimate basis of authority, in Paul's mind, lay in his experience of Jesus as God's son. But once that acceptance was granted, the tradition derived from Jesus was also authoritative.

Chapter seven of 1 Corinthians provides a good example of the authority Paul accords a traditional saying of Jesus. He cites Jesus' prohibition of divorce (7.10, 11), which is similar to what can be read in the Synoptic Gospels (see below). But Paul then faces up to the question of people married to pagan unbelievers (7.12–16): if the unbelieving spouse separates, that is to be accepted. Separation should not be sought by Christians, but if it happens, believers are not bound by the marital union (7.15). In this instance, Paul attempts to apply Jesus' view of marriage to a situation in the Hellenistic world which the Palestinian Jesus did not address; what results is strong counsel against divorce, but not an absolute prohibition. Paul here develops and applies Jesus' teaching much as a Pharisee might have interpreted Torah, because traditional teaching had then (as now) to be addressed to ever new situations. When Paul gives advice to the unmarried (7.25–40), however, he has to admit, 'I have no command of the Lord' (v. 25). That is, he recognizes that Jesus said nothing that can be applied to their situation, and so gives his own opinion (v. 25) as one who has God's Spirit (v. 40b).

Paul's advice against marriage is thoroughly uncongenial to most people today. It also seems out of keeping with the primeval commandment that human beings should 'be fruitful and multiply' (Genesis 1.28); Jesus himself based his teaching about marriage on the positive statement in the Torah that male and female form a single unit in marriage, or 'one flesh' (see Matthew 19.4–6 and Mark 10.6–9, with Genesis 1.27; 2.24). For Paul, however, believers of his day faced a radically new situation, 'the appointed time is shortened' (1 Corinthians 7.29). The 'time' or 'moment' (*kairos*) Paul has in mind is the future coming of Christ to judge the world, in comparison with which any ordinary relationship pales into insignificance (7.26–35).

In common with other Christians, Paul believed that the resurrection of Jesus was not the end of his ministry, but the beginning of a triumphant victory (see 1 Corinthians 15.20–6). The risen Christ was but the 'first product': those who belong to Christ are to be raised when he comes again and destroys every force which resists him (15.23–5). As will be seen in chapter three, this vivid teaching of a grandiose future judgement was not unique to Paul. It was part of the traditional Christian preaching, and was even believed by Jews, although without reference to Jesus. As a Pharisee, Paul may already have expected God to judge the enemies of Israel in an ultimate manner, and his call caused him to see that any such event must occur through God's son, the Jesus he preached. Paul's advice about marriage is therefore not based on any stated aversion to sexuality, but is derived from a firm conviction that the end of ordinary life is so near that worldly connections of any sort are only an unnecessary encumbrance (see 1 Corinthians 7.29–35). To him, the impending end was distressful enough (v. 26); further anxieties were to be avoided (vv. 32–5).

In his preaching of Jesus, the teacher who was killed, rose again, and who will judge everyone, Paul represented the main stream of the apostolic message. Although he stressed his independence of other apostles in order to insist on the revelatory basis of his apostolate, the content of his teaching had a traditional basis, and he professed to have seen the same Lord who appeared to the other apostles (see 1 Corinthians 9.1 as well as 15.5–8). Just as Jesus' first followers had been sent to heal on behalf of the kingdom, as well as to preach it (see Matthew 10.1–15; Luke 10.1–12, discussed in chapter one), so Paul claimed that 'signs' attended his ministry (see 2 Corinthians 12.12). Of course, the shift in the content of preaching, from the kingdom of God to Jesus' future coming, was a radical one. But this shift, which was largely based on the experience of Jesus' resurrection, was not Paul's invention. It nonetheless has implications which will concern us in chapter seven, and Paul was no less radical for sharing his stance with others. Readers of Paul, no matter what their belief or unbelief, simply must bear in mind the author's belief that he saw the risen Jesus, who died for our sins and rose according to God's promise, and that the same Jesus will judge the world. This radical appraisal of the ultimate significance of Jesus, and of the complete insignificance of worldly ties, is a fundamental assumption of Paul's thought.

Paul's conflict with other Christian teachers

Paul's radicalism, however, does not only lie in his passionate acceptance of a profoundly supernatural belief in Jesus as God's son. He is also to be considered radical because his particular interpretation of that faith brought him into conflict with other Christians in his time and left its imprint on Christianity thereafter. The letter to the Galatians again provides the clearest evidence of why Paul felt compelled to make a radical break with some of his contemporaries.

After his fifteen-day visit with Peter, and his meeting with James, Paul reports that he continued preaching (Galatians 1.21–4), and then returned to Jerusalem fourteen years later (2.1). The precise occasion of the second visit is not spelled out; some scholars identify it with the meeting recounted in Acts 15, where Paul and Barnabas arc sent from Antioch to Jerusalem in order to settle the question of whether Gentiles who become Christians should be circumcised according to the Mosaic custom (Acts 15.1, 2). Certainly, Paul says Barnabas accompanied him in Galatians 2.1, but the immediate purpose of the visit, in his opinion, was to describe his gospel and have it confirmed by notable Christians in Jerusalem (2.2). Circumcision, however, was also an issue, as was only natural. The cutting away of the foreskin from the penis of every male was laid down in the Torah as the means by which God's covenant, his agreement with his people, should be recognized by Jews (see Genesis 17.9–14). On this point, there could scarcely be equivocation; any failure to circumcise is said to break God's covenant, to refuse the divine promise (Genesis 17.14). It was perfectly reasonable that those who saw in Jesus the fulfilment of God's covenant with Israel should demand that all Christians, Gentiles and Jews alike, should bear the mark of the covenant. However reasonable it may have seemed to some, it was not the opinion of Paul.

Paul does not here defend his own position at first, but lets the facts of his visit to Jerusalem tell the story of his deeply felt antipathy to any requirement that Gentile Christians should be circumcised. He says that Titus, who was a Greek believer he brought along, was not compelled to be circumcised (Galatians 2.3). Within Greek culture, of course, the human body was considered a beautiful form, and circumcision seemed a kind of maiming. It was not unknown for Jewish athletes, who – like their Gentile colleagues – competed naked, to undergo painful operations to cover the embarrassing marks of their circumcision. For Paul however, to remain uncircumcised was not a matter of taste, but a fundamental freedom guaranteed by his true gospel to Gentiles; those who argued Titus should be circumcised are condemned as 'false brothers' (Galatians 2.4, 5). Paul takes it that these Jewish Christians, who were doubtless sincere from their own point of view, were defeated. James, Peter, and John, the very 'pillars' of the community, accepted Paul's gospel as one which should be preached to the uncircumcised, while Peter concentrated on those who were circumcised (2.6–10).

Such an agreement could not have lasted very long, under the best of circumstances. In principle, one can distinguish between Christians who keep the Torah and those who do not, but in practice the two groups are bound to meet. That, according to Paul, is precisely what happened at Antioch (Galatians 2.11–16). At Antioch, Christians of both groups were represented, and – as was the habit in the early Church – they ate together. Common meals were a particular sign of the intimate fellowship felt among believers, and a way of deepening that fellowship. But Jews who ate with Gentiles, whether in or out of a Christian context, were breaking with their own customs. Because Torah condemned anyone who refused circumcision and said he should be 'cut off from his people' (Genesis 17.14), eating with such a person was wrong. He was 'unclean', and any food he prepared was probably 'unclean', as well. The language of 'clean' and 'unclean', which is central to much rabbinic literature, strikes many people today as arbitrary, and even superstitious. But 'clean' in ancient Judaism referred to what could approach God within his covenant, while anything 'unclean', be it a person or an object, was alien to God and his promises. Under the ordinary understanding of what it meant to live by the divine covenant, therefore, eating with

Gentiles was wrong and dangerous. Apparently, the teaching of Jesus himself was not understood to have overturned this aspect of Jewish religious sensibility.

The Jerusalem meeting had not settled this issue, but Paul clearly felt that the agreement about circumcision implied that Gentiles and Jews could eat together. If the great 'pillars' of the Church gave him and Barnabas 'the right hand of fellowship' (Galatians 2.9), how could fellowship be denied to the Gentiles Paul and Barnabas evangelized? The custom of mixed table fellowship became established in Antioch, and Paul says that even Peter fell in with the habit when he went there (2.12a). But then some people came who were associated with James, and Peter separated himself from mixed fellowship (2.12b). Paul was outraged, and, as he says, 'opposed him to his face' (Galatians 2.11). His anger does not seem to have mellowed much over time, because he still insists that Peter acted out of mere fear of those who were for circumcision and its implications for table fellowship (2.12b).

Peter does not give his side of this argument anywhere in the New Testament, but it seems very harsh to write him off as a frightened coward. Those from James' circle may well have convinced Peter by argument that the agreement about circumcision did not set aside normal Jewish rules of fellowship at table. As a matter of fact, Paul admits that 'the rest of the Jews', and even Barnabas, were – as he says – 'implicated in the hypocrisy' (Galatians 2.13). What Paul called hypocrisy could be seen as a sensible compromise. In fact, Paul seems to have been in a minority of one, and divided from his own missionary colleague (Barnabas), in resisting the compromise. The majority – including Peter and Barnabas, who had assented to the agreement made in Jerusalem – obviously did not feel that the principle of including the Gentiles in the Church should be taken to override covenantal ordinances for Jews. Peter and Barnabas may have felt a tension between the two principles (which caused them to vacillate), but they did not wish one to set aside the other completely.

Paul reacted so negatively to any such compromise that he publicly confronted Peter (Galatians 2.14a). His first objection was that Peter acted hypocritically; he gave Gentiles the impression he was one of them, and then expected them to tolerate his separation according to Jewish customs, and therefore to accept such customs (2.14b). But Paul's second point is far more profound, and expresses the nub of his position (Galatians 2.15, 16). Even Jews who accept Jesus, Paul argues, know that they are not made righteous by observing the law; their righteousness, their acceptability to God, comes solely from their faith in Christ. That is the basic truth of the gospel which those who sided with Peter falsified (2.14a), and which Paul claimed consistently to maintain (2.5). In effect, Paul makes his own experience a model for Christian believing generally. Both before and after his commissioning as an apostle, he saw Jesus and the law as antipathetic; from that point onward, however, any claim of Torah was relativized by the absolute revelation of God in his son. Just as Paul had to give up his devotion to the law, the Torah as written and interpreted, in his recognition of Jesus as God's son, so all those who professed Christian belief were to renounce any authority apart from that of Jesus Christ.

Up to this juncture in Galatians, Paul's case rests almost entirely on his own experience, and on his readers' acceptance of his apostolic authority. Clearly, however, the Galatians had good reason to wonder whether Paul was right; he was, by his own admission, a relatively recent convert to the faith he once persecuted, and he was opposed by Peter, associates of James, and Barnabas. Paul required to back up his position with other arguments in order to prevail, which is what he proceeds to do. In an exposition which is as brilliant as it is difficult to follow, Paul rests his case on Abraham, the very patriarch with whom God made his covenant (Galatians 3.6–22).

He observes that God considered Abraham righteous because he believed in the promise that all the nations of the earth would be blessed through him (Galatians 3.6–9, see Genesis 12.3; 15.6). It would have strengthened the argument at this point to remind the readers that circumcision only appears later in Genesis as a sign of an already established faith; in a less hectic state of mind, Paul later said precisely that (see Romans 4.10, 11). Nonetheless, Paul is able to establish that faith was the basis of the covenant made with Abraham, and he takes that covenant to be in the nature of promises which cannot be annulled (3.15–18). Certainly, the law of Moses does not annul them; that came at a much later stage (3.17), and is subsidiary to the initial promise. To Paul's mind, the covenantal promise of a blessing for all nations finds its fulfilment in Christ (3.16).

Paul is here attempting to establish, on the basis of Scripture, a radically new understanding of the covenant with Abraham. Instead of a promise which Jews keep faith with by observing the law, the covenant becomes those promises addressed to Abraham, and now being fulfilled in Christ. The obvious question is: then why was the law given at all? Paul poses just that question to himself in Galatians 3.19, and goes on to give an answer (vv. 19b–22). Law in his argument is an additional feature, provided through angels at the hand of Moses (3.19). Jews commonly believed the law was given to Moses by angels, but Paul applies that belief in a creatively fresh way: because God is one, anything which passes through the hands of a mediator is derivative, not directly from the single God himself (3.20). Indeed, he claims that the law was given so as to make it clear that human action is always in the category of sin (3.22). Only the promise of the covenant, which comes directly from God, escapes the condemnation of sin. And that promise is realized by faith in Jesus Christ alone (3.22).

Paul therefore describes the Torah he once served in an extremely negative way. The law actually curses those who do not perform all the commandments (3.10, see Deuteronomy 27.26), and even the prophet Habakkuk admitted, 'The righteous man shall live by faith' (3.11, see Habakkuk 2.4). In other words, Scripture itself points beyond the law, beyond itself, to that righteousness which is based on faith in God's son. The proof of this, for Paul, is to be found in a passage from Deuteronomy 21.23, 'Cursed be everyone who is hung on a tree' (Galatians 3.13). Christ came under the curse of the law in his crucifixion in order to confirm that Abraham's blessing for the nations could be fulfilled only by faith (3.14). The precise means of Jesus' death, that is, precluded any notion that he was righteous because he conformed to legal requirements. His righteousness was either purely a matter of faith, or it was not righteousness at all.

Paul compares believers as a whole to a person who is to come into an inheritance at maturity: while a child, such a person is treated as a slave, and is under the usual chain of command in the house (4.1, 2). In the same way, he argues, we were once under the control of the ordinary forces of the world (4.3). But when God sent his son, to live under the same natural and legal conditions that impede us (4.4), he offered us the possibility of becoming sons ourselves (4.5). That is why at baptism a believer can cry, 'Abba, father!' (4.6). 'Abba' is the Aramaic familiar word for father, and Paul here refers to the well known fact that Jesus addressed God in this direct way (as in the Lord's Prayer). Christians imitated Jesus' speech, especially when they were baptized. The point was that they accepted Jesus' relationship to God as their own; each believer became a son of God in that sense (4.7). Having reached that position, Paul maintains, there is no turning back again to any other authority (4.8–11); freedom from law is the only proper condition of Christians (see 5.1).

The ethical teaching of Paul

Paul's preaching has proven to be a strong and heady new wine. The example of Marcion was given in the Introduction; he went to the extreme of maintaining Pauline theology implied that even the God of the Old Testament, as well as its Scriptures, had to be rejected in favour of Christ and the true God who is his father. Paul's statements about law seem open to the interpretation that Christianity is at base a religion without rules, in which each believer may do what is right (or enjoyable) in her or his own eyes. Shortly after he wrote to the Galatians, Paul had to address such an understanding of his teaching. In Corinth, a cosmopolitan city which was open to the many cultural influences which trading brings, an obviously free and easy morality prevailed. To Paul's disgust, Christians were sexually loose; it was even reported that one man was sleeping with his father's wife (1 Corinthians 5.1). On a charitable reading, the woman concerned was the man's step-mother, rather than his genetic mother, but Paul abhors this implicitly incestuous union. In a solemn but obscure passage, Paul instructs his Corinthian readers to meet and, when his spirit is present with the power of the Lord Jesus, 'to hand over such a one to Satan, for destruction of the flesh' (5.4, 5).

The precise meaning of Paul's language continues to provoke debate. If taken literally, it could imply capital punishment, but there is practically no possibility that the small Christian community at Corinth exercised any such power. Paul was prone when upset to use expressions which were so colourful as to be of questionable taste; his suggestion that the partisans of circumcision should castrate themselves (see Galatians 5.12) is the most notorious example. In the present case, Paul may have had no more in mind than the expulsion of the immoral Christian from the community. Expulsion is what Paul recommends for any brother who is immoral (1 Corinthians 5.11); one is not to mix or eat with any such person. God will judge all those who are outside the community (5.13); in the final judgement, they will be in Satan's power (as in v. 5). Despite his passionate language, Paul holds out some hope for the wayward brother at the end of 5.5. His spirit, at least, might be saved in the dreadful day of the Lord. But this slim hope is probably conditional on the brother's repentance, and a consequent return to community life.

Because the Church consisted in Paul's eyes of those who are on God's side in the day of judgement, expulsion was a most serious discipline. Indeed, Paul demands the withdrawal of fellowship at table in view of immorality (1 Corinthians 5.11); the discipline of James' partisans which he condemned in Galatians (2.11–13) is now recommended. Clearly, he felt that there were limits to what could be tolerated by Christians, but not the limits Peter and Barnabas agreed to. But if law was no longer to be regarded as the means of righteousness, why should such limits be set?

'Everything is permitted me,' was the slogan of those who tolerated immorality at Corinth (1 Corinthians 6.12a). That is only a half truth, Paul replies. What is permissible may not be useful, and one must never fall under the power of any authority but God's (6.12b–d). God raised Jesus, just as he intends to raise us (6.14), so that we really belong to Christ. Our bodies are, in effect, parts of Christ, as members of a body, and it is unthinkable to prostitute the members of Christ (6.15). The metaphor of believers forming Christ's body is pursued further later in

1 Corinthians, in order to argue for a co-ordinated organization of life in the Church (12.12–30). Despite the difference in ethical issues between chapter six and chapter twelve, Paul operates on the basis of a single insight about Christian ethics generally. In baptism, he argues, we accepted the pattern of Jesus' faith as our own. For all our differences, all of us, whether Jew or Greek, slave or free, accepted a single spirit (12.13), the same spirit which cried, 'Abba, father' (see Galatians 4.6). Just as we enjoyed one spirit, we were baptized to join Christ's body (1 Corinthians 12.13).

It is easier for us today to grasp the thought of believers partaking of one spirit than to understand what Paul means precisely by Christians being the body of Christ. So far, two leading features of the metaphor are plain. It is used in 1 Corinthians 6 to insist that freedom must not be used as a pretext for licentious living; immorality involves us in enslavement to impulses which do not derive from God. In 1 Corinthians 12, the metaphor is applied as a model of social harmony: our common baptism implies that egotism must be overridden by our care for and honour of one another. Scholars continue to discuss the source of Paul's metaphor of the 'body'; he may have been influenced by Hellenistic philosophy, by Jewish thought, or by some combination of antecedents. In any case, it is reasonably clear why Paul is using this language. At baptism, he argued in Galatians, Christians identified themselves with Jesus' faith in his heavenly father (see 4.6). In this sense, they became one with Christ, or were joined to his body.

The joining of believers with Christ has been variously described, sometimes as a kind of 'mysticism' or 'participation in Christ'. Such descriptions can be useful, but they have an esoteric ring about them, while Paul is arguing on the basis of a common experience of baptism which all Christians should be able to understand. It may be more helpful to think of baptism as the time when believers are *identified* with Jesus, taking his faith as their own. They would not all necessarily think they were mystically united with Jesus, or entering into a new spiritual dimension created by him; they might do so, but they could be expected to agree that, whatever else happened, they were joined with the faith of Jesus. With him, they could address God as

'Abba'. Such a profound experience of being included in a new relationship with God through Christ, the fulfilment of the covenantal promise, might well be described both as receiving a new spirit and as inhabiting a new body. Christians continued to be themselves, in all their diversity. But, from the point of view of faith, they shared a single spirit, and belonged to the body of the man whose belief they accepted.

The testament of Paul

The theme of believers' identification with Christ in baptism is pursued by Paul in his letter to the Romans. This is the most systematic of Paul's works, because it was written to a community he had not yet visited, but hoped to meet (see 15.22–5). The letter was probably written after the Corinthian correspondence, around AD 57, and represents a new maturity in Paul's position. The passionately controversial style of Galatians, and the tone of outraged dignity in the Corinthian letters, are muted, as Paul attempts to set out in a coherent manner his understanding of how God's grace in Christ is both a confirmation of the covenantal promise to Abraham (see 1.18–4.25) and a powerfully ethical force (see 5.1–8.39).

On both fronts, Paul is much more lucid than in the earlier letters, largely because he is not responding to local issues (with which his readers' familiarity is assumed), and because he is not on the defensive. In the latter part of the letter, Paul offers crucial explanations of his position. In chapters 9–11, he makes clear his absolute fidelity to the promise of the covenant, even though he no longer regards the law as a means of fulfilling it. 'All Israel will be saved' (11.25, 26), despite Jewish rejection of Christ. Paul compares Israel to an olive tree (11.16b–24); some of the branches have been cut off, and wild Gentile grafts put in their place, but the natural branches can be grafted in again. By this operation, the fundamental election of Israel (the tree originally planted) is vindicated, and – despite the question of the law – Paul still does not imagine that Christianity and Judaism are separate plants. They have a single, holy root (11.16b). The one promise to Israel is in his mind fulfilled for all peoples in Christ (see 15.8–12). On the ethical front, Paul shows that he can think in positive terms, not only in response to abuses such as those at Corinth. He develops, to some extent by means of his metaphor of Christ's body (12.3–8), a rather comprehensive recommendation to seek God's will (12.1, 2) in the organization of the Church (12.3–8), in the pursuit of caring relationships with others (12.9–21), in the acceptance of secular government (13.1–7), in the enactment of Christ's love to all (13.8–14), in regard for the conscience of others (14.1–23) and in whole-hearted generosity (15.1–13). It therefore becomes crystal clear that ethics belonged to the very essence of faith in Paul's understanding.

The engine of Paul's ethical thinking is, once again, his observation of what happens in baptism. In Romans he spells out the identification of believers with Christ even more clearly (6.3–11) than in his earlier letters. The pattern of Jesus' death and resurrection is repeated in the believer (vv. 3, 4). Just as Jesus' faith involved dying, so we who were baptized, Paul says, were crucified in regard to sin (vv. 6, 7). And Christ was raised from the dead so that we might conduct ourselves 'in newness of life' (v. 4). Our baptism means we accept a faith over which death's power has been broken (v. 9); our life of faith through Christ Jesus is directed to the service of God alone, without regard for the constraints of sin (v. 11).

Paul seems to have been very familiar with Jesus' teaching on the primacy of love (see Galatians 5.14; 1 Corinthians 13; Romans 13.8–10). Love was not to Paul's way of thinking a general attitude; and it certainly was not a matter of sentiment. Rather, the fact of accepting Jesus' faith in baptism, of being incorporated into his body, freed believers from every external authority – and every private impulse – to enact the power of Christ's love within them. As early as his letter to the Galatians, Paul could command, 'Carry one another's burdens, and so complete the law of Christ' (6.2). Such an injunction seems odd, coming in a letter which attacks devotion to law. But 'the law of Christ' is for Paul no external authority, no impediment between the believer and God, but 'faith working through love' (Galatians 5.6). The love taught by Jesus, and appropriated by accepting his faith in baptism, has a logic of its own, a ruling force which might be called 'law'. To preach anything more, any other principle, was to enslave Christians to a new external master; to act under any impulse but Christ's love was to be enslaved by one's internal oppressor, the power of sin (see Romans 6.12–23).

Paul is without question the most demanding writer in the New Testament. A passionate intellectual, he forged an account of salvation in Christ which was true to his own experience, to his evaluation of God's covenantal promise to Israel, and which addressed the challenges of Christian mission on the basis of faith as he understood it. His theology was not worked out fully in advance of his preaching ministry; rather, it was developed in the crucible of success and failure, acceptance and dispute. The letters which have here been considered manifest a considerable evolution in Paul's position. That evolution appears even greater when one takes into account letters written before (1 Thessalonians), during (Philippians, Philemon) and after (Colossians, if Paul indeed wrote it) the period of the correspondence here cited. Nonetheless, the central conviction that in Christ the believer enjoys the fulfilment of God's covenant, and acts accordingly, belongs to the essence of Paul's thought.

The honour in which Paul was held in the early Church is attested by the books which bear his name, but which he himself did not write: Ephesians (and perhaps Colossians), 2 Thessalonians, 1 Timothy, 2 Timothy, Titus. The last three documents are known as 'the Pastoral Epistles', in view of their fatherly tone and their attention to the order of the Church. The quiet, settled authority of these letters contrasts with the lively polemic of Paul's major works, and the style is much simpler. To some extent, the fact that these letters are addressed to specific friends might explain the change in tone and style, but their focus on administrative matters seems strange for Paul. Even more strikingly, the author of the Pastorals has some rather un-Pauline things to say: 'And we know that the law is good, provided one uses it lawfully' (1 Timothy 1.8). In the end, of course, such a statement is not out of keeping with Paul's position, since he believed Christian love fulfils the law (see Romans 13.10). But he normally shied away from making the law in itself a positive ethical standard, as in 1 Timothy. The Paul of 2 Timothy 1.3 announces that he serves God 'with a clear conscience from my ancestors'. One might say that, with advancing years, Paul came to a new confidence about his relationship to God after his commission to preach Christ, but where is the agonized conscience of the man who confessed he had persecuted the Church in his zeal for ancestral tradition (see Galatians 1.13, 14)? Niggling doubts about expressions in the Pastorals, together with their distinctive tone, emphases, style and setting, have brought many scholars to the conclusion that Paul did not dictate them directly to a secretary, as in the case of the authentically Pauline letters.

Documents which inventively claim to be written by a great authority are called 'pseudonymous', which means 'falsely named'. It frequently comes as a shock to be told that, in fact, documents included in the New Testament were not written by their putative authors. But many Jewish documents of the period, some of which will be mentioned in chapter three, were pseudonymous, and pseudonymity is also a feature of Hellenistic literature. By means of this technique, an author imbued with regard for the thought of an authoritative teacher could address new situations and defend his master against possible misunderstandings. That appears to be the programme of the Pastorals in particular, where Paul's reputation is vigorously defended. No one reading them could easily believe the charge that Paul was simply a rebel against the law who was unconcerned with ethical issues. To say a document is pseudonymous in no way diminishes its value for an understanding of the New Testament; a pseudonymous book is a later development of the teaching originated by the person under whose name it has come to us.

Paul's radical account of Christian faith was such that, once it was accepted, a break with Judaism became inevitable. Even as Paul wrote, Jews were laying the basis for that thoroughly Torah-orientated understanding of the covenant which he attacked (see chapter five). It is notable that, by the time of the Pastorals, the adjective 'Jewish' can be used without explanation of teaching which is to be avoided (see Titus 1.14). Usages of that kind betray a situation very different from Paul's, when the unity of all people in a single covenant, given to Abraham and fulfilled by Christ, was the apostle's dominant concern. The easy assumption that Judaism and Christianity are just totally different religions is challenged by Paul's radical thinking.

By the same token, Paul's vehement rejection of law as a

sufficient force in ethical living was not a mere plea to use a new law carefully; he insisted that neither Jews nor Gentiles should serve any master but God (see Galatians 3.23–9 and 4.8–11). There would be nothing Pauline about spurning the Torah in order to erect a new edifice of law. The Pastorals to some extent, in their address of a new situation, give comfort to an anti-Semitic tendency: everything that is negative is ascribed to the Jewish law, while the Church is permitted to develop its own code. Of course, this tendency is not fully expressed in the Pastorals, but they represent a development which could lead in that direction.

In the event, the second century saw the emergence of Christian anti-Semitism. Whatever the appeal of that tendency, and whatever nurtured it, it represents a betrayal of Paul. Paul understood clearly that the problem posed by law is faced by everyone, because it is endemic to humanity (see Romans 2.12–16), and he certainly did not portray law as a merely Jewish alternative. Baptism for him represented the call to be a new sort of person, for whom the old legal divisions into Jew and Greek, slave and free, male and female, no longer have any real meaning (see Galatians 3.27, 28). Fundamentally, Paul did not reject Judaism, any more than Jesus did, and to see him as anti-Jewish is a travesty of his teaching. It cheapens his radicalism to imagine that his only concern was to dispute with Jews in order to found a new religion based on its own legalism. For him the root (or *radix* in Latin, from which the term 'radical' is derived) of faith is that promise to Abraham which is confirmed in Christ. Jesus' faith in his father, sealed by his obedient death on the cross and vindicated by the resurrection, offered to all people the prospect of becoming children of Abraham, sons of God. To accept that faith by baptism implied a radical rejection of every authority which attempts to mediate between the believer and God, and an equally radical commitment to life in the spirit and body of Christ. Paul's thought is not easily appreciated by any religious group which regards its own customs and rules rigorously, as expressions of God's will; in essence, it is no more threatening to Judaism than to any institution which is based on law. Apparently, it was even difficult to grasp for Peter and Barnabas, which is a measure of its radicalism.

FOR FURTHER READING

A readable introduction to Paul's theology and letters is provided by J. A. Ziesler, *Pauline Christianity*: The Oxford Bible Series (Oxford and New York: Oxford University Press, 1983); a still more accessible treatment of Pauline themes is M. D. Hooker, *Pauline Pieces* (London: Epworth Press, 1979; in America, the work was published as *A Preface to Paul* in New York: Oxford University Press, 1980). Issues particularly related to the Corinthian and Galatian correspondence are addressed by J. W. Drane, *Paul: Libertine or Legalist? A Study in the Theology of the Major Pauline Epistles* (London: SPCK, 1975). On the general question of Pauline thought, a work which has become standard, despite its difficulty, is D. E. H. Whitely, *The Theology of St. Paul* (Oxford: Blackwell, 1974). A simpler treatment is L. E. Keck, *Paul and His Letters*: Proclamation Commentaries (Philadelphia: Fortress Press, 1979). A more biographical treatment is provided by G. Bornkamm, *Paul* (London: Hodder and Stoughton, 1975).

Useful commentaries (in the last case, an exposition) on the letters mentioned in this chapter include C. E. B. Cranfield, *Romans. A Shorter Commentary* (Edinburgh: T. & T. Clark, 1985); F. F. Bruce, *1 and 2 Corinthians*: New Century Bible (London: Oliphants, 1971); C. K. Barrett, *Freedom and Obligation. A Study of the Epistle to the Galatians* (London: SPCK, 1985).

The vexed question of Pauline chronology is addressed in two recent, technical studies: R. Jewett, *Dating Paul's Life* (London: SCM Press, 1979 and Philadelphia: Fortress Press, 1979); G. Lüdemann, *Paul, Apostle to the Gentiles: Studies in Chronology* (London: SCM Press, 1984 and Philadelphia: Fortress Press, 1984).

3

The Church Awaiting the Lord

The Pastoral Epistles, for reasons mentioned in the last chapter, are widely considered to represent later developments of Paul's thought, perhaps near the turn of the first and second centuries. Even at this period, however, there was a keen expectation that the order of the world was to pass away in the face of God's judgement. 'Know this,' the author of 2 Timothy warns, 'that in the last days hard times will arrive' (3.1), and he goes on to describe the dreadfully inhuman attitudes and the dangerous teachings he anticipates (3.2–9). But this anticipation does not derive from a generally pessimistic fear that things are getting steadily worse. The point is that degeneration is the sign that these really are the *last* days before the judgement. After them comes the rule of Christ, who is 'about to judge the living and the dead' (4.1). In 2 Timothy (see 4.8), as in 1 Corinthians (see 5.5), the 'day' of the Lord is the longed for moment of judgement, when a divinely righteous order will supersede the decadent injustice of this world. The word for 'last' or 'end' in Greek is *eschaton*, and the name 'eschatology' is given to teaching of God's final judgement. The eschatology of the New Testament is one of its most striking and persistent features, and no account of its religious character can reasonably ignore it.

Vigorously eschatological teaching is already to be found in the Old Testament, among the Prophets. The New Testament's hope for the end of all things cannot be understood apart from earlier, Jewish developments. The last chapter of Isaiah promises the appearance of God himself in fire in order to judge (66.15, 16). Idolatry is to be punished by destruction (66.17), but those who support Israel – even Gentiles – are to be involved in a glorious procession to Jerusalem, the place of God's holy mountain (66.18–21). The universal aspect of this promise is stressed in

66.23, in the statement that 'all flesh will come to worship before me', but Jerusalem is the consistent focus of the promised vindication. At the same time, God's judgement is not limited to the terms and conditions of this world; it is also a new creation, involving new heavens and a new earth (66.22).

The last chapter of Isaiah is a mature expression of prophetic eschatology, and belongs to a section of the book (chapters 56–66) which was composed well after Isaiah's death, perhaps around 530 BC. But the passage cited articulates the abiding belief in God's justice, his intolerance of evil and commitment to good, which underlies biblical eschatology in general. The God of Israel was indeed conceived to be the creator of all things, light and darkness, good and bad (see Isaiah 45.7), but he was no impersonal force to which morality did not matter. On the contrary, God's choice of Israel as a people to manifest his righteousness was in the nature of a covenant, a binding agreement to bless those who keep faith with him (see Isaiah 61.8, 9). The final judgement of God was to be in keeping with his just nature, and his commitment to Israel, but it also – if necessary – could include a new creative act by God. Because God was the ultimate and moral power behind all things, total destruction and new creation were seen to be part and parcel of his judgement. Eschatology normally involved a transcendent hope, one which looked beyond the ordinary limits of life in its focus on God's future vindication.

Apocalyptic eschatology

Just before, and during, the period of the New Testament, Jewish eschatology entered a new and exciting phase. The book of Daniel represents this development most clearly within the Hebrew Bible. The transcendent theme of eschatology is still there, but it is expressed in a new key. One reason for the change of key involved in Daniel is that the historical conditions of Israel had become almost intolerably inconsistent with God's promise of blessing. In 167 BC, the king from the Seleucid dynasty (which derived from Alexander the great) took possession of the Temple, prevented the appointed sacrifices, and offered a pig on the altar in homage to his own god. This was a cruel blow to those who hoped God's vindication would be centred on the Temple, particularly because it came after a long, slow build-up in Israel's national status. The events of the real world seemed totally out of keeping with God's promise.

The book of Daniel offers reassurance that the old eschatological hope is still valid, despite experiences to the contrary. It is pseudonymously written in Daniel's name, a figure allegedly from the sixth century BC, and so takes the perspective of the distant past. Daniel is presented as having a vision of the future in chapter seven. There, four beasts represent the great empires which were to rule from Daniel's time (Babylon, Persia, Media, and Greece). The last beast is particularly dreadful, and different from the rest; it has many 'horns', which represent individual rulers who owed their power to Alexander, including the Seleucids (7.7, 8). By means of Daniel's vision, the experiences of the present were put in perspective, and its final note is one of victory. After the beasts are seen, a description of God on his throne follows (7.9, 10), and the beasts are said either to be destroyed or to be set on the brink of destruction (7.11, 12). 'One like a son of man', a human being, is then presented to God (7.13); to him total dominion is given (7.14). The meaning of the entire vision is then explained to Daniel: the beasts are the great kings who are to rule, and after them dominion will belong to the people of God (7.17–27). By taking the perspective of a figure from the past, the book of Daniel conveys the sense that history between the time of the seer and the present has been under divine control, despite its unpleasantness. Moreover, because the events described are a visionary prediction made in the past, credibility is gained for the new hope that foreign domination is about to be destroyed, to the benefit of God's people. The most striking feature of the eschatology taught in Daniel is its visionary expression. Certainly, the prophets of Israel had from time to time claimed visionary experiences (see Isaiah 6.1–13), but here almost the entire content of the teaching is claimed to derive from a vision. And while the prophets were generally concerned with the immediate application of God's will to Israel, the Danielic seer is rather consumed with the elements of the vision itself. Indeed, the point of the vision is that, as long as the beasts' power endures, the dominion of God must await its consummation. Victory is to be won, not in immediate, historical struggle, but in faithfully enduring hardship until the visionary conflict is ended. The belief that historical events correspond to heavenly realities is not an innovative teaching in Daniel. Even in the book of Judges, for example, Deborah's victory is said to be occasioned by God's involvement (5.4, 5). But in Daniel the vision is not a mere glimpse of an image, as in the Old Testament generally. The vision rather forms a coherent (if cryptic) whole, which the reader must understand to grasp the message of the book.

In essence, the vision of 'Daniel' comes as a divine revelation, complete in itself, not as a prophecy which demands immediate action. Such a work is called an 'apocalypse', from the Greek word for 'revelation', and teaching of this sort is known as 'apocalyptic'. Daniel presents several features which are normally characteristic of apocalyptic works: they are frequently pseudonymous, filled with symbolic or heavenly images, and ascribed to angelic mediation. It should be stressed that apocalyptic writings were not exclusively concerned with issues of eschatology. Their 'revelations' might refer to the foundations of the world, the constitution of the universe, or the lay-out of the angelic court around God. Concerns of this kind cannot be explained completely with reference to the strain put by historical conditions on the prophetic hope in God's judgement. Alongside that factor, there is another, more positive influence. By the time apocalypses came to be written, Jews had come to acquire the religious vocabulary of Babylonia, the place to which many were exiled after the destruction of the Temple in 587 BC; there the heavenly realm was described as a reality distinct from the human world (see 1 Enoch). When this language was applied within Jewish eschatology, the result was a lively hope that the divine and human realms would one day coincide: 'And those who teach wisdom will shine as the firmament, and those who make many righteous as the stars, for ever and ever' (Daniel 12.3).

Belief in the ultimate coincidence of the divine and human realms implied that existence itself would be altered: resurrection was a common feature of apocalyptic teaching (see Daniel 12.2), while it was not a promise developed fully by the prophets. In the Synoptic Gospels, Jesus is said to have compared resurrected people to angels (see Matthew 22.30; Mark 12.25; Luke 20.36), and this is but one example of the deep influence of apocalyptic teaching on him, and on Judaism generally. But apocalyptic eschatology has another, more esoteric aspect. The book of Daniel had predicted to the discerning reader the global domination of Israel after the slaughter of the Seleucid 'beast'. However reassuring that may have been during the second century BC, it proved to be an embarrassing statement: the ebb of Seleucid power brought in its wake the domination of Rome. And although Herod, the client of Rome, renovated the Temple, in AD 70 it was set ablaze by the legions of Titus. The specificity of apocalyptic teaching left its claims vulnerable to the bruising impact of history. However comforting the world of vision was when taken on its own terms, its claim to predict hard reality never proved very successful.

The work known as 4 Ezra (2 Esdras 3–14 in the Apocrypha) places itself some thirty years after the destruction of Jerusalem (3.1), and was probably composed in its final form near the end of the first century AD. Explicit mention is made of Daniel in 12.11, 12, in order to claim that additional explanation is being given to 'Ezra', the pseudonymous seer of the book. The visionary imagery of 4 Ezra is even more complicated than what we find in Daniel, but the evident reference is to Roman rule, at the end of which the triumph of the Messiah from the seed of David is promised (see 4 Ezra 12.31–4). The next chapter centres on the vision of a heavenly man who comes with the clouds of heaven (13.3); he is identified as a figure kept by 'the Most High' (13.25, 26), his own son (13.32, 37, 52) who will rule from Zion (13.35, 36) by the power of the law (13.38). The figure is clearly to be associated with the 'son of man' in Daniel 7, who also comes with clouds (7.13) and is the seal of victory for 'the saints of the Most High' (7.18), but the additional features of the Ezran 'man', and his virtual equation with the Messiah of chapter twelve, are innovative. As will be seen later in this chapter, the Danielic figure of the 'son of man' also makes its appearance, with innovative features, in the New Testament. The vision of 'Ezra' proved no more durable in its particulars than that of 'Daniel'. A Jewish revolt in AD 132, which lasted three bloody years, resulted only in yet another conquest, the systematic redesign of Jerusalem by the imperial forces, and the dedication of a Roman temple there. Nonetheless, 4 Ezra clearly demonstrates that the power of apocalyptic teaching, and its appeal to the religious imagination, could endure catastrophic failures.

The Revelation of John

Of all the books in the New Testament, none is more apocalyptic than the Revelation (also known as the Apocalypse). There are, however, certain traits which make the Revelation stand apart from Jewish apocalyptic literature, even without our taking its Christian stance into account. First of all, it is not pseudonymous, at least not in the sense that Jewish apocalypses are. The 'John' identified as the recipient of the vision (Revelation 1.1) is not an ancient worthy, but a contemporary (or nearly contemporary) Christian. The intention of the text may be to identify the seer with the 'beloved disciple' of the fourth Gospel, but that is far from certain. If such a claim is intended, the style, tone and content of the Revelation are so distinctive that it must be doubted. But even so, the Revelation would be pseudonymous more in the sense 2 Timothy is than in the sense Daniel is. For this reason, it might be useful to say that the Jewish apocalypses are 'pseudepigraphic', written at a long chronological remove from the people they are attributed to, while the Revelation is at most pseudonymous, written by a near contemporary of the John it is ascribed to. Secondly, the Revelation takes the form of a letter (see 1.4), which by the time of writing was apparently a fairly standard form of communication among Christians. More specific advice is given to particular communities than is normally the case in apocalyptic writings (see chapters two and three), and this ethical emphasis gives point to the book's claim to be 'prophecy' (1.3). But, even after these unusual elements are considered, the book's substance must be seen as apocalyptic: it is the work of an inspired seer (1.10–16) whose angel (1.1) makes known to him visions which are replete with the symbolic and heavenly figures, the angelic wars, and the scheme of God's final triumph, which are the stock and trade of the Jewish apocalypses. As in the case of 4 Ezra, the Revelation appears to have been written (probably near the end of the first century) after the destruction of the Temple in AD 70. In the light of recent events, the seer can confidently say there will be no temple in the new Jerusalem which comes from heaven (21.22). Apocalyptic works, whether Jewish or Christian, seem typically to have been produced as a consequence of serious assaults on the Temple. Threats to the ordinary intercourse between God and his people were seen to call for new, extraordinary revelations.

John's initial vision is of one 'like a son of man' (1.13), which is reminiscent of Daniel 7 and 4 Ezra 13. But this human-like figure is described in far greater detail in the Revelation (1.12–20), and at times the imagery used implies his divine status. For example, the mention of 'white hair' in 1.14 corresponds to the description of God himself in Daniel 7.9. Because this vision is John's opening revelation, it sets the tone of the book as a whole, and the authority of this one like a son of man is the basis on which John writes to the seven churches in chapters two and three. The figure therefore dominates proceedings more than in Daniel and 4 Ezra, where it is more an image of what will happen than an authority in itself. The reason for this substantial difference is made plain in 1.18: the one like a son of man is he who died, and yet is alive, the risen Jesus. On this basis, the seer claims to write 'a revelation of Jesus Christ' (1.1, and see vv. 2, 5), in which the Lord himself speaks (22.16).

As in the Jewish apocalypses, the one like a son of man is not merely a visionary figure, but bears the promise of future vindication. In Revelation 14, a climax is reached in a series of visions (contained in chapters twelve and thirteen) which predict the divine victory over Satan and the Roman Empire. The latter is in mind when the fall of 'Babylon' is spoken of in 14.8; 'Babylon' is attested as a cipher for Rome in apocalyptic circles, which was used in order to avoid giving the impression that revolt against imperial authorities was being openly encouraged. (The agent of the Temple's fall in 587 BC had been Babylon, which made 'Babylon' a good designation for Rome in its capture of Jerusalem in AD 70.) The counterpart of this destruction, which engulfs all the adherents of the 'beast' of Rome (14.9–11), is the blessing of those who 'keep the commandments of God and the faith of Jesus', including those who are dead (14.12, 13). As in

Daniel 7, their victory is signalled by the triumphant appearance of one like a son of man (14.14). But in the Revelation, this figure – whom the reader knows is the risen Jesus – has an openly regal aspect. He bears a golden crown, as well as a sharp sickle of judgement, and is *seated* in the manner of a monarch, rather than standing (as an attendant would be). The keen expectation that the risen Jesus is soon to come in victorious splendour is underlined at the end of the Revelation as the central hope of the entire work: 'The one attesting these things says, "Surely, I come quickly." Amen, come, Lord Jesus!' (22.20).

The parousia of 'the son of man'

The Greek word which normally refers in the New Testament to this second coming of Jesus is *parousia*, which means 'presence' or 'arrival'. Curiously, the term is not used in the Revelation, although the work is imbued with the idea of Christ's impending judgement. In Matthew, Jesus himself is said to speak of his own parousia (24.3, 27, 37, 39). His disciples ask the sign of Jesus' glorious coming, and of the end of the present age (24.3). He responds by warning of deceptive teachers, of strife and tribulation as the setting in which his gospel is preached (24.4–14). A mark of the final act in the drama of the world is to be the desecration of the Temple, such as is predicted in the book of Daniel (24.15, see Daniel 9.27; 11.31; 12.11). This is to be taken as a sign to flee Judaea (24.16–22), but no prophecy that Christ is in a particular place is to be heeded (24.23–6), because 'the parousia of the son of man' is to be evident as lightning in the sky (24.27). Indeed, the very forces of nature are to be dissolved (24.29) before the son of man comes 'upon the clouds of heaven' (24.30, see Daniel 7.13) to judge by means of angels (24.31). The cataclysm will be comparable to what happened in the days of Noah (24.37–41). The combination of visionary elements with predictions of the final events, in what amounts to a scenario of the end, marks out this section of Matthew as an apocalyptic discourse. Moreover, the reference to '*the* son of man', coming as it does with other allusions to Daniel 7, clearly points the reader

82

back to the Danielic figure who is 'like a son of man' (Daniel 7.13). Here, as in the Revelation (which was written shortly after Matthew), Jesus' glorious judgement is described by identifying him with imagery borrowed from Daniel.

The question now emerges: did Jesus predict his own parousia as part of an apocalyptic scenario, in the way Matthew indicates? Jesus is only portrayed as using the term parousia in Matthew among the Gospels, and then only in chapter twenty-four. It would seem that a word which was central to early Christian belief has been projected back to the usage of Jesus himself. The case seems similar to the interpretation of the parable of the sower, which was discussed in chapter one: there, too, teaching given privately to Jesus' disciples became an occasion for them to introduce their own view of the significance of Jesus' words (compare Matthew 13.10, 11 and 24.3). The word 'church' (see 16.18; 18.17) is another case in which Matthew alone among the Gospels has Jesus employ the language of the community he brought into existence. It seems particularly to have been a tendency of the first Gospel.

While Matthew uniquely attributes use of the term parousia to Jesus, all three Synoptic Gospels present an apocalyptic discourse in Jesus' name (Matthew 24, 25; Mark 13; Luke 21.5–36) which climaxes in a reference to the Danielic 'son of man' (Matthew 24.30, 31; Mark 13.26, 27; Luke 21.27, 28). As in the case of the interpretation of the parable of the sower – in fact even more so – there are significant differences of wording among the first three Gospels, and each has unique elements; the material added in Matthew (see 24.37–25.46!) is particularly distinctive. It is not surprising that we find more variety among the Gospels in the apocalyptic discourse than we do in the interpretation of the earlier parable, because the passage is much more extensive. Nonetheless, the discourse is presented much as the interpretation of the parable is. After Jesus makes a somewhat public statement (Matthew 24.1, 2; Mark 13.1, 2; Luke 21.5, 6), he is asked for explanation by his disciples (Matthew 24.3; Mark 13.3, 4; Luke 21.7). This explanation suits the apocalyptic style of early Christian teaching, such as it is represented in the Revelation, rather well. But Jesus himself seems to have resisted the temptation to link his preaching of the kingdom to a precise apocalyptic timetable; he insisted the kingdom 'does not come with observation' (Luke 17.20).

Even within the 'little apocalypse', as the discourse within the Synoptics is known, a clear warning against overly precise eschatological speculation is given. In Matthew (24.36) and Mark (13.32), Jesus bluntly states that neither any angel in heaven nor the son knows 'the day or hour' of the son of man. Luke presents a different saying at this point (21.34–6), but it expresses the same message: the day of the son of man cannot be calculated. Paul passes on explicit teaching concerning the parousia (1 Thessalonians 4.13–18), but says of its time only that it comes suddenly (5.1–3). If Jesus had really given a specific timetable of the last events, it is nearly impossible to understand why he would have warned against apocalyptic speculation. Moreover, his own timetable would surely have been authoritative for those who believed in him; on that basis, the 'little apocalypse' should determine the content of Paul's teaching, and that of the Revelation. In fact, Paul refers only to the suddenness of the parousia, not to the sequence of events in the 'little apocalypse'. And the series of visions in the Revelation follows its own course, and cannot be understood as providing mere interpretations of what we read in the Synoptics. For these reasons, it seems clear that Jesus himself was not an apocalyptic teacher, but that his message about the impending kingdom was interpreted in an apocalyptic fashion by some of his followers. This explains the variety of apocalyptic scenarios in the New Testament.

The identification of Jesus with the 'son of man' figure in Daniel 7 seems to have been a central element in Christian apocalyptic teaching. That is an importantly common feature in the Revelation and the 'little apocalypse'. The identification was by no means universal, however; Paul, for example, makes no use of it, despite his interest in eschatology. But those responsible for compiling the 'little apocalypse' appear to have used the Danielic identification of Jesus as their starting point, and an apocalyptic discourse with several allusions to Daniel was composed out of various sayings attributed to Jesus. In principle, the mechanism of compilation differs little from the way in which Matthew's 'Sermon on the Mount' was framed. When the apocalyptic discourse was produced, however, the result was to make Jesus the teacher of an eschatological scenario which he himself never subscribed to, and which many of his sayings do not accord with.

In the case of the interpretation of the parable of the sower, we saw in chapter one that Jesus' followers permitted their missionary experience to influence their presentation of what Jesus said the parable meant. But at least their innovative teaching derived from what Jesus himself taught, the parable itself. On what grounds did they associate Jesus with the figure of the 'son of man' in Daniel 7? Unless that question can be answered, we would have to say that Jesus' followers invented the connection. That would not be an impossible contention. After all, the figure in Daniel 7 exercised an important influence on the inventive speculation of apocalyptic teachers, and it would have been natural for apocalyptically inclined Christians to associate the figure with Jesus, the one in whom they saw God most decisively at work. On the other hand, the idea that the association was simply invented is out of keeping with the normal procedures which seem to have governed the process by which Jesus' sayings were handed on.

In the event, there is clear evidence that Jesus did refer to himself by means of the usage, 'the son of man'. By itself, however, the phrase does not refer to Daniel 7. In Aramaic, 'son of man' simply means 'a human being', or humanity in general; because the equivalent of the definite article is much more common in Aramaic than in English (or Greek), the phrase also appears as 'the son of man'. An Aramaic speaker, such as Jesus, could speak of 'the son of man' in order to refer to people in general, including himself. An example of this usage is provided in the Jerusalem Talmud (Shebiʿith 9.1, see also Midrash Rabbah, Genesis 79.6 and Ecclesiastes 10.8) under the name of a rabbi of the second century AD: 'Not even a bird perishes without the will of heaven. How much less the son of man.' Rabbi Simeon is here seen to make a general statement, but it applies particularly to himself, as a fugitive from Roman persecution: on the strength of his belief in divine protection, he departs from the cave in which he has been hiding.

To refer to 'son of man' in the sense of 'mankind' is precedented in the Hebrew Bible, and so comes as no surprise as a rabbinic idiom. Psalm 8.4 provides the best known example:

'What is man, that you remember him, or a son of man, that you attend to him?' There is even some biblical precedent for an individual being referred to in this way; the book of Ezekiel consistently has the prophet addressed by God as 'son of man'. But the Aramaic idiom, instanced in the last paragraph, is the nearest analogy to some of Jesus' sayings in which 'the son of man' is referred to. As in the case of Rabbi Simeon, a general application, as well as a self-reference, is implied by the usage.

Somewhat in the manner of Simeon, Jesus urged his followers to see that God's care reached even to sparrows, so that they should not fear (Luke 12.6, 7). In this case, however, 'the son of man' idiom is not used. On other occasions, however, Jesus did employ it. A prominent instance is the saying, 'Foxes have dens, and birds of heaven have nests, but the son of man has nowhere to lay his head' (Matthew 8.20; Luke 9.58). The degree of self-reference achieved by the phrase is greater than appears in the saying of Simeon, because it only makes sense as applying first of all to Jesus. And Jesus' usage cannot be applied in a thoroughly general sense, since there are, obviously, people who do have places to lie down. But the saying has some general applicability, because it is directed to potential disciples (see Matthew 8.19; Luke 9.57); they, too, must be prepared to share the homelessness of Jesus, and therefore to forego what we can precisely call creature comforts such as human beings might normally expect. In sayings of this type, Jesus seems to have adapted an Aramaic idiom to speak of himself, and of those who followed him.

Not all of the 'son of man' sayings in the Gospels can be explained on the basis of Jesus' adaptation of the Aramaic idiom. Aside from the sayings which allude to Daniel 7, there are some which challenge any general application. An example is Matthew 11.18, 19; Luke 7.33–5, where Jesus contrasts himself (and no one else) to John the Baptist; in this case, self-reference seems to be the only point of the usage, not only the main point. Allowing for this sort of exception, among others, there is nonetheless ample evidence to maintain that Jesus called himself 'the son of man' as a matter of course (see also Matthew 16.21; Mark 8.31; Luke 9.22). He probably did not use it to associate himself with any particular figure, but to mark himself out as a human being chosen and sent by God. On that basis, Christians with apocalyptic inclinations took 'the son of man' Jesus referred to as the equivalent of 'one like a son of man' in Daniel 7. The progression seems perfectly natural, once the usage of Jesus and the apocalyptic tendency of the early Church are taken into account. Research and debate on this question must continue, but a growing tendency within the New Testament to apply Jesus' idiom in an apocalyptic sense does seem evident.

The 'little apocalypse' in the Synoptics is attached to Jesus' prediction of the Temple's destruction (Matthew 24.1, 2; Mark 13.1, 2; Luke 21.5, 6). That Jesus spoke against the Temple seems evident; it even figured in the charges brought against him before the authorities in Jerusalem prior to the crucifixion (see Matthew 26.61; Mark 14.58 and, in a different context, John 2.19). But the events leading up to and including the actual destruction of the Temple in AD 70 occasioned a flowering of apocalyptic work, as in the instances of the Revelation and 4 Ezra, much as the desecration of the Temple in 167 BC had occasioned the vision of 'Daniel'. The 'little apocalypse' seems to be a part of that development, which resulted in Jesus' sayings being welded into an apocalyptic scenario.

Eschatological reserve in early Christianity

The Revelation and, to a lesser extent, the 'little apocalypse' give expression to the sort of eschatological fervour which also gripped Jewish groups of the same period. Jesus' refusal to commit himself to a single apocalyptic scheme resulted in a variety of schemes being taught by early Christians. But the bulk of the New Testament refrains from apocalyptic speculation, even when the issue at hand is eschatological. That reserve may derive from the reticence of Jesus, and stands in some contrast with the highly specific teaching of both Jewish and Christian apocalypses.

Among the later documents of the New Testament, reserve in respect of apocalyptic speculation is manifest in the first letter of Peter. Although this communication to a series of churches in Asia Minor is ascribed to Peter (1 Peter 1.1), it appears pseudonymous in its present form. The author quotes freely from the

Septuagint, while we would expect Peter to show at least some familiarity with the Bible in Aramaic, even if he could write in Greek. And the literary style of the letter is remarkably fluent in comparison with the standard of the New Testament generally. By a frequent use of participles, the author is able to achieve the long, flowing sentences which were a hallmark of good Greek style, and he employs more forms of verbs and more participles than are found when writers used Greek only as a second language.

In fact, the author occasionally overreaches himself in his attempt to attain an elevated style. He sometimes uses participles when a form of the imperative would be appropriate, and elects clumsily to begin some sentences with relative pronouns ('who', or 'which'). When he instructs his readers, 'gird up the loins of your mind' (1.13), it is difficult to escape the impression that a metaphor has got the better of him. The author also has an interest in Church order (see 5.1–5) which is reminiscent of the Pastorals (see 1 Timothy 3.1–13; Titus 2.1–6). Although the extent to which 1 Peter reflects the disciple's teaching is difficult to judge, since there are no writings which come directly from Peter's hand, the letter seems at best a derivative version of his position. This impression is confirmed by the observation that 1 Peter seems to betray the influence of expressions incorporated in other books in the New Testament, such as Matthew (5.11, 12, see 1 Peter 4.13, 14), John (20.29, see 1 Peter 1.8), and Romans (13.1–7, see 1 Peter 2.13–17). On the whole, the letter presents the author's understanding of Petrine teaching in attractive Greek, using the established language of Christian belief. The letter is normally dated near the end of the first century, during the general period in which the Revelation was composed.

At the close of the letter, the author states his purpose: he wishes to urge his readers to stand fast in the grace of God (1 Peter 5.12). The 'grace' he has in mind is not merely the present experience of God's support, but the specific assurance that God will exalt believers after they endure suffering (5.6–10). The emphasis on suffering is explicable once it is realized the letter addresses a context in which Christians are persecuted (see 3.14–16; 4.12–16), as does the Revelation. The purpose of these trials, according to the author, is that believers' faith – as metal refined by fire – might be rewarded 'in the apocalypse of Jesus Christ' (1.6, 7). It is precisely in this apocalypse that God's 'grace' will be manifest (1.13); 'grace' is, once again, an eschatological reality.

The author understands the reward of believers to be stored in heaven, and awaiting revelation in the final moment of history (1.3–5). To him, it is evident that 'the end of all things has come near' (4.7), and that the ordeal of Christians (4.12) is but the beginning of God's judgement (4.17). The convictions that the hope of faith is already in heaven, and that contemporary events represent the unfolding of God's judgement, are features common to 1 Peter and the Revelation. But the author of 1 Peter does not engage in a visionary depiction of the heavenly reality he is sure exists, nor does he specifically relate such visions to historical experience. At both points, 1 Peter is crucially different from the Revelation, and it distances itself from central features of apocalyptic writing generally.

The eschatology of writings such as 1 Peter definitely involves an expectation of God's imminent judgement, and is expressed by means of features also familiar to us from apocalyptic literature. But the absence of anything remotely similar to the visionary scenarios of Daniel, the Revelation, and 4 Ezra makes 1 Peter seem non-apocalyptic, even though vividly eschatological. A similar stance is taken up by Luke in Acts, especially when he has Paul speak. In Acts 17.30, Luke presents Paul as insisting that the previous ignorance of the Gentile audience has been overlooked by God, so that the present is a moment for repentance. But repentance is not merely motivated by the assurance that the past is no longer an obstacle to acceptance by God: there is also an element of threat in the statement that God has set a day to judge by means of the same Jesus he raised from the dead (v. 31).

Luke's statement, attributed to Paul, is illuminating in two respects. First, in that it is directed to a Gentile audience, the suggestion may be made that eschatology was of wider interest than one might at first imagine. Indeed, the Paul of Acts uses the threat of an eschatological 'day', warranted by the resurrection, as the linch-pin in an argument designed to bring about his Athenian hearers' repentance, which is the very object of his preaching (see 17.16–21, 34). Educated citizens of the Hellenistic world are therefore expected to give attention to eschatological teaching. Second, there is a remarkably restrained quality in the language of Acts 17.31. Although definite expression is given to a firmly eschatological hope, there is no hint of apocalyptic imagery, much less an apocalyptic scenario. The statement is much more bare than the teaching of 1 Peter, and also lacks the full description Paul was willing to engage in (compare 1 Thessalonians 4.15–18; 1 Corinthians 15.20–8). The reserve is so heightened that even the imminence of the judgement is not emphasized: the fact of the judgement is presented as more important than its time.

The appropriation of eschatology in a Hellenistic setting is also portrayed by Luke in his description of the response to Paul of the Roman governor named Felix (23.24; 24.10). Felix can be addressed as 'honourable' (23.26; 24.3), the very word Luke himself uses when addressing 'Theophilus', the alleged recipient of the Gospel (1.3) and Acts (1.1). Felix is, therefore, the sort of person the literary work as a whole has in mind as someone who might be sympathetic to the preaching about Jesus. When he summons Paul to hear about the Christian faith (24.24), Paul is said to speak about 'righteousness and self-control and the coming judgement' (24.25a). The reference to a future judgement seems eschatological, but the emphasis of this account of Paul's message falls on its ethical aspect. Although the reference to eschatological judgement gives bite to Paul's ethical teaching, and is sufficiently vivid to frighten Felix (24.25b), there is no apocalyptic embellishment in the passage.

What Felix is told in Acts therefore amounts to an eschatological teaching, shorn of apocalyptic imagery, which is closely linked to ethical instruction. His reaction to Paul is mixed. He is chastened (24.25b), but he also hopes for some payment from his prisoner (24.26a). Although unconverted, he engages in frequent conversation with the apostle during the two years prior to the replacement of Felix by Festus (24.27). Luke, writing around AD 90, portrays by means of Felix the kind of intelligent, but sceptical, reaction which Christians might expect from their Hellenistic neighbours. Although Luke is aware that Paul was handed over to the Roman authorities with execution in mind (see the prophecy of Agabus in Acts 21.10, 11), he ends Acts with a picture of Paul in Rome supporting himself, receiving guests, preaching the kingdom, and teaching about Jesus (28.30, 31). Authorities such as Felix do not become Christians, but they are tolerant enough to permit Christian teaching. By addressing his two-volume work to 'Theophilus', an actual or imaginary official, Luke argues that the kindly treatment of Paul amounts to a precedent which should be followed. The meeting of Felix with Paul is interesting because the governor is both frightened and intrigued by the combination of ethical and eschatological teaching. Luke therefore portrays Felix's mixed reaction to Paul in part as a response to eschatology.

Conclusion

The settings of documents in the New Testament can to some degree be deduced by considering the type of eschatological teaching they espouse. Jesus' confident expectation of the kingdom was sometimes expressed in vivid images, some of which are similar to what can be read in apocalyptic literature. But the 'little apocalypse' in the Synoptic Gospels and the Revelation manifest the creative introduction of an apocalyptic scenario into the teaching of Jesus. Jewish apocalyptic books such as 4 Ezra indicate that certain groups cherished scenarios of the end, and confirm that they thrived in the period after the Temple was burned. On the other hand, the apocalyptic strain in the New Testament is far from dominant. 1 Peter attests a vividly eschatological orientation which may express itself in apocalyptic imagery, but which declines both the scenario of the end time and the convention of the seer's vision which are essential features of apocalyptic eschatology. A strongly ethical stress is also expressed in 1 Peter, as the author offers comfort, support, and warning to Christians who are under severe pressure for their beliefs. Luke, particularly in what he has Paul say to Gentiles in Acts, demonstrates that eschatology had a place in early Christian preaching, even when the conventions of Jewish apocalyptic teaching exerted little or no influence. The ethical emphasis becomes dominant in this sort of Christian eschatology, and the future is described in much more sober language.

The variety possible within eschatological teaching in the New Testament undermines any attempt to discover a single eschatology which could be described as the standard. To make the Revelation the measure of what Jesus taught would cause us to ignore his refusal to trade in apocalyptic scenarios, which seems to have been a characteristic feature of his teaching. By the same token, there is an apocalyptic richness in the Revelation which demands to be read in its own terms, as vision, letter, and prophecy; there is no way responsibly to limit the seer's message to those few elements he happens to share with Jesus' sayings about the kingdom. Originality is also apparent in the eschatological teaching of 1 Peter and Acts; the hasty resort to a standard, be it Jesus' view or the Revelation's, would only tend to reduce our sensitivity to original features. Each document, or tradition within a document, must be permitted to express its particular eschatology.

The eschatology of the New Testament is not only various. It is also resilient. The fact that many speakers and authors felt free to shape their own eschatological teachings does not mean that eschatology was an optional component in early Christian preaching. The case is very much the opposite. There is no major document in the New Testament which does not press a clear eschatology, usually one which approximates to one of those described in this chapter. It is all too easy for modern readers to enthuse over the ethical teaching of Jesus or Paul, Luke or the author of 1 Peter, and to leave aside their eschatological teaching. Eschatology is frequently ignored altogether, or treated as a category quite distinct from substantive matters such as how people come to be saved. The Revelation is difficult to read precisely because its eschatology cannot be bracketed out as one reads. Yet a consistent feature of eschatology in the New Testament, as expressed in sayings of Jesus, the 'little apocalypse', the Revelation, 1 Peter, and Acts, is its close connection to ethical teaching.

The teachers and writers who were responsible for the New Testament did not see 'the last time' as a moment for abstract speculation regarding what would happen next. Rather, their conviction that God was about to act in a definitive way gave their ethics an edge, and their teaching an urgency. Their understandings of how and when God was to intervene did vary considerably, so that contrasting, even contradictory, attitudes towards apocalyptic conventions can be perceived. But such diversity only underlines the consensus shared by Christians (and many Jews) that the world as they knew it would dissolve. Comparison of their expectation is sometimes made with today's scenarios of nuclear war, which can seem almost apocalyptic in their complexity. Indeed, some Christian teachers in the United States have recently produced apocalyptic scenarios of their own, occasionally by identifying the visionary beasts of Daniel with powerful modern nations. Whatever the appeal of such schemes, the frequently heard claim that they bear the authority of the New Testament is a figment either of ignorance or of deception. The simple fact is that the eschatology of the New Testament is too diverse to be comprehended in any one scheme, and a good deal of Jesus' teaching is not patient of apocalyptic treatment. Moreover, the historical reference of Daniel to Seleucid power, and of the Revelation to Roman power, cannot be wished away by the desire to see in them, for example, prophecies of Soviet influence.

Eschatological or apocalyptic literature can no more be understood correctly by refusing to see it in its historical setting than can any other sort of literature. If, for example, the 'little apocalypse' associates the parousia with the fall of the Temple, the task of the reader is to discover why that association is made, not to pretend the fall of the Temple was a symbol for another, later event; attempts of the latter sort are more designed to vindicate the New Testament than to understand it. Christian readers particularly quite often feel challenged by the apocalyptic element in the New Testament, because predictions were made which evidently did not come to pass. Rather than face up to the challenge of critical reading, some students will instinctively try to make their text predict some event which is not referred to, but which did occur. The price of such a programme is that the meaning of texts is sacrificed to the meaning readers wish texts to have. The fundamental hope of eschatology in the New Testament is that God will bring this world to a close. That expectation was not simply a cause for dread, as in the case of nuclear war; it was a matter for fervent anticipation. In the minds of the teachers and writers who contributed to the New Testament, God was remaking the creation. The manner in which that claim was made may strike us as strange, and may even seem to have been contradicted by the two thousand years of surprising, but ordinarily ambiguous, human history that lies between the texts and us. But eschatological fervour was a prominent feature of early Christian faith at every level; both its forceful vigour and its naively erroneous predictions belong to what any reader must learn to appreciate.

FOR FURTHER READING

The range of approaches to apocalyptic thinking is represented by P. D. Hanson (ed.), *Visionaries and their Apocalypses*: Issues in Religion and Theology 2 (London: SPCK, 1983 and Philadelphia: Fortress Press, 1983). For a fuller, historical study, see W. Schmithals, *The Apocalyptic Movement, Introduction and Interpretation* (Nashville: Abingdon, 1975) and the simpler, more restricted work of P. S. Minear, *New Testament Apocalyptic*: Interpreting Biblical Texts (Nashville: Abingdon, 1981). G. W. E. Nickelsburg, *Jewish Literature Between the Bible and the Mishnah: A Historical and Literary Introduction* (Philadelphia: Fortress Press, 1981) offers a useful introduction to much of the ancient literature involved in the discussion of apocalyptic teaching.

The challenges of interpreting the Revelation have proved too great for many commentators, but G. R. Beasley-Murray, *The Book of Revelation*: New Century Bible (London: Oliphants, 1974) may be recommended. Discussion of the 'son of man' idiom is necessarily complicated. The treatment of B. Lindars, *Jesus, Son of Man. A Fresh Examination of the Son of Man Sayings in the Gospels in the Light of Recent Research* (London: SPCK, 1983 and Grand Rapids: Eerdmans, 1984) is remarkably lucid, despite its technicality. A more accessible, but now somewhat dated, summary is given in the seventh chapter of G. Vermes, *Jesus the Jew. A Historian's Reading of the Gospels* (London: Collins, 1977).

1 Peter is usefully treated, along with other writings of interest on this topic, in J. N. D. Kelly, *A Commentary on the Epistles of Peter and Jude*: Black's New Testament Commentaries (London: A. & C. Black, 1969). In the case of Acts, see F. V. Filson, *Three Crucial Decades: Studies in the Book of Acts* (London: Epworth Press, 1963 and Richmond: Knox, 1963).

4

Which Translation?
And How to Use It

English-speaking readers have recourse to many versions of the New Testament in their native language. A recent estimate puts at seventy-five the number of fresh editions which have appeared during the twentieth century alone. Of course, ever new English versions are devised partially in order to satisfy the tastes of consumers. In addition to wanting their Bibles in different sorts of binding and with various kinds of print, people also have preferences for distinctive styles of English. What seems stately to one person may appear archaic to another, and vigorous writing is praised by some readers as 'relevant', only to be denounced as 'trendy' by others. But disputes of that kind are less important from the point of view of understanding the New Testament than they are from the point of view of assessing the likes and dislikes of modern readers. The first question on a critical reader's mind is whether the translation to hand is accurate, not whether it is attractive.

Accuracy has in fact been the primary goal in the great projects of translation engaged in by British and American scholars since the fourteenth century. During that time, changes have had to be introduced in the critical understanding of the text of the New Testament. There have been three principal reasons for such changes. First, the stock of ancient manuscripts of the New Testament available to scholars has been increasing, sometimes at a very quick rate; discoveries are still being made, and much ancient material in libraries awaits proper cataloguing. At the moment, some five thousand Greek witnesses (as early manuscripts of an ancient text are called) may be consulted, and altogether they disagree in many thousands of readings. Almost all the best manuscripts were collected after 1611, when the Authorized (or King James) Version was published. Obviously, the cataloguing and evaluation of new readings has a profound effect on the Greek text a translator begins with, and so on the translation which is produced. But the second reason translations have been altered is that the English language has changed. When readers of the Authorized Version are told by Paul in Romans 13.13 to avoid 'chambering', they are probably perplexed. The translation happens to be excellent, and its gist can be appreciated when it is remembered that, in the seventeenth century, the main (or only) piece of furniture in a 'chamber' was a bed. But no version can be considered adequate when the language it translates into has ceased to be understood. Finally, translators have had to reckon with the emergence of different theories of translation. Whatever theory one adheres to will directly influence one's practice in translation.

Policies of translation

This third factor in translation, the translator's own understanding of what she or he is doing, requires further consideration. It seems straightforward to say that discoveries of manuscripts might alter the text of the New Testament which is translated, and also that changes in the English language may require adjustments in translation. But many people believe that the process of translating itself does not change. In their minds, the translator's business is simply to put the words of one language into the words of another. Basically, that procedure is indeed the ideal, but there is nothing simple about it. Anyone who has studied a foreign language knows all too well that English words do not equate directly to, say, German words or French words. Every term has a range of meanings and uses in its own language which may partially – but not completely – correspond to the meanings and uses of another term in a different language. The lack of direct equivalents between one language and another requires that words be translated variously, according to their contexts. Does '*der Mensch*' in German mean 'human being'? The answer to that question is 'yes', provided the meanings 'person' and 'one' are kept in mind. A more subtle example of the difficulty is provided by '*ça va*' in French, which may indeed be translated 'it goes', but the phrase is more frequently used to say 'I am well' in response to a question. In view of the complex relationship between any language and any other language, translators are very wise to ask, 'Just what is expected of us?'

The question of a policy of translation is especially pressing because languages can be so fundamentally different from one another. They not only have different words which mean different things in different contexts. They also relate those words to one another in different ways: the order of speech in Greek, for example, is notoriously difficult for speakers of English to adjust to. And even matters which seem basic, such as tense, can fluctuate from language to language. By means of various tenses, we refer in English to past, present, and future actions. But in Greek, tense seems to have been as much a way of speaking of *how* action was done, as when it was done: the result is that two perfectly competent translators may put the same Greek form in a given passage into different English tenses. Generally speaking, Greek tenses can be assigned English equivalents without much strain, but there are enough difficult cases, where Greek forms in context can be variously construed, for translators to wonder how best to proceed.

Enough has already been said to indicate that, in the nature of the case, a translation cannot be truly 'literal'. Because there is no precise equivalence between one language and another, any attempt at exact, word-for-word translation will only result in the production of nonsense. On the other hand, it is quite reasonable for a translator to discover formal correspondence between the language she or he is translating from and the language she or he is translating into. By 'formal correspondence', translators mean similarities in words and other linguistic structures. But they realize that these similarities are not identities; considerations of context will cause them to adjust their translations. Translators of the New Testament will bear in mind that the Greek term *logos* frequently corresponds to 'word' in English, but they must remember at the same time that 'account', 'speech', and 'reason' are other possible renderings. Similarly, they will know that the Greek tense known as the 'aorist' generally corresponds to the simple English past tense, but that the aorist is sometimes used of emphatic action in the present. The discovery of such 'formal correspondences' between one language and another therefore does not reduce the translator's task to recognizing the functional equivalents between two languages. Rather, she or he must constantly bear in mind the range of correspondences which a given formation might have, and be guided by a consideration of context in making a final decision.

The limits involved in discovering formal correspondence are most obvious when it comes to the translation of idioms. An 'idiom' is a usage which is peculiar, or nearly peculiar, to the language in which it appears, so that it has no formal correspondent in the language one is translating into. In the Gospel according to John, when Jesus' mother tells him that wine at a wedding had run out, he replies with an idiomatic expression. A formally correspondent, or 'literal', rendering would give us, 'What to me and to you, woman?' (John 2.4). Uses of this phrase elsewhere in the Old and New Testaments indicate that it is a Semitic idiom which speakers used in order to put people off. Aware of the usage, the translators of the Revised Standard Version (which will be discussed below) render the passage, 'O woman, what have you to do with me?' Their translation is partially based on the awareness that 'to you' in Greek can suggest possession ('what have you?'), and 'to me' is not distinguishable from 'with me' in that language. But they have shaped the wording so that it reads as a negative retort to Mary, which is indeed the appropriate rendering in context.

Although the translation offered in the RSV has a negative ring, it does not represent an idiomatic English usage. For this reason, it succeeds as a formally correspondent rendering, but fails to deliver the punch which a Greek reader would have felt behind the usage. After all, the expression is elsewhere used by demons to ward off Jesus (see Mark 1.24; Luke 4.34, and Matthew 8.29; Mark 5.7; Luke 8.28), by a woman to rebuke the prophet Elijah (1 Kings 17.18), and by an Egyptian ruler to ridicule Josiah, king of Judah (2 Chronicles 35.21). Faced with the task of representing the force of this idiom, the translator might well decide to dispense with formal correspondence, and try instead to use an English idiom of similar vigour. Such a procedure might be described as dynamic transference, and is employed both in the New English Bible and Today's English

Version (both of which will be discussed below). The translators of the NEB therefore render the idiom in John 2.4 as 'Your concern, mother, is not mine,' while the translators of TEV opt for the still tougher phrasing, 'You must not tell me what to do.'

Attempting dynamic transference is obviously a less objective procedure than pursuing formal correspondence. As in all instances of translation, the translator must make decisions based on an experience of both the language she or he translates and the mother tongue. In instances of dynamic transference, which is frequently required in the rendering of idioms, the job of translation also takes the translator into the subjective realm of deciding how the impact made by a phrase in one language can be approximated in another language. Such a dynamic transference is hardly objective, but it is often necessary. Otherwise, the rendering offered might be 'accurate' only in the sense it is relatively free of error, and seem dry and laboured as compared to the original wording the translator is supposed to be representing. Both the NEB and TEV seem to succeed better than the RSV in the case of the idiom in John 2.4.

The attempt at dynamic transference, however, must not be confused with paraphrase. 'Paraphrase' describes the attempt of a translator or reporter to put someone else's idea into new words. Paraphrases can often be found in newspaper articles and more popular works of history. Inevitably, such reports convey what the original speaker or writer was thought to mean, rather than the exact sense of the initial communication. When a politician makes a speech which is reported in newspapers of different political complexions, readers will probably differ on what the speech amounted to. Reporters and editors shape our impressions of current events by what they omit, explain, quote directly, or put into their own words. The reported form of a speech is usually more exciting than the original, and is almost certainly briefer, but the politician who made it might very well be surprised with the end result. For the purpose of critical reading, paraphrases of the New Testament should be avoided. They are more concerned with conveying translators' impressions of texts than with rendering those texts themselves.

An example of the paraphrase of John 2.4 is provided by the Living Bible. In that paraphrastic version, Jesus' abrupt statement is weakened almost beyond recognition. When he says to his mother, 'I can't help you now,' the rebuke contained in the Greek text is transformed into a promise for the future. Linguistic justification for the rendering is absent; the meaning has been arrived at by attending more to the way the translator wished to see Jesus than to what the text actually says. In fact, the Living Bible did not begin as a fresh rendering of the original Greek manuscripts of the New Testament, but as a freshly worded retelling of the English Bible according to the principles of conservative Evangelicalism. Obviously, the rendering of John 2.4 has the advantage that Jesus' hard words to his mother need not be explained; they are homogenized into what the gentle Jesus of pious imagination might have said. Such an approach is at odds with the task of critical reading, and for this reason the Living Bible cannot be recommended for study.

The weaknesses of paraphrase are by no means limited to the versions which are openly paraphrastic. The translation of the Living Bible, 'I can't help you now,' may sound excessively pious, but the translation of the New English Bible, 'Your concern, mother, is not mine,' would be worthy of an old-fashioned British schoolboy. The translators were apparently moved by the desire not to make Jesus appear harsh, because they render the expression in a much more direct fashion when the speaker is anyone other than Jesus. The rendering of the NEB at 1 Kings 17.18 ('What made you interfere?'), or at 2 Chronicles 35.21 ('What do you want with me?'), are much better examples of the principle of dynamic transference in action. The latter expression is in fact used as the model by the translators for rendering the use of the same expression by demons. The identical model is used in Today's English Version, except when Jesus is the speaker. As has been mentioned, John 2.4 is instead rendered by the somewhat softer command, 'You must not tell me what to do,' and the address 'woman' has been omitted from the initial translation of TEV, presumably to avoid the charge that Jesus was a sexist. Clearly, those responsible for both the NEB and TEV modify the expression suggested by dynamic transference when Jesus is the speaker. In this case, the translators have introduced a degree of paraphrase into their work. To the extent that the practice of dynamic transference leads to such lapses, it should be practised with care. In John 2.4, the expression, 'What do you want from me, woman?' (an expression commonly found in American English), is perhaps the best idiomatic counterpart of the original idiom. In North America, particularly New York City, 'What do you want from me?' is not a genuine question; it is a rhetorical refusal to deal with the person addressed.

The ways in which formal correspondence is pursued, dynamic transference is practised, and paraphrase slips into them both, can perhaps be seen most easily in the translation of difficult idioms. But cases of that kind are only the tip of the iceberg. The same principles and habits which translators develop in order to render an idiom are the basis on which they render the whole of the New Testament. Their techniques determine how their readers see and understand the text, especially because the majority of those who are interested in the documents do not read Greek. For this reason, it is vitally important to appreciate the technique of translation which resulted in the version one reads, and the purpose that version was written to serve.

Some widely used versions

By way of considering some versions which are widely in use, their renderings of Romans 13.10b will be assessed. Translated according to formal correspondence, that text would read simply, 'therefore love is law's fulfilment'. Curiously, none of the translations most widely in use follows that straightforward model.

The Authorized Version, or the King James Version, was published in 1611. Its aim, under the guidance of the Hampton Court Conference in 1604, was to secure a translation of the Bible on which the various factions of the English Church could agree. A broad spectrum of scholars collaborated to refine the work of their predecessors in the English tradition of biblical translation. The dedication of the translators to the principle of formal correspondence was such that words were printed in italics when the English rendering did not represent a term in the Greek text consulted. At Romans 13.10b, the AV gives us, 'therefore love *is* the fulfilling of the law'. The use of italics, however, can only be a rough and ready guide to what is and is not present in the Greek text. In Greek, the verb 'is' frequently is implied, rather than stated, so that there is no reason why attention should be called to it here. On the other hand, there is nothing in the original which explains why 'the' should be introduced before 'fulfilling' and 'law', and why the word should be 'fulfilling', rather than 'fulfilment'.

The questions about 'the' and 'fulfilling' are answered, however, when the sentence is read in context. In chapter thirteen of Romans, Paul addresses ethical instruction to his readers. They are urged to support civic systems of justice and taxation, since such authorities enjoy the warrant of God himself (13.1–7). In the last analysis, however, Paul insists that love is the only basis on which we can be said truly to owe anyone anything (13.8a); the act of loving one's neighbour is what fulfils 'law' (13.8b). To this point, regulations of a civic nature have been the focus of Paul's argument, so that 'law', or 'custom' (as the term might also be translated), presumably refers to such requirements of an ordered society. But in 13.9, he goes on to quote from the Torah in order to identify these requirements, both as prohibition (against adultery, murder, theft, and covetousness, see Exodus 20.13–17 and Deuteronomy 5.17–21) and demand (for love, see Leviticus 19.18). The 'law' Paul thinks of as fulfilled is associated with the Torah, as given to Moses; it is '*the* law' he has in mind, not custom in general. Likewise, the fulfilment he speaks of in 13.10b is not a generality, but the completion of the commandments he mentions; it is 'the fulfilling', the act of putting love into practice. The Greek word 'fulfilment' (*plērōma*) may refer either to the action of completing or the fact of completion; the translators of the AV made the appropriate contextual decision in accepting the first alternative.

The Authorized Version was by no means a faultless product when it was first published. Thousands of small changes were made during the seventeenth and eighteenth centuries in order to produce a smoothly flowing translation, which – together with Shakespeare – was until recently a standard of good, written English; but the achievement embodied in the AV became all the more apparent when efforts were made during the nineteenth century to revise it. Two principal considerations made revision necessary. First, the Greek text rendered in the AV is known as the Received Text, which is attested in manuscripts from the medieval period. After the AV was published, textual discoveries made it increasingly plain that the Received Text could not be accepted as original in many cases. Second, the language of the AV had become so unfamiliar to many readers over the course of time that a thorough modernization was urgently needed.

To answer these needs, the Revised Version of 1881 (New Testament) and its American counterpart of 1901 were produced. Unfortunately, they were only partially successful. The translators often retained the outdated phrasing of the AV; when they did depart from their model, their commitment to formal correspondence resulted in the production of an often stilted and dry style of English. On the other hand, the Revised Version and the American Standard Version (as its North American counterpart was called) reflect the practice of textual study in their time, while the translators of other major versions have generally tended not to engage as seriously in textual questions. The advances of both versions were largely preserved in the Revised Standard Version, of which the New Testament appeared in 1946. The translators of the RSV had more textual evidence available to them than had been accessible ever before. Unfortunately, a consistent policy was not adopted for coping with the evidence, so that the textual value of the RSV is uneven. The language of the RSV is, however, superior to that of the RV or the ASV. The dedication to formal correspondence is less slavish and the translators were willing to return to the wording of the Authorized Version (and other translations) in order to render the original in vigorous, readable English.

The actual wording of the Revised Standard Version at Romans 13.10b is, in the event, identical with that of the Authorized Version. Indeed, in 13.8–10 as a whole, the two versions differ primarily because the verbal forms of the RSV are modern (without such wording as 'worketh' and 'shalt', as in the AV), and its language is both more up to date and slightly more explanatory. The success of the RSV in capturing the sense of the original in fluent English is demonstrated by its ecumenical usage. American Protestant churches initially commissioned the translators, and the Apocrypha was not rendered as a matter of course. But in 1952, the Episcopal Church formally requested that the Apocrypha be included, and the way was paved for a Catholic edition of the RSV, which appeared in 1966. In 1973, the Common Bible was published, in which works regarded as canonical in Orthodox churches were also included. There was certainly a price to be paid for widening the appeal of the RSV. The rendering of some passages was altered in the light of doctrinal considerations, and the Received Text was increasingly permitted to override critical study of the manuscript evidence. Jesus' 'brothers', who are referred to in Matthew 12.46; Mark 3.31; Luke 8.19; John 7.3, become 'brethren' in the Catholic edition, to avoid giving offence to those who hold to the perpetual virginity of Mary. And the so-called 'longer ending' of Mark (16.9–20) is accepted in the later editions. Both steps, which are only examples of many similar moves, represent a retreat from critical acumen. The meaning of 'brother' in Greek is clear; to alter its sense just because Jesus is involved goes far beyond the linguistic procedures proper to translators. And the 'longer ending' of Mark (discussed below) has been recognized since the nineteenth century as a late pastiche of elements taken from the other Gospels. The Gospel originally ended with the stunned silence of the women at the tomb (16.8); the desire for a fuller account, complete with appearances of the risen Jesus, arose when Christians felt that Mark was lacking something which other Gospels provide. That the RSV has become the basis of an ecumenical English Bible must be welcomed. It represents a point at which critical discussion from almost any Christian perspective may begin. But its obvious faults and compromises clearly demonstrate that, while it may provide a focus for critical reflection, it is certainly not to be taken as the definitive rendering of the most primitive manuscripts of the New Testament.

The New Testament of the New English Bible was first published in 1961, and represents a new policy of translation as compared to the RSV. The NEB is a fresh rendering, not a revision, and it is guided by the attempt of its British translators to express the original text intelligibly. Their technique therefore relies more on dynamic transference than on formal correspondence. They achieved an attractive, literate style which makes the NEB extremely popular among educated readers. In the Authorized Version and the Revised Standard Version, clarity had been attained, but often at the expense of not communicating in idiomatic English. Even the statement, 'therefore love is the fulfilling of the law,' while clear enough, is hardly the way most speakers of English would express themselves. Accordingly, the translators of the NEB put Romans 13.10b into their own words: 'therefore the whole law is summed up in love'.

From the point of view of formal correspondence, their translation seems very daring. The adjective 'whole' does not appear in any manuscript of the Greek text, the noun 'fulfilment' has been made into the verbal phrase 'is summed up', and the verb 'to love' becomes a preposition with a noun ('in love'). Each transformation, however, is defensible as an account of the sense which the Greek statement would have in English. Because Paul has been speaking of discharging both civil responsibilities and the commandments of the Torah, he is clearly using 'law' in 13.10 in a broad sense, to include the requirements of justice generally. Just that breadth of meaning is communicated by saying 'the whole law'. 'Is summed up' may at first seem an odd way of rendering 'fulfilment', but the translators are here trying to put across the impact the noun has in its context. Because Paul presents love as the force which 'does not work evil to one's neighbour' (13.10a), it is what effects the maxim, 'You shall love your neighbour as yourself.' That statement from Leviticus 19.18 is, according to Paul, what sums up the commandments as a whole (13.9). Love is the power within the statement which summarizes the Torah; it is, in effect, itself the summary of law. That is the contextual logic of Paul's assertion which the translators of the NEB have managed brilliantly to convey. Having committed themselves to emphasize that sense by means of the verbal phrase 'is summed up', they avoided the possible redundancy of rendering 'love' as a verb, as well. 'Love' in any case appears as a noun at the beginning of v. 10, so that it appears as Paul's principal category of thought at this point. 'In love' at the end of the verse in the NEB carries the thought through Paul's statement as a whole, and rounds the statement off nicely.

A possible objection to the translation of Romans 13.10b in the NEB is that love is made to appear as the formal replacement of law in Paul's thought. As we saw in chapter two, that clearly is not the case. In Paul's understanding, love is the seal of believers' identification with Christ; by accepting Jesus' faith as their own, they enact the love which law could point to, but which they could not effect by means of law alone. Love becomes the governing impulse in their lives, the fulfilment of that covenantal blessing which the law attested, but did not deliver. The extent to which love can rightly be styled the summary of the law in Paul's thought is therefore limited: it 'sums up' the essence, without addressing each and every particular. As he himself puts it, love does no wrong (13.10a), and in that overarching goodness, specific commandments find themselves fulfilled (13.10b). If one is aware of the immediate context of the passage in the NEB, and of its wider context in Paul's thought, one will avoid taking the translation up in the wrong way. As a rule, readers will have to rely more on appreciating context, and less on the meaning of individual words, when they come to interpret translations which are based more on dynamic transference than on formal correspondence.

The desire to achieve idiomatic English style may, however, result in a translation which is misleading, no matter what context it is read in. In 1966, the American Bible Society published *Good News for Modern Man*, the New Testament of a rendering of the Bible known as Today's English Version. The translation is deliberately less literary than that of the NEB, because it is designed, not merely for native speakers of English, but for all those throughout the world who must rely on that language, however well they know it (perhaps only as recently acquired), for their knowledge of the Bible. The vocabulary of TEV is accordingly simple, and its grammar direct. Less attention is given to literary context than in the NEB, and much more to the discovery of punchy English equivalents of the original Greek phrasing. The result, in the case of Romans 13.10b, is the most direct rendering available: 'to love, then, is to obey the whole Law'. Unfortunately, that translation is almost certain to mislead ordinary readers of English. The use of 'whole' is legitimate, as in the case of the NEB, and 'then' sounds more straightforward than 'therefore', but it is surely unfortunate to introduce the notion of obedience here, and to limit the statement to Jewish law (the apparent implication of the capital 'L'). It makes Paul appear to say that the law defines the content of love, when only Christ does that in his thought. And the usual sense of the verb 'obey' in English has to do with adherence to an external authority, which is emphatically not Paul's understanding of the informing power of the love released in baptism.

The great virtue of the TEV, even here, is its clarity. It is not only linguistically more direct, it is also conceptually simpler than any other major rendering. Unquestionably, the idea of love being a matter of obedience is easier to grasp than that of love being the fulfilment or summary of the law. The trouble is that those who contributed to the formation of the New Testament, including Paul, were not always easy to understand. Paul would have avoided a tremendous amount of conflict if he could have equated Christian love and obedience to the Torah. That he did not do so presumably reflects his profound commitment to the radical insight that the covenantal promise to Abraham is fulfilled by Christ, not the law. No doubt, those responsible for TEV never intended to imply otherwise, but their search for the simplest rendering has here interfered with the basic accuracy of their work.

In another respect, however, TEV has a great advantage over the NEB, although it is not apparent in the rendering of Romans 13.10b. The translators of the NEB made reference to a wide variety of variant readings in the many manuscripts of the New Testament, but they did not have a coherent policy for deciding which readings to accept, and which to reject. Through its successive editions, TEV has been brought into line with the Greek text of the United Bible Societies, which has been the fruit of years of co-operation by an international panel of scholars following a reasonably consistent programme. The challenge of textual criticism will be discussed later in the present chapter, along with the reasons for which no existing text of the New Testament in Greek can claim the universal assent of scholars. For the moment, it should be stressed that those responsible for TEV have performed a signal service in basing their translation on sound and accessible textual work. For far too long, translators have contented themselves with occasional reference to variant readings; very often, unlikely readings have been noted, and important readings have been ignored. Considerable textual work stands behind the NEB, but it is often difficult for readers to understand the evidence and logic applied to particular cases. TEV does not cite anything like the full range of evidence, but it does direct the reader to the printed Greek text which is its basis, where such evidence may be considered. Hopefully, that procedure will prove to be a standard which future translators will at least try to attain.

The same year, 1966, in which the New Testament of TEV was published also saw the publication of the Jerusalem Bible in English. The work on which this translation is based was originally done in French, at the École Biblique in Jerusalem. The French rendering, published in 1956, was designed to express the meaning of the Bible in contemporary language, and the English version follows the lead of the original. Unfortunately, the translators' desire for clarity sometimes causes them to cross the line between dynamic transference and paraphrase. The rendering of Romans 13.10b is an example of this tendency: 'that is why it (love) is the answer to every one of the commandments'.

The overall construction selected to convey the thought, 'that is why . . .', is indeed idiomatic, and gives the correct impression that Paul is here rounding off an argument better than the other translations we have considered. But the remainder of the rendering in the JB, particularly the words 'answer' and 'every one of the commandments', suggests there is a direct correlation between love and individual precepts. One might argue that, since Paul believed love fulfils the law generally, he implied that there is a correspondence between love and the specific requirements made in the law. But the task of spelling out implications is better performed in commentaries than in translations, since otherwise the primary meaning of a text might be obscured. In the present case, the JB could be taken to mean that love constitutes a new code for Christian behaviour, rather than being the informing force Paul takes it to be.

A victory of paraphrase over translation was marked by the publication during the 1960s of the New Testament within the project called the Living Bible. This version is not a rendering of the Greek New Testament, but an attempt to put the English of the American Standard Version into more accessible language. The result is frequently stunning, and the LB has proved to be extremely popular among Protestants, but some of its renderings are seriously inaccurate. Romans 13.10b provides a case in point: 'That's why it (love) fully satisfies all of God's requirements. It is the only law you need.' Curiously, there is a marked similarity between this rendering and that of the Catholic Jerusalem Bible. The governing syntax of the opening ('That's why . . .') is the same, and the close association between love and specific commandments is evidence of the paraphrasing policy of both. But the finale of this verse in the LB, in which love is made formally to replace the law, represents Protestant doctrine more than Paul's thought. As we saw in chapter two, law points to a fulfilment of itself in Christ according to Paul, and is not merely set aside by baptism. The LB dispenses with the nuances of Paul's thought, and opts for the easier idea that the Jewish law belongs to a dispensation totally different from the rule of love. Whatever the merits of such a view, it cannot seriously be claimed as Paul's understanding, because he insisted that law had a definite, although partial, role to play in the salvation of all people. In this case, as in others, the original meaning of the New Testament serves the LB more as pretext than as text.

In 1973, the New Testament was published within the now complete project to produce the New International Version of the Bible. Stylistically, the Protestant translators sought to produce a rendering which was not tied to national idioms, but might easily be understood by speakers of English anywhere in the world. Moreover, the NIV represents a retreat from the ideal of dynamic transference, and a fresh attempt at formal correspondence. In both respects, the project succeeded. The NIV is generally clear, straightforward, and accurate, as the rendering of Romans 13.10b illustrates: 'Therefore love is the fulfilment of the law.' This phrasing may seem stolid as compared to the wording of other recent versions, but it corresponds well to the Greek text, and is easily understood. 'Fulfilment', in fact, is even more formally correspondent to *plērōma* than 'fulfilling' in the AV and the RSV. On the other hand, the translators have here perhaps given too little weight to the use of the term in context. After all, Paul is not speaking of love as an abstract concept which fulfils law, but as an activity; in this sense, 'fulfilling' is more accurate, as well as more fluent.

Despite their generally successful commitment to formal correspondence, the translators of the NIV have permitted a tendency towards making abstract statements to influence their renderings. The use of 'fulfilment' is one example of the tendency; another is the use of 'the' with 'fulfilment' and 'law'. The formally correspondent translation, 'love is law's fulfilment', is perfectly understandable as English, and avoids a misimpression which some readers might derive from the double use of 'the'. In English, to say 'the fulfilment' may imply that all the validity of what is fulfilled is taken over by the thing that fulfils. For example, when modern Christians say Jesus is the fulfilment of Israel's messianic hopes, the implication is that no other Messiah should be looked for. But Paul does not believe that the mere fact of love totally eradicates law; indeed, he can describe the force of love as 'the law of Christ' (Galatians 6.2). The translators of the NIV turn Paul's ethical assertion, that love is the power which enacts law, into an abstract statement to the effect that love takes over the law's validity. And by specifying 'the law', when the Greek text does not, the translators point the reader much more directly to the Jewish law than Paul does. Obviously, the NIV is here nothing like as misleading as the LB, but its stated commitment to accuracy does give the impression that words are in the Greek text which in fact cannot be found there.

As the present volume goes to press, a new edition of the Jerusalem Bible has been released, whose wording at Romans 13.10b corresponds almost exactly to that of the NIV: 'and so love is the fulfilment of the Law'. Apart from the initial two words, the new JB accords with the NIV, although 'law' is capitalized, as in TEV. Precisely the observations which have already been made in respect of the NIV and TEV, therefore, obtain in the case of the new JB. But it is worth noting that the new translation is the direct result of criticism that the JB relied too much on paraphrase, and reflected the French translation more than the Greek original of the New Testament (see the General Editor's foreword, p. v). In other words, further considerations of translational policy, such as we have offered, have directly influenced the wording which has been chosen. Although the new JB is not free of the doctrinal nuances which we have already detected in TEV and the NIV, it represents a clear return to the principles of formal correspondence. At the same time, its similarity to more recent Protestant versions reminds us that the critical task is essentially an ecumenical one.

Choosing a version

In the nature of the case, no single translation of the New Testament can be recommended as a completely clear and accurate rendering. What makes for clarity does not necessarily make for accuracy, and vice versa. But even a brief review of versions currently available suggests some rules for guidance in the choice and use of a translation.

The first rule is that critical reading requires a translation, not a paraphrase. The Living Bible, or the condensed version offered in the recently published Reader's Digest Bible, should be avoided. They are readable, often inspiring, and serve as an initial introduction to the Bible for many people. But they reflect too many of the translators' concerns, and too little of the New Testament's nuances, to be used in serious study.

Even those versions which are translations in the proper sense must be used with care. There is no such thing as the New Testament in English; there are only renderings in English, in which translators have tried as best they could to convey the sense of the original. For that reason, it serves no useful purpose to ponder the various possible meanings which an English word used in a translation might have without reference to the context in which it is actually used. After all, the writing does not employ that word; it employs a Greek term which is not the exact equivalent, but a formally correspondent or dynamically transferred usage. To consider the etymological meaning of words in the Authorized Version, for example, might help us to understand the sense of the translation better, but is a waste of time from the point of view of understanding the New Testament itself.

Readers should select a translation in accordance with their own needs. Some will wish to have the explanatory guidance offered within the Jerusalem Bible; others will be attracted to the literary sensibility of the New English Bible. The idiomatic vigour of Today's English Version will recommend itself to many, while the stricter technique of formal correspondence as practised in the New International Version has also yielded great benefits. The Authorized Version resonates with the learning and language of another age, although at the price of precision for some modern readers, while the Revised Standard Version retains much of the stately prose of its predecessor, but with greater accuracy and a more modern style.

Whichever rendering is chosen, an edition with a preface should be sought, so that the reader can be informed of the principles of translation which were followed. If formal correspondence was the guiding principle, a certain artificiality in the wording is to be expected from time to time. The reader will have on occasion to refer to the wider context of a statement in order to see just what sense the translators were attempting to convey. To call love the 'fulfilling', or 'fulfilment' of the law, as in the AV, the RSV, and the NIV, for example, is only a sensible statement when one has regard to Paul's entire argument in Romans 13. On the other hand, those versions which take dynamic transference as their preferred procedure will often introduce wording which is vivid in English, but susceptible of being taken in an incorrect way. When love is said to be a matter of obedience (TEV), or the answer to every commandment (JB), or a summing up of the law (NEB), readers of English could easily get the impression that in Paul's mind there is a direct equation between legal requirements and God's love in Christ. Again, reference to the wider context of statements is necessary. But a formally correspondent rendering often needs to be put in context to be understood at all, while a dynamically transferred rendering sometimes needs reference to context in order not to be understood wrongly.

In addition to a statement of the basic procedures which translators carried out, a good preface should also contain information as to the standard of English they have aimed to write; whether language is intended to be colloquial, idiomatic, simplified, or literary, to be used in public reading or for private reflection, will obviously influence the wording and style chosen. By being aware of these factors, readers will more easily distinguish between the tone and texture of the original writing and those of the translation they happen to be reading.

In order to keep beginners aware that translations are renderings, not originals, there is a great deal to be said for encouraging the use of different translations by the members of a given group. If it does not cause confusion, there is even a case for having various translations of a single passage read aloud. That procedure may help students to avoid developing interpretations which are too dependent on the English wording of a particular version. But those at the very beginning of their study can easily be put off or perplexed by exercises of that kind; for them, it is better to refer to a common translation, whose principles are clearly explained. Among scholars, the Revised Standard Version has long been accepted as the best rendering for use by students. It is generally clear, its cadences are reminiscent of some of the best prose in the Authorized Version, and its commitment to formal correspondence is tempered by a sound sense of literary context. It is not always as lively or straightforward as it might be, and its textual base is occasionally suspect, but the overall result is quite satisfactory. The other translations mentioned in this chapter, along with some which have not been named, can also be used responsibly. As in the case of the RSV, their limitations should be explained to students, and they do not enjoy the degree of scholarly approval which the RSV does.

The Greek text of the New Testament

In the end, of course, the surest way of approaching the meaning of the New Testament is by means of the Greek text. Knowledge of Greek has gone out of fashion in western education, even though it was the basis on which learning flourished from the time of the Renaissance. For good or ill, it is no longer possible – as it once was – to insist that students in higher education read the New Testament only after they have acquired a sound grasp of classical languages. Today, those who read the New Testament in Greek generally acquire linguistic competence while they are being grounded in the subject. The task is difficult, but quite possible. As in the learning of any language, memorization and a disciplined approach to the structure of Greek are

113

required, and there is the additional hurdle that the grammar involved is more complex than in most modern languages.

Without question, competence in Greek is the single most important tool a student can acquire in the study of the New Testament. Until it is acquired, she or he will always be in danger of reading a meaning into an English translation which is quite out of keeping with the Greek text. Although there are ways of reducing the hazards of that pitfall, for example by consulting commentaries while reading, in the end knowledge of Greek is the only way of eliminating them. While it would be unrealistic to insist that beginners should arm themselves with competence in Greek before they commence study, it is most uncritical to pretend that the original wording of the text can safely be ignored. In the present chapter, Romans 13.10 has provided a clear instance of how variously the language of the New Testament has been rendered; those different renderings would generate many divergent interpretations if they were discussed only in their own terms. The Greek text is the standard which introduces some consistency into our discussion of meaning. It is how we measure the adequacy of translations and interpretations. While every student cannot reasonably be expected to have access to this standard, every professional teacher should have some recourse to it.

Among scholars working in higher education, use of the New Testament in Greek is assumed to be regular practice. As they teach on the basis of their own renderings, their students are able to discuss divergences from printed translations. Those students who are also learning Greek have the opportunity to see the results of linguistic competence in action. Teachers in secondary schools also have elementary grammars of Greek available to them; consistent work with one of them, and a dictionary, greatly enhances the precision and depth of their teaching.

Recent advances in the presentation of Greek language enable readers at large, not merely professional teachers and students, to make a sound beginning in acquiring familiarity with the Greek text. Even the ability to look up words in a Greek dictionary greatly reduces one's dependence upon the translation at hand. Many 'interlinear' editions of the New Testament have also been published; in them, the Greek text is printed in alternative lines with an English translation, so that it is possible for those who do not read Greek fluently to see what precise words the English rendering is supposed to convey. Armed with all these aids, there is no excuse for teachers (or preachers) at any level to believe that the original wording of the New Testament is inaccessible to them.

Aside from the tremendous advantage a knowledge of Greek has for understanding the original sense of the New Testament, there is another benefit. No translation gives anything like a full range of textual variants, the actual differences of wording among the many manuscripts of the New Testament. The decision to prefer certain of these variants to others can profoundly affect one's interpretation of the text overall. It is true that a majority of them may seem so slight as to be negligible, but with the manuscripts presenting so many variants, only a tiny proportion needs to be significant for the textual criticism of the New Testament to constitute a crucially important discipline for every scholar. By way of example, the ending of Mark's Gospel might be mentioned, because there are three distinct options available, and a preference for any one of them will influence one's judgement of the literary shape of the Gospel as a whole. In some manuscripts, as has been mentioned, the Gospel closes with a bare reference to the silent fear of the women at the tomb (16.8) after a young man has told them that Jesus is risen (the first reading); in others, brief mention is then made of the women informing those around Peter of the wonderful announcement, and of the successful preaching authorized by Jesus (the second reading); in others still, an account of Jesus' appearances after his resurrection is offered (the third reading). Obviously, one's decision about the text will here influence one's literary judgement of the Gospel, as well as one's historical understanding of how stories of Jesus' resurrection came to be told.

Textual criticism cannot be practised by merely counting the manuscripts in order to see which reading the majority of them favours. Most of the existing manuscripts were written down from earlier copies in the Middle Ages; their readings are only as good as the documents which the copyists used. If a reading is the result of an error during the process of copying, its mere repetition does not make it any more acceptable. Textual critics

115

are therefore normally concerned to describe 'families' of manuscripts. A textual family is formed when manuscripts share a preference for many variants. Once a family attests a variant, it can be taken seriously as a possible reading of the text, and not merely a possible mistake (or deliberate change) made by a single scribe and transmitted to later manuscripts. Attestation of a variant by a family is a weightier consideration in textual criticism than the number of witnesses within the family. After all, the later a document was produced, no matter how accurate or inaccurate it was, the more likely it is to be available today.

As it happens, there is support from textual families for all three endings to Mark. Support for the second reading, however, is not as strong as it is for the other two, because the family involved seems to be from a period after the fourth century AD. Nonetheless, attestation by any major family should be considered sufficient to make a variant worth thinking about further.

The next step is to determine whether the variant suits the style of the document in which it is alleged to appear. Just at that hurdle, the second ending to Mark falls. It uses vocabulary which does not appear elsewhere in the Gospel, and evokes themes which are not developed within Mark as a whole. The problem of vocabulary is not as acute in the third ending, but the content of this account of Jesus' resurrection is extremely suspect. Each appearance is mentioned in a very brief way, and appears to be a summary of what can be read at greater length in the other two Synoptic Gospels, and even Acts. There are condensed references to stories concerning Mary Magdalene (vv. 9–11, compare Luke 24.9–11 [and 8.2]), two disciples (vv. 12, 13, compare Luke 24.13–35), the eleven (vv. 14–18, compare Matthew 28.16–20 and, for v. 18, Acts 28.3–6), and Jesus' ascension (v. 19, compare Luke 24.50, 51 and Acts 1.9–11). Since the condensation of stories from other Gospels does not appear to be the procedure by which Mark as a whole was compiled, the longer ending would seem to have been a later compilation which was designed to bring the Gospel into conformity with the others.

Selecting a reading as one's preference, in this case the close of the Gospel at 16.8, is not the end of the task for a textual critic. In order to be convincingly shown to be original, the preferred reading should help to explain how the other readings were generated, as mistakes or secondary alterations. The abrupt ending of the original text of Mark at 16.8 certainly could have caused perplexity to readers who knew that other Gospels contained full stories of Jesus' appearances after his death. The shorter addition alludes to Jesus' own direction of the later preaching of his followers, while the longer addition summarizes favourite stories from other sources. It is much easier to imagine a progression from an abrupt ending to two additions than it is to explain why, if one of the more extensive endings was original, it was left out.

The fact that a variant appears to be secondary does not mean it is worthless. The two additions to Mark evidence the fervent belief of the early Church that the account of Jesus' resurrection went on from the story of the empty tomb to actual appearances of the man himself. That sort of belief would need to be appraised in any assessment of the resurrection. But Mark's message does not focus on the particulars which brought Christians to belief: the picture of frightened, silent discipleship in the face of the mysterious fact of the resurrection is the last image of the Gospel.

The responsible practice of textual criticism requires far more detailed discussion than is possible or desirable in this volume. The example of Mark's ending is intended only to illustrate certain principles of textual criticism, and the analysis itself accords with the judgement of most scholars. By working with a good edition of the New Testament in Greek, and accepting sound advice from a manual of textual criticism, students will find in variant readings a rich resource, on the basis of which they can more clearly understand both the New Testament and the rise of early Christianity.

Just as good commentaries indicate areas of difficulty or ambiguity in translation, they also deal with textual matters, often in a way which can fairly easily be understood by the beginning student or the general reader. Although the time is passed when a working knowledge of Greek can seriously be demanded of every critical reader of the New Testament, a willingness to appreciate linguistic and textual questions does remain an absolute requirement for progress to be made. By being open to the suggestion that one's translation is not an unchanging norm, but only a possible rendering, the reader is in a position to see the richness of meaning which the English versions only intimate.

FOR FURTHER READING

The Authorized Version was revised several times after its initial publication in 1611: the corrected edition of 1762, which is widely available, is considered standard. The Common Bible, the ecumenical edition of the Revised Standard Version, was published in 1973 (London and New York: Collins); 1978 saw the publication of the complete New International Version (by Zondervan of Grand Rapids), which has also appeared in London (Hodder and Stoughton, 1982). A revised version of the New English Bible appeared in 1972 (Cambridge: Cambridge University Press; London and New York: Oxford University Press). See also Today's English Version (London: Collins, 1976; New York: the American Bible Society, 1976), and the Jerusalem Bible (London: Darton, Longman and Todd, 1966; Garden City: Doubleday, 1966; the same two publishers released the New Jerusalem Bible in 1985). The Living Bible, paraphrased by K. N. Taylor, is published in London by Coverdale (1973), and in Wheaton by Tyndale House (1971). The Reader's Digest Bible appeared in 1982 (Pleasantville: Reader's Digest Association). The abbreviations used in the present chapter have become conventional, and it is usual to refer to versions in ordinary type, not in italics or within quotation marks. Fuller discussion is available in S. Kubo and W. F. Sprecht, *So Many Versions? Twentieth-century English Versions of the Bible* (Grand Rapids: Zondervan, 1983); a more limited, but also more readable, treatment, is F. F. Bruce's *History of the Bible in English* (London: Lutterworth, 1979).

Two widely available editions of the New Testament, which present substantially the same text, are those of the Bible Societies, *The Greek New Testament* (London and New York: Collins, 1976), and K. Aland (with others), *Novum Testamentum Graece* (Stuttgart: Deutsche Bibelstiftung, 1979), the latter of which is more complete in the variants presented, but also more difficult to read. An innovative introduction to the Greek of the New Testament is offered in E. C. Colwell and E. W. Tune, *A Beginner's Reader – Grammar for New Testament Greek* (London and New York: Harper and Row, 1965). B. M. Metzger, *The Text of the New Testament: Its Transmission, Corruption, and Restoration* (London and New York: Oxford University Press, 1968) has become something of a standard work of textual criticism. For anyone considering

advanced study of the New Testament, the indispensable dictionary is
W. Bauer's, *A Greek – English Lexicon of the New Testament and Other
Early Christian Literature* (London and Chicago: University of Chicago
Press, 1979); condensed editions are also available.

5

The Worlds of the New Testament
Judaism and Hellenism

Most readers of this volume will probably approach the New Testament with a knowledge of Christianity in their backgrounds. Whether or not the faith of the Church is their own, they will be familiar with some of its leading ideas. And as they study, the question will naturally arise whether the Christianity they know is consistent with the claims of the New Testament. Did Jesus believe he was God's son? Did he preach a message of forgiveness which only the Church can mediate? Are human beings portrayed as naturally sinful, and in need of a special power from God in order to find salvation? Owing to the world in which we live, questions of that kind inevitably emerge; they are symptoms of the relationship between studying the New Testament and thinking theologically within the Christian tradition.

In the final chapter, some of the theological issues raised by reading our texts critically will be discussed. For the moment, it is only necessary to bear in mind that, as we read, questions of that sort can arise. But where do they come from? Why do questions about Jesus' sonship, about sin and forgiveness seem natural, while the issue of eschatology, say, appears foreign to most of us? Of course, the texts we read relate to the questions in our mind, but the text is by no means necessary for us to pose them. We can – and often do – ask about God, Jesus, sin, and matters of that kind, quite outside the context of reading the New Testament. In other words, such questions are a part of the world we live in; they belong to the stock of theological issues which are embodied in our culture. We might not think of them in particular, or even know much about them, but we know the questions are there.

When the term 'world' was used in the last paragraph, it obviously did not refer to the physical earth. The human world is not composed only of what we can see; our world includes how we imagine the earth is placed in the solar system, what we believe is most important in life, and why we think we are alive. Just as physical space has three dimensions, so does our social world. We relate to people from the past as our predecessors, to our contemporaries as we try to make decisions and undertake actions in the present, and to those who are to be in the future we expect to come. While human beings may be said generally to behave in this way, they nonetheless inhabit different worlds. A person living in Calcutta is likely to have a different view of the human past, present, and future from that of someone living in Denver. There may even be significant distinctions between the social worlds of people living in the same basic civilization, for example in Britain and America.

One of the tasks of interpretation and theology is to relate the New Testament to our world, which involves an appreciation of the issues involved in contemporary living. But the documents of the New Testament derive from and address, not our world, but their own. Particularly, they do not presuppose the development of scientific thinking in the West, or even the full emergence of Christian theology. The business of formulating creeds and liturgies, even of deciding on the books of the canon, was undertaken in a systematic way only after our documents were composed. Such issues as the Trinity, and the precise powers of bishops, were basic for those thinkers who followed the period of the New Testament. Teachers of that time are known as the Fathers of the Church, and their works can illuminate how the Scriptures were understood within early Christianity; indeed, their concerns sometimes intersect with those of the New Testament. But on the whole, they proceeded on the assumption that the Church was quite different from Judaism, and a distinctive minority movement within the Roman Empire. During the first century, Christians were still working out the identity of the new faith, so that its relation to Judaism and the Empire was a matter of discussion, sometimes of debate. The world of the New Testament is different from that of the later Church and our own, both philosophically and religiously. The understanding of that world is basic to critical reading.

The faith spoken of in our documents did not even address one

121

single, coherent world, but two: Judaism and Hellenism. The very existence of the New Testament testifies to the intersection of those two worlds. A Palestinian teacher who taught in Aramaic and gathered disciples in the manner of a rabbi was the basis of a movement whose most ancient documents are written in Greek and follow conventions of Hellenistic writing. Obviously, the New Testament could not have been composed as it was if Judaism and Hellenism had been hermetically sealed from one another. There were Jews who lived and worked outside Palestine, and were educated within Hellenistic culture, just as some non-Jews were avid readers of the Jewish Scriptures, and even attended worship in synagogues. Judaism and Hellenism were, however, sufficiently distinct from one another to involve different social worlds.

Judaism

Judaism was, in its own understanding, grounded in the promise of the one God, who made heaven and earth. The primeval promise had been made by God himself to Abraham, the supreme patriarch of all Israel: his descendants were to inherit the land 'from the river of Egypt to the great river, the river Euphrates' (Genesis 15.18). This binding agreement, or 'covenant', was solemnized when Abraham made a sacrifice according to God's command (Genesis 15.7–11), and sacrifice was a typical occasion on which Israel remembered the covenant. Indeed, Abraham's willingness to sacrifice his son Isaac, who was replaced at the last moment with a ram (Genesis 22.9–14), was taken as a sign that he was worthy of the promise which had already been given (Genesis 22.15–18).

The nature of God's covenant was such that it involved responsibilities, as well as blessings: particularly, circumcision was the divinely ordained means of staying within the covenant (Genesis 17.9–14). Judaism has perennially been marked by a sense of obligation in daily life to abide by the terms of God's promise. A story is told of Jacob, the grandson of Abraham, concerning the time he returned to the promised land after a long sojourn with his uncle in the vicinity of the Euphrates. He is beside himself with fright at the thought of how Esau, his brother, will receive him. In his distress, he is said to wrestle with a mysterious, unnamed man (Genesis 32.24–32). The man seizes Jacob on the inside of his thigh, but Jacob fights on. Jacob only lets his antagonist go on condition he blesses him; the man replies, 'Your name will no more be called Jacob, but Israel, because you contended with God and man, and prevailed' (Genesis 32.28). The name 'Israel', of course, was taken by the people of the covenant to refer both to themselves and to their land. Moreover, they avoided eating the part of an animal's body which corresponded to where Jacob was injured during the heavenly combat (32.32). The story of God's covenantal promise was not only to be remembered mentally; the community recalled and enacted its very conditions, so as to join itself to the blessings which were to come. God's covenant and Israel's faithfulness are the axioms of the Hebrew Bible.

The covenantal obligations of Israel were most fully spelled out within the Hebrew Bible through the ministry of Moses. After the exodus from Egypt, Moses is portrayed as the leader of 'elders', whose function was to judge disputes among the people (Exodus 18.25, 26). He derived his authority from God himself, who demanded faithfulness to the covenant by means of obedience to his own voice as it was made known by Moses (Exodus 19.3–9). The following chapter sets out what have become known as the 'Ten Commandments' (20.1–17). In fact, of course, the books of Exodus, Leviticus, Numbers, and Deuteronomy (all of which focus on Moses' ministry) teach many more than ten precepts; in the rabbinic understanding, 613 was the count. But what Christians call the Ten Commandments do express the dual obligation of Israel both to God and its own members, which became a hallmark of the covenantal community. The two sorts of obligation were inextricably entwined. The famous commandment, 'you shall love your neighbour as yourself', is immediately followed by a divine prohibition against mixing different breeds of cattle, or different sorts of seed or cloth (Leviticus 19.18, 19).

To those who restrict the application of religion to ethical matters, Israel's widely ranging conception of covenantal law can seem odd. Not infrequently, Christians characterize Judaism as legalistic, in that every aspect of life seems to come under its law.

But Israel's Torah, the law of guidance which kept the community within the promises of God's covenant, was not intended as a special way of righteousness which a few pious individuals might keep. Rather, the Torah was the very constitution of Israel as the elect people of God. The community as a whole bore covenantal responsibility, just as it was to enjoy the fulfilment of God's promise. The laws of what is 'clean', and what is not, are especially eloquent reminders that the entire community was to keep itself in a fit state to enter into the promises of God through the covenant.

During the centuries of Israel's existence as an autonomous state, two foci of national life emerged: the monarchy and the Temple. Both institutions are given prophetic warrant in 2 Samuel 7.4–17, and became axiomatic features in the life of Israel. But in 63 BC, the general Pompey entered Jerusalem, and established Roman rule there. From that time, we may speak of the emergence of Judaism, or more precisely, of early Judaism. Judah, named after Jacob's son, had long been the most prominent area in Israel, and now the chief focus of national identity, the king, was no longer at the centre of community life; the name 'Judaism', as distinct from 'Israel', refers to the religious impulses which focus on a geographical promise without benefit of a clearly national institution. In the absence of the monarchy, Jews looked to other quarters for leadership. Some turned to the apocalyptic seers whose heritage was described in chapter four. Small minorities from time to time chanced rebellion against Rome, in order to establish government under God's chosen ruler, often called his Messiah. Others sought refuge in the aristocracy, which attempted accommodation with the Romans and, at the same time, maintenance of the cult in the Temple. Others still, who withdrew to places such as Qumran, tried to lead communal lives in purity and detachment from a world which seemed hopelessly corrupt. All of these movements had their beginnings in the period before 63 BC, but the dissolution of the monarchy gave them a new prominence; in effect, they were battling amongst themselves for the right to define what Judaism was.

In the end, the Judaism which emerged after this formative period was dominated by rabbinic discussion. The rabbis traced their roots back to Ezra, who had long before (during the fifth century BC) helped to reconstitute Israel after a long period of exile. Ezra had based his ministry on teaching the Torah, and explaining it, in which he had many assistants (see Nehemiah 8.1–8). The rabbis also represented a focus on the law as written in the Bible, and as interpreted and supplemented by their own discussion. Such a focus on Torah was the sole orientation which stood the test of time. Movements of national revival, which sought to replace Roman government with messianic rule, were crushed; apocalyptic expectations of imminent vindication were disappointed; withdrawal into the wilderness meant relinquishing real power. Finally, the Temple itself was taken by the Romans in AD 70, after a failed revolt. With that catastrophic fall of a sacred institution, the Torah remained as the only viable warrant of the covenantal promise, and the rabbis were vindicated as the most faithful interpreters of Torah.

Jesus taught, and Christianity emerged, as the ferment of early Judaism gave way to the triumph of rabbinic Judaism. But the fact that Jesus is addressed as 'rabbi' on numerous occasions in the Gospels does not mean he can be equated directly or uniquely with the professional teachers who were later dominant. As was observed in chapter four, there was such an eschatological edge to Jesus' message that some of his followers were able to develop an apocalyptic scenario from what he said. Passages such as that concerning Jesus' temptation (Matthew 4.1–11; Mark 1.12, 13; Luke 4.1–13) suggest moreover that he had, or was understood to have had, some affinity with those who advocated withdrawal from the world at large. Finally, the crucifixion itself, a Roman method of execution reserved for serious criminals, indicates that Jesus could be perceived as a dangerous threat to the established order of his time. The varieties of early Judaism are reflected in the portraits of Jesus which the Gospels convey, and they can also be traced in the development of early Christian theology.

The method by which Jesus taught his disciples, which was discussed in chapter one, is reminiscent of rabbinic practice. Rabbis passed on their teaching to disciples first of all by word of mouth. A rabbi's lesson was called his 'mishnah', which refers to what he repeated. A valid mishnah was equated with the Torah given to Moses; it was held to offer the guidance of God for the community. Gradually, by the end of the second century AD, lessons were collected in the document known as Mishnah, in which the oral Torah – that is, the teachings of rabbis – is explicated in view of the new conditions which Judaism faced. Midrash is another basic form of rabbinic teaching; here, lessons are related to biblical books, and arranged in a sequential fashion. They resemble commentaries, but frequently the leading theme is provided by the teaching itself, rather than by the biblical book concerned. Some Midrashim (the plural form) were collected during the second century, but most of the documents which exist today were assembled at a much later period. Rabbis were also involved in the production of Targums, which are paraphrases of biblical books in Aramaic (the language of Jesus' day, which is quite different from Hebrew). Because Targums are paraphrases, rather than translations, they frequently present notable expansions and interpretations of the Hebrew text. The Targumic documents available today were produced over a very long period of time, and none seems to have been completed during the first century.

Given that Jesus taught his disciples in a somewhat rabbinic way, we may ask: is the New Testament (in the case of the Gospels in particular) comparable to rabbinic literature? Initially, the answer to that question must be a firm 'no'. The Mishnah represents the lessons of many rabbis; only one is at issue in the New Testament, and no document within it focuses merely on Jesus' teaching (to the exclusion of stories about Jesus). Similarly, no document within the New Testament is merely a commentary (midrash) or an explanatory paraphrase (targum) of a biblical book.

Having said that, however, we might observe that there are elements of Jesus' teaching as presented in the Gospels which might be styled 'mishnaic', 'midrashic', and 'targumic'. When Jesus sent out his disciples to preach and heal (see Matthew 10.1–15; Luke 10.1–12, which are discussed in chapter one), he armed them with his mishnah, an account of what to say. When he discussed the question of marriage and divorce (see Matthew 19.1–9; Mark 10.2–12), he did so by contrasting two biblical passages. Genesis 2.24 speaks of husband and wife becoming a single unit, while Deuteronomy 24.1–4 seems to envisage divorce as a routine procedure. Jesus resolves this apparent contradiction by arguing that divorce was only a concession in view of 'hardness of heart', and not the intention of God. The technique of discovering a coherent message in contrasting biblical passages is well known in the Midrashim. When Jesus announced 'the kingdom of God', he used a concept which is also found in the Targums, where it refers to God's final, personal intervention on behalf of his people. It may well be that Jesus chose his central message with an awareness of what people were accustomed to hearing in the course of their worship in synagogues. The distinction between *halakhah* and *haggadah*, which was described in chapter one, is also tenable in the case of the Gospels: Jesus' teaching is handed on directly, and stories about him illustrate his message. Most of the genres of rabbinic literature present both direct, *halakhic* teaching, and illustrative, *haggadic* stories.

The earliest teachers of what became known as Christianity grew up, lived, taught, and died in the milieu of early Judaism. For that reason, some familiarity with Judaism is indispensable for the study of the New Testament, and Jewish literature remains an unavoidable area of research. But even the Gospels cannot be explained fully as documents of Judaism: their concentrated focus on Jesus, and their use of continuous narrative, rather than isolated *haggadoth*, mark them out as distinctive literary forms. And the documents of the New Testament become less influenced by the conventions of Judaism, naturally enough, as their intended readers include more and more Greek-speaking Gentiles. For those reasons, early Judaism is a necessary topic of inquiry, but it is not sufficient in itself to explain the documents we seek to understand.

Hellenism

Hellenism is sometimes portrayed as a direct alternative to Judaism; its polytheism, its appeal to rational discourse in fluent Greek, and its enthusiasm for foreign religions indeed give it a very distinctive view of the world as compared to what we find in the Hebrew Bible or rabbinic discussion. The temptation arises to make a hard and fast distinction between Jesus and his first disciples, Aramaic-speaking Jews who lived in Palestine, and the exponents of the Church who followed them, Greek-speaking inhabitants of the Mediterranean basin. There are good reasons why that temptation should be resisted. First of all, many Jews lived in what was known as the 'Diaspora', the dispersion from Israel. The Diaspora was partially involuntary, in that Jews were from time to time deported from their homeland by foreign powers. But once settled outside Israel, many Jews proved themselves educated citizens of the Hellenistic world, and some left Israel voluntarily. Jewish thinkers such as Philo of Alexandria explained Judaism in terms which those familiar with Greek philosophy might understand, and Josephus, the Jewish historian, recounted the history of his nation by means of conventions he learned from the Greek writers who preceded him. The Hebrew Bible in its Greek guise, the Septuagint, was highly regarded – among other religious writings – in the Hellenistic world generally, and Jerusalem stood in high repute as a holy city. Commerce and Roman military control also facilitated the interchange between Judaism and Hellenism, even though tensions between them erupted occasionally in the bloody revolts of Jews, and even more violent repressions by Gentile soldiers and mobs.

Accommodation between Judaism and Hellenism was possible because Hellenism was not based on a single set of religious impulses, as Judaism was. Rather, its genius was its ability to tolerate and absorb many different cultural elements. Hellenism is usually dated from the time of Alexander the great, who conquered the civilized world of his day, before he died in 323 BC. Alexander was not only a military figure; he also imposed Greek language and culture on the lands he dominated. Alexander had been tutored by the Greek philosopher, Aristotle, and widespread knowledge of the philosophies of fourth-century Athens was perhaps Alexander's greatest (although largely unintentional) achievement. The library established after his death at Alexandria, a city named in his honour, was among the greatest monuments to his stature, and the discussion which went on within the categories of Greek philosophical thought, there and elsewhere, was enormously influential. The world's learning began to be assembled, and that learning was understood on the basis of Greek philosophy.

Hellenism (a term which derives from the original word for 'Greek') may be defined as the attempt to understand and order the civilized world according to ideals developed in ancient Greece. Plato, who lived in Athens during the fifth and fourth centuries BC, was probably the most influential thinker of the entire period. He developed the technique used by his teacher, Socrates, in which questions were posed and answered on the basis of a reasoned interaction between different points of view. That technique, and the implicit appeal to reason alone as the final arbiter in argument, remains fundamental within philosophical disciplines in the West. Plato's particular contribution, however, was his rational defence of idealism. An idealistic philosophy is one which locates the substantial reality of our world, not in what our senses perceive, but in the ideas our perceptions relate to. So, for example, it was argued that there is no such thing as a wise person apart from an idea of perfect wisdom already present in our minds; a wise person is only a partial representation of an underlying reality. Plato's philosophy was by no means accepted universally. Most notably, Aristotle argued for a view of knowledge which was much more oriented to the experience of our senses. Aristotle still provides basic reading for those engaged in political thought, and other branches of Greek philosophy were so concentrated on the physical world that they eventually developed into the method of thinking which we today call science. Nonetheless, Platonic idealism, in one form or another, was basic to popular philosophy in the Hellenistic period.

Alexander's empire was a startling military achievement, and led to an enduring philosophical triumph, but it was a political fiasco. Almost immediately after his death, Alexander's generals carved up his dominion amongst themselves, and each region went its own way. In the western part, Rome gradually emerged as the dominant force in the midst of warring local régimes, and the Roman Empire came to be the most significant power over the whole of the Mediterranean basin. Rome granted conquered territories a remarkable amount of local autonomy, and even bestowed its citizenship on some inhabitants; this unusually tolerant policy ensured a comparative peace which had not been known before, and which has rarely been seen since.

Pragmatic though that achievement was, it must have seemed a gift from the gods; by the time of Augustus, at the dawn of the period of the New Testament, the Emperor could even be known as 'son of God'. Sacrifice was offered to the Emperor, which is a symptom of the conviction during the Empire that a single, divine force lay behind the political settlement, nature, and the human mind. Roman pragmatism for the most part prevented Imperial worship from becoming too onerous; Jews were generally exempted from it, and were permitted peaceably to practise their religion. Christianity posed a nagging problem once it was perceived as a movement distinct from Judaism, because at that point Christians could not legally claim exemption from the duty to offer sacrifice to the Emperor. Christians were persecuted from the second century AD, in view of their intractable refusal to perform what was seen more as a public obligation than as an act of piety. But it is eloquent testimony to the pragmatic genius of Rome that, once the durability of the new faith was proven, it was (by the fourth century) tolerated, and even officially embraced.

Popular philosophy during the first century was a growth industry. There were many schools of thought which competed for attention and engaged in debate; people could make a living wandering from city to city, offering instruction and public discourse. Just as the varieties of Judaism are to some extent reflected in the New Testament, so the range of Graeco-Roman philosophy merits, and presently receives, close attention from the point of view of its influence on Christianity. Of all the schools, Stoicism possibly best represents the temper of the Empire. Stoicism takes its name from the *poikilē stoa*, the 'painted portico', where the founder of the school, Zeno, taught at Athens, shortly after the time of Alexander. Zeno considered that a principle of reason underlies the whole of existence, at the levels both of the universe and individual human beings. That principle might at a given point dictate the destruction of all things, but in due course new structure and restoration would follow, much as a fire can be seen to flare up, nearly burn out, and settle itself progressively. Whatever the fire of reason might do, however, the sole good of human life was to live in accordance with its dictates. The essential harmony of existence, natural, political, and individually human, lies at the heart of the Stoic orientation. Its doctrines were related to the Platonic appeal to reason, and suited ideally a world in which obedience to authority had become a paramount virtue. It is scarcely coincidental that one of the most prominent Stoic teachers of the second century AD was Marcus Aurelius, himself a Roman Emperor.

The dutiful morality of Stoicism was developed by Seneca, tutor and adviser to the Emperor Nero, during the first century. His conviction that an underlying reason was the key to existence led him to pursue a metaphor of the body: 'All this, which you see, in which the divine and the human are included, is one; we are members of a great body' (*Moral Letters* 95.52). The development of this motif within Stoicism near the time of Paul is notable, because the apostle also – as was seen in chapter two – insistently applied a metaphor of the body to believers. But the similarity does not imply that Paul merely appropriated a Stoic form of thought, because Seneca's conception of the 'body' is pursued for different ends than Paul's. The Stoic metaphor is applied to describe the substantial reality available to people in the universe: its 'body' is perceptible by reason, and is (in principle) accessible to every reasonable person. Paul, on the other hand, is concerned to describe an identification with Christ by an act of faith, not a feature of the natural order. He can also refer to this act of incorporation into Christ as a 'new creation' (2 Corinthians 5.17); it is very far from a principle already obvious from the existing conditions of life.

The development of the two ethical metaphors of the body, Stoic and Christian, might be called parallel, but only on condition that one remembers parallel lines do not touch. The metaphors are indeed analogous, but they convey different meanings within distinctive systems of discourse. Very often, the study of Hellenistic philosophy aids our understanding of how Paul's message could have been approached by his contemporaries, and of the categories of thought he may have used to articulate his message. But care must be taken not to confuse the meaning of a category, be it a metaphor or a phrase, in one tradition of thought with its meaning in another. The danger of such confusion is particularly acute because neither Paul nor any contributor to the New Testament was a professional philosopher.

Some awareness of popular philosophy was part and parcel of Christian activity in the Mediterranean basin, and Christian teachers used the vocabulary of their own world to explain the faith they fervently held. But the transition of the Church from a local movement to a more globally Hellenistic enterprise did not involve replacing faith with philosophy. The central focus on Jesus as the only mediator of God's grace (see 1 Timothy 2.5) became all the more emphatic as Hellenism emerged as the primary context of Christianity; a firm resolve developed to guard against religious speculation, by applying the words of Jesus as a criterion of sound teaching (see 1 Timothy 6.3–5). The Hellenistic teachers of the Church were reserved in respect of philosophical debate, and condemned what they saw as the immorality of their age (see 1 Timothy 1.8–11). The attitude of Christians towards the discussion and customs of their time did nothing to enhance their reputation in some quarters of the Empire. Tacitus, a Roman historian who wrote very early in the second century, blandly remarks that Christians were a despised group (*Annals* 15.44). This routine antipathy was fostered by false and scandalous rumours about the practices of the new faith, but it was also the result of the emerging consciousness of Christians of being apart from the world in which they lived.

Paul was a primary contributor to an exclusive attitude in the early Church. In Philippians 3.2, he warns his readers against 'the dogs, the evil-doers', with practitioners of circumcision chiefly in mind. But a reader in the Hellenistic world would perhaps have associated 'dogs' with another movement which began in fourth century Athens, and became widespread. The Cynics earned their name for being dog-like (from the Greek word *kuōn*); dogs in the ancient world were seen, not as friendly, but as dirty, anti-social, and dangerous. The Cynics were noted for their ceaseless questioning and refusal of normal customs. Their quest for a morality which was not merely a matter of convention led them to be considered socially obstreperous, although their search for ethical integrity was generally sincere. Paul seems to have used the abusive association of the term 'dogs' in applying it to another group, which he saw as dividing the community of Christians. Of course, the association was active in a Jewish context, as well (see Matthew 7.6); but it has its own tenor within the Hellenistic world.

A superficial awareness of contemporary philosophy is also evident in 1 Corinthians. There, Paul attacks the notion that, in the absence of hope in the resurrection, one might as well say, 'Let us eat and drink, since tomorrow we die' (15.32). The quotation itself derives from Isaiah 22.13, but Paul is using it to attack a school of thought founded by Epicurus, a philosopher who had settled in Athens by 306 BC. Epicureanism was indeed a materialistic teaching, which denied immortality. But Epicurus held that his doctrine freed people from the fear of death, since there was no rational fear of any punishment afterwards; Epicurus' followers were to cultivate peace of mind by concentrating on their experience of the present, which was the only experience they expected ever to have. Both Jews and Christians associated this philosophy with mindless sensuality. (Even today, an 'epicurean delight' refers to a good meal. The polemical stance of early Christianity has to some extent shaped our language. In a similar way, 'cynicism' today refers more usually to a sceptical attitude towards people than to the original philosophy.) Paul refutes the alleged position of Epicurus with a line he knows from a Greek writer, 'Bad company ruins good behaviour' (1 Corinthians 15.33, an apparent quotation of Menander's lost comedy, 'Thais'). His attack is far from a serious discussion of a philosophical system, but is more a passionate outburst against second-hand, popular ideas.

As portrayed in Acts, Paul has a more positive approach to pagan philosophy. In chapter seventeen, he addresses the men of Athens in a public discourse (17.22), in the course of which he quotes the poet Aratus, who said of Zeus, 'we are his offspring' (Acts 17.28). Aratus was essentially Stoic in outlook, and the argument of Acts 17 runs on in a manner reminiscent of Stoic teachers (and, of course, the Old Testament) by insisting that the divine cannot be reduced to any object people might make (17.29). The setting of the speech in Acts calls attention to the philosophical interests of Athenians (17.16–21), and specifically mentions Stoics and Epicureans in their midst (v. 18). But while the Stoic position held that reason was the only means of access to the divine, Acts 17.30, 31 presses the argument against idolatry into a call for repentance in the face of God's judgement by means of Jesus. As in the case of the metaphor of the 'body', similarity in language may at first sight conceal a profound difference in thought and orientation between Christianity and Stoicism.

The relationship between the New Testament and Hellenism is as curiously ambivalent as the relationship between the New Testament and Judaism, but for different reasons. Primarily on the basis of Jesus' teaching, Christianity emerged as a distinct movement within early Judaism. Its consistent, almost unique focus on Jesus as the standard and means of any access to God was increasingly at odds with the rabbinic view, which saw in the Torah the essential guarantee of the covenant. Hellenism provided the context in which the distinctive faith of Christians was articulated. Its concepts, fashions, and vocabulary were part of the mental equipment which Christians used to understand themselves and God. There is no question of their adopting Hellenistic thought; it was the very basis on which they perceived and communicated. Yet their faith in Jesus was such that both their conception of God and their ethical attitudes changed radically in comparison with what their contemporaries held dear. God for them was no longer a general force of reason or matter which permeated nature and people; he was a single, personal being who could be known only by means of revelation in the person called Jesus. Good behaviour could no longer be construed as simple conformity to the customs of the Empire; Hellenistic Christians distinguished themselves from others as a community in which the peculiar demands of their faith were practised.

Hellenism therefore joins Judaism as a world to which early Christians belonged, and yet did not belong. It was once fashionable to refer to the 'background' of the New Testament, in order to speak of the Jewish and Hellenistic features which are prominent within it. Such a designation gives the false impression that the Church was basically unlike Judaism and Hellenism, something which might be understood in its own right. The background of a painting is, after all, only there for the sake of contrast, in order to emphasize the features of the main subject. What makes the Church such an exciting development, histori-

cally speaking, is that its faith was articulated *within* the ferment
of early Judaism and the debates of Hellenism. Its adherents were
Jews, Greeks, and sometimes both; they spoke and thought
according to the conventions of their own time, and yet fashioned
a message and style of living which grew to be at odds both with
Judaism and Hellenism.

The difficulty of the early Christian position was to some
extent that of all compromises: they seldom satisfy both sides
fully. For many Jews, the relaxation of the Torah's demands
seemed unacceptable; for many Hellenists, the consistent focus
on the Hebrew Bible and the teaching of a single rabbi from an
obscure part of the Empire seemed parochial. But had Christianity merely been a compromise, it would not have evoked the
negative reactions it did. Judaism was capable of making room for
Gentiles in its midst, and Hellenism was noted for its absorption
of foreign religions. The scandal of Christianity lay more in its
claim to represent the single truth about God, as revealed in
Jesus. The Church could no more accept Torah alongside Christ
than it could accept Seneca alongside Paul. It grew up within the
categories of Judaism and Hellenism, expressed itself in terms a
Jew or a Greek could understand, and then turned on both of
them. Christians did not merely preach a possible view of God,
but claimed to know the full truth about him, and demanded
repentance as the only acceptab.e response to their message. The
new faith was nurtured in two worlds, and proclaimed the coming
of a world to come, where their teacher, their Lord, alone would
rule. That persistent message, in the face of conflict and persecution, is what makes the early Church seem an alien within the
two worlds of which it was also a citizen.

Jewish, Hellenistic, and Christian stories

The fact that Christian teachers developed their message within
their own world, or worlds, implies that their perception of Jesus,
and their expressions of his significance, were influenced by the
conventions of their time. Those Jewish and Hellenistic conventions included, not only religious vocabulary, but also stories told
about religious figures. Many of these stories relate what we

would call 'miracles': marvellous events which do not accord with our view of what is possible in the natural order. Such events are referred to so frequently in the New Testament as to perplex modern readers. Did they actually occur? Were they believed to have happened as they are related, but, at the same time, might they be susceptible of natural scientific explanation? Or again, were they related as symbolic portraits of the faith they were intended to generate, without pretending to make claims of physical reality? Questions of that sort come irrepressibly to mind when stories about miracles are read, but they need to be held in abeyance for the moment. They belong to the study of how the New Testament stands with the world of our own day (chapter six). Stories about miracles are not nearly as unusual when they are judged by the standards of Jewish and Hellenistic religious discourse.

A story is told about a rabbi named Ḥanina ben Dosa in the Talmud (Berakhoth 34b), a collection of teaching compiled during the fifth century AD. The son of a famous teacher is mortally ill with fever, and his father sends two rabbis to ask Ḥanina to pray for the child. Ḥanina ben Dosa goes into an upper room (a quiet place commonly associated with prayer), and prays for him. He then comes down, and confidently says 'Go, the fever has left.' The emissaries ask Ḥanina whether he is a prophet, but he replies emphatically that he is not. Rather, he insists, his statement is made on the basis of experience, 'If my prayer flows easily, I know it is accepted; if not, I know it is rejected.' The bemused scholars make a note of the time of Ḥanina's statement, and return to their chief. He, in turn, swears that at the very moment they noted, the fever had left his son.

Ḥanina had a great reputation for effective prayer, and several stories in the Talmud illustrate his ability. Typically, however, he avoids the personal credit which his prayer might bring him. The immediate question of the emissaries in the present story, 'Are you a prophet?', is turned aside by Ḥanina. Within rabbinic thought generally, prophecy was held to have passed with the generation of Ezra, so that a claim to prophesy would have amounted to the assertion that God had made his Spirit specially available to an individual. Ḥanina does not make any such assertion about himself, but bases his confidence on his humble prayer. As a result, the triumphant success celebrated at the end of the story redounds to God's glory, rather than primarily to Ḥanina's reputation.

A somewhat similar story is told in the Gospel according to John (4.46–54). The setting is Cana of Galilee, where – in another famous passage – Jesus was said to have provided drink at a wedding (see John 2.1–11). An unnamed royal official approaches Jesus, asking him to come with him and heal his mortally ill son. Jesus' answer seems designed to put the man off, 'Unless you see signs and wonders, you will not believe.' But the distraught father makes it clear he is concerned only about his son, and again asks Jesus to come. Jesus' reply is terse, but accepting, 'Go, your son lives'; and the man returns, full of hope. On the way back, the father is met by his servants, who give him the happy news that his son has revived. He then learns that the fever departed at the very hour Jesus had said, 'Your son lives.'

There are certain clear similarities between the stories concerning Ḥanina and Jesus. Both relate the effect of a cure at a distance, the disease is a fever, the victim is the son of a prominent man, and underlings are involved in the narratives. But while the conventions of the stories may be compared, their content is different. The father in John is not a famous rabbi, but an official of an administration sanctioned by the Romans, and he comes into direct contact with Jesus, rather than sending emissaries. (A similar, but quite distinct, story is related in the Synoptic Gospels; see Matthew 8.5–10; Luke 7.1–10.) More importantly, the story in John has quite a different impact from the story in Talmud; it focuses on Jesus, rather than on any prayer of Jesus.

Indeed, John's Gospel does not even portray Jesus as praying at this point. The emphasis falls instead on the authority of Jesus himself. The reference at the beginning of the story to what happened earlier at Cana prepares us for an unusual event, and the close underlines the point: 'This, again, was the second sign Jesus did when he came from Judaea into Galilee' (4.54). The purpose of such 'signs' may be said to be the theme of the story, because Jesus, quite unexpectedly, raises the issue with the father, 'Unless you (a plural form) see signs and wonders, you will not believe' (4.48). Jesus therefore addresses, not merely the royal official, but those who might seek miraculous signs as a prior condition of their faith. But the man, by his simple, unconditional request (4.49), makes it clear that his approach to Jesus is not a test, but a genuine plea for help. The happy ending of the story therefore signals that Jesus' healing comes as the seal of faith, not as its precondition. Only those who appreciate the one who heals can claim access to his healing. Both the man and his household are said to believe at the close of the story (4.53); the healing intensifies and broadens the scope of a faith which was already there in germinal form. But the 'sign' did not produce faith, as the demonstration of overwhelming power to a sceptic might do.

Of course, the emphasis on Jesus in John's story should not be construed as a claim of any unique status apart from God. The same Gospel has Jesus insist that the son can do nothing aside from what the father does (5.19, see 5.30; 8.28), and he avoids the crowd's acclamation of him as a prophetic king after the feeding of the five thousand (6.14, 15). The reserve about Ḥanina in the Talmud is not altogether unlike John's portrait of Jesus' healing; Jesus is associated closely with God, but he is no autonomously divine figure. But Ḥanina is the vehicle for the praise of prayer; the focus in John is irreducibly on Jesus himself. To that extent, the similarities of the stories only serve to highlight their pursuit of differing aims.

The comparability of the two stories does nothing to establish whether they are historically accurate. As was explained in chapter one, the interpretative development involved in the production of John's Gospel is such that it cannot be read as an immediate chronicle of events. And although Ḥanina was a figure of the first century, the interpretative contribution of rabbis to the Talmud was no less influential than that of Christian teachers to the New Testament, and it extended over a much longer period. Moreover, the underlying question of how stories of miracles are to be taken affects our reading of both texts. For all that, there is a positive gain to be won by comparative study. We cannot be certain we are dealing directly with 'the historical Jesus', or 'the historical Ḥanina', but we do know we are dealing with the perceptions of both figures within Christianity and Judaism. Distinctive religious orientations are expressed by the two stories, and they serve to illustrate the peculiar features of their respective worlds. In all probability, neither story was a source of the other; Jews had as little interest in having Hanina imitate Jesus as Christians did in having Jesus imitate Hanina. The two rabbis, each with a reputation for healing, were perceived and spoken of in similar conventions of story-telling, and those conventions came to reflect the religious impact both teachers exercised.

The interpretative reworking of material concerning an earlier hero is also characteristic of some Hellenistic literature. An example of what might be called philosophical romance is the *Life of Apollonius of Tyana*. The work was written during the third century AD, by Philostratus, but Apollonius himself was a first century figure, and Philostratus alleges that he used the diary of Damis, an immediate follower of Apollonius. The number of historical and geographical errors in the work, however, make the author's claim suspect.

The *Life* is no sober biography, but propaganda in favour of the Pythagorean tradition, in which Apollonius was a hero. Pythagoras lived during the sixth century BC, and his name is still associated with mathematics. (In geometry, the formula that relates the sides of a right triangle is known as the Pythagorean Theorem, although it was developed after Pythagoras' time.) It is not straightforward to distinguish Pythagoras from the school which developed in his name, but it is evident that, for him, numbers were not merely abstract entities. They were the basic principles of the real world; by attending to their study, and practising asceticism, a person could be free from the weary cycle in which human souls moved from body to body in successive lives. Pythagoreanism was also associated with the study of music, which was closely related to mathematics in the ancient conception, largely owing to the influence of Pythagoras. In its comprehensive claim to address many different aspects of human life, his movement came to acquire a considerable reputation as a practical philosophy.

Apollonius, as depicted in the *Life*, is a man of remarkable purity. He lives simply, clothed in linen and draped in uncut hair; he practises his arduous, itinerant ministry without the financial means he might have accepted, wearing crude sandals, and abstaining from sexual contact, meat and wine (see 1.7, 8, 13; 6.11; 8.7.6). His dedication to the rule of Pythagoras derives from his conviction that he is near to God, possessed of divine virtues (8.7.7). His divinely bestowed wisdom gives him an extraordinary knowledge of languages, without having to learn them (1.19), the power to see into the future (5.11; 6.32), the ability to heal (3.39; 4.45) and to exorcize demons (3.38; 4.10, 25). Philostratus insists that Apollonius was not a magician (7.39); he did not acquire delusive techniques which he practised commercially. His powers derived rather from his attention to the rule of life fitted to ultimate reality.

Certain stories about Apollonius in the *Life* are reminiscent of those about Paul in Acts. By means of his foresight, Apollonius escapes a shipwreck (5.18); in a far more elaborate narrative, Paul's similar ability is brought into play in Acts 27.9–44. Like Paul, Apollonius is subject to official persecution and arrest, but on the charge of being a magician. While in prison, he is said, without special effort, to remove himself from a chain, thus proving that he transcended the bounds people are normally restricted to (7.38). To the mind of 'Damis', this event made Apollonius seem all the more divine: he is seen truly to be of superhuman nature, and to accept imprisonment voluntarily. Apollonius' proximity to divine wisdom is such that his wonder-working is a natural result of his philosophical advancement. Although Pythagoras is his guiding star, Apollonius' appeal to reason as a ruling moral and natural principle owes something to Stoicism. Hellenism was characterized by a synthesis of various philosophical and religious trends, as well as by a fascination with foreign civilizations and occult phenomena. The *Life* also accommodates a thirst for the unusual, although the charge of magic is specifically refuted on Apollonius' behalf. He wanders through many remote lands and cultures, and employs a variety of esoteric techniques by means of his wisdom.

The story of Paul's deliverance from a prison in Philippi (Acts 16.11–34) is told by means of conventions that may well have delighted a Hellenistic audience. The narrative is recounted in its first part as what happened to 'us', as if the narrator was one of Paul's company. That technique lends the vivid tone to Acts 16 which the *Life* enjoys in view of the diary of 'Damis'. Paul and his friends are entertained in the city by a merchant (vv. 13b–15), much as Apollonius enjoyed the hospitality and lavish offers of noble people (see *Life* 5.27–38). The passage in Acts takes a new turn when, unsolicited, Paul exorcizes a spirit by means of which a slave gives oracles (vv. 16–18). Her owners are annoyed, because the slave's cure represents a loss of income for them, and they have Paul and Silas put into prison (vv. 19–24). Apollonius was also reputed to have exorcized without being asked to do so (see *Life* 4.10, 25), and his ministry landed him in legal trouble (see 8.3). Finally, Paul and Silas are freed from prison by a miraculous earthquake, which releases doors and fetters, but leaves them unharmed (vv. 25, 26). But, like Apollonius, Paul does not use the opportunity of release in order to escape (vv. 27, 28). The jailer is so astounded, he asks for salvation and is baptized with his household (vv. 29–34). In due course, in a sequel to the story, Paul is exonerated by the due (and apologetic) process of law (vv. 35–40).

The jailer's response to the miraculous earthquake highlights a principal, and innovative, feature of the story in Acts. The jailer does not attribute Paul's release to any special virtue, as 'Damis' did in the case of Apollonius. Rather, he asks what he must do to be saved (16.30). That is, he sees the events described as proof that his entire way of life is leading to destruction; he feels he requires access to God in order to redeem it. Paul demands his belief in Jesus (vv. 31, 32), and the baptism of the jailer and his household is the climax of the story (vv. 33, 34). The focus of the narrative shifts from Paul to the faith preached by Paul; that faith is the hero of the story, more than any individual. Even the earlier parts of the narrative manifest just this subtle alteration of the expected focus. Paul finds a patron, not because of his own eloquence, but because 'the Lord opened her heart to attend to what was said by Paul' (v. 14). Similarly, although Paul acts in a sudden, authoritative manner to rid the slave of her spirit, he does not do so on his own account, but 'in the name of Jesus Christ' (v. 18). In the story as a whole, Paul is more the agent through whom Christ acts than a hero in his own right. Moreover, there is no attempt to argue that Paul is especially wise, or that he operates on the basis of his perception of philosophical truth; the narrative relates a divine incursion into human life, not the virtue of perceiving a reality which underlies the ordinary world. A similar incursion is the motif of several stories in Acts, which are told of Peter (5.17–42; 12.1–19). The repetition of the motif of a release from prison, directed by God, serves further to diminish any focus on Paul in himself in Acts 16.

Particular care must be taken in comparing the *Life* with the New Testament, in view of its date and its evident dependence, from time to time, on Christian theology. The appearance of Apollonius after his death to a young man (8.31), for example, may be an instance of Philostratus' desire to claim the glory of Jesus for his hero. The actual title of his work in Greek shows his purpose is to speak *Regarding Apollonius of Tyana*, and there is scarcely a page of the book which does not accomplish the aim of praising him by drawing on some philosophical, literary, or religious motif which Apollonius is held to exemplify. Indeed, it is conceivable that Philostratus may have been inspired partially, if only indirectly, by familiarity with Acts. Clearly, sources such as the *Life* must not be used as providing a literary pattern into which Christian writers simply inserted Jesus and Paul.

As in the case of the Talmud, however, a literary source from the Hellenistic world need not antedate the New Testament in order to illuminate it. Although the *Life* must not be treated as a source of Acts, neither does it derive entirely from Acts. Most importantly, whatever the literary contacts between them, Acts and the *Life* illustrate how similar conventions can be pursued to differing ends. Comparative analysis enables us to see that, although Apollonius and Paul were held to have been involved in similar miracles, the significance of those miracles was construed in markedly distinctive ways. A Hellenistic, non-Christian reader might have read Acts with a degree of familiarity with the conventions employed in it, but the theme of those conventions would certainly come as a surprise. The notion of an underlying principle, at once reasonable and divine, beneath the tapestry of life is abandoned, and its place is taken by the conviction that God is actively intervening, by means of faith in Jesus, in human affairs.

The prologue of John's Gospel

An appreciation of the worlds of the New Testament can greatly enhance our sense of how its message was understood in its own time. The first eighteen verses of John provide a case in point. The passage is known as the 'prologue' of the Gospel, because it sets forth themes in poetic terms which are developed by narrative means later on. The stylistic differences between the prologue and the bulk of the Gospel have led many scholars to question whether it was composed by the person or persons who were responsible for John as a whole. Moreover, there is considerable scholarly disagreement concerning the world of discourse to which the prologue belongs.

John speaks of the *logos*, a Greek term which has a range of meanings, running through 'word', 'saying', and 'statement', to 'account', 'resumé' and 'defence', depending on the context in which it is used. The prologue speaks of this *logos* as being with God, and as the agency of creation. Within a Jewish context, Wisdom – conceived of as a woman – was held to be God's companion in the beginning (see Proverbs 8.22–31, and the identification of the speaker in vv. 1–3). 'Wisdom' in Jewish circles was probably not thought of as a figure distinct from God, but as an image of God's wise creativity, and some scholars would associate John's *logos* with her. Others rely more heavily on the use of *logos* in Stoic circles, in order to refer to the rational principle of human and natural life; for them, the prologue speaks in a thoroughly Hellenistic idiom. Others still, in a more speculative fashion, relate the prologue to the conceptions of Gnosticism. Gnosticism was a movement which flowered fully in the second century AD although its roots are much earlier, and its influence was long felt. (In the Introduction, the thought of the Christian Gnostics Marcion and Valentinus was discussed.) The central motivation of Gnosticism was generally a quest for 'knowledge' (*gnōsis* in Greek), but knowledge of a specific kind. Gnostics believed that the world we live in is an illusion of matter, quite unrelated to divine reality. The true God can therefore not be known except by a special gift of knowledge, which is what Gnostics sought. They explained the illusive appearance of earthly life by positing that, from the true God, partially divine figures emerged; the term *logos* can be applied to such a force in Gnostic circles. Given the wide range of meanings of *logos* in Greek, none of these three proposals for understanding the setting of the prologue can be excluded at the outset.

The question of where the prologue was composed, and within which point of view, remains a matter for discussion. Indeed, to proceed further in discussing that issue would require a greater degree of technicality than can be accommodated in the present volume. But more straightforwardly, and perhaps more fruitfully, we can say that, whatever the sources of the prologue, it was quickly read by Jews, Hellenists, and Gnostics. Those from all three groups might have felt comfortable with the word *logos*, but what the prologue claims about it must have struck them as unusual.

For those Jews who spoke Aramaic, the term 'Memra' would have been familiar from the Targums. 'Memra' may be translated 'word', but it is even more difficult to define than the Greek term *logos*. 'Memra' is used in contexts which speak of God's address of Israel, and of Israel's reaction to God. So, for example, the Targum promises, 'If you are willing and attend to my Memra, you shall eat the good of the land' (Targum Isaiah 1.19); in that case, 'Memra' is what Israel might respond to. A similar meaning is evoked by passages which speak of 'the wicked who transgressed his Memra' (see Targum Isaiah 28.21). But then there is the threat, 'If you do not attend, his Memra will become among you as an avenger' (Targum Isaiah 8.14); here, 'Memra' is an activity of God. The divine side of 'Memra' can also be expressed in creational terms, 'I stretched out the heavens by my Memra' (Targum Isaiah 44.24). Obviously, no single word in English will do justice to all these meanings (and there are other contexts of usage, as well). We can only say that 'Memra' refers to God's activity, his commanding address of Israel, and to Israel's response to God.

Clearly, there can be no assumption that the prologue was composed originally in Aramaic, or that many people with a first-hand knowledge of the Targums knew it in its present, Greek form. But the comparability of 'Memra' in the Targums and *logos* in the prologue does invite consideration from the point of view of how God relates himself to his people, which is an issue addressed in many ways within the Scriptures of Judaism. The creational associations of both terms are evident, and even the statement that the *logos* was rejected by its own people (John 1.10, 11) is reminiscent of the Targumic complaint that Israel failed, and could again fail, to obey God's 'Memra'. The promise, however, that the *logos* gives power to those who receive it to become children of God (1.12, 13) takes the term out of the range of usual meanings of 'Memra'. The Aramaic term is used within the covenantal relationship of God with his people, not, as in John, to speak of the creation of a new relationship. Finally, the assertion that 'the *logos* became flesh' (1.14) identifies it with a human being, Jesus. And this human being is said to make God known, as a son manifests his father, in a way the law could not (vv. 16–18). That claim, which is the central argument of the prologue, could only have seemed an unacceptable denigration of the Torah to Jews.

From the point of view of Stoicism, the explicit link in the prologue between the *logos* as a principle within all things (1.1–3) and the *logos* as available in life to people (1.4, 5, 9) may have seemed congenial. Even at this early point in the text, however, the Johannine *logos* appears distinct from the Stoic understanding of reason. The prologue does not assert that the *logos*, as reason, is available directly to people; rather, 'life' appears as the field in which people may operate (1.4). Because life is determined by the *logos*, it can serve as the 'light' of human beings. Illumination is available, not as the gift of reason, but as involvement in living. By implication, the ordinary conditions of life are more important in the prologue, and the *logos* is less intellectually accessible, than in Stoicism. Indeed, the *logos* is sufficiently obscure so that people can reject it (vv. 9–11); accepting the *logos* is an unusual event, which involves becoming – for the first time, not by intellectual nature – children of God (vv. 12, 13). Finally, the close association of the *logos* with a particular human being contrasts with the Stoic view of reason as transcendent, particularly because Jesus' relationship with the father is expressed in terms which are derived from Judaism (vv. 14–18).

The possibility of interpreting the *logos* as an obscure entity appealed to the proponents of Gnosticism, and they devoted considerable attention to John during the second century.

Because the Johannine *logos* is not directly accessible to human beings, rejected by them, and contrasted to what Moses made available (v. 17), it was attractive to Gnostic thinkers. They could claim support for the view that the revelation of the true father was quite other than the inferior world made by the creator (who was identified by some with the God of the Old Testament). In the end, the father could be known only by a special disclosure of the *logos*, and even that could not be identified fully with the father himself, who remained aloof from human conditions. To be saved meant being generated as a new being (vv. 12, 13). In order to pursue this line of argument, however, Gnostics had to ignore, or explain away, central features of the text. The bald statement that the *logos* was the very centre of life (v. 4), in which people's 'light' was to be discovered, was embarrassing to the hard and fast separation of divine reality and human existence among Gnostics. Indeed, 'light' is said in the prologue to enlighten every person (v. 9), rather than to be a gift withheld from all but a few. Those who receive the *logos* select themselves by their willingness to receive it (v. 12); they become 'begotten' (v. 13) by God as a result of their choice, not as a result of a constitutional difference in their ability to know God. The father is made directly known by the *logos*, who is his unique representative (v. 18); God comes directly and intimately into human affairs, rather than remaining an alien truth. All this is possible because the *logos* actually 'became flesh' (v. 14), which is a statement at odds with the Gnostic contempt for material existence.

Comparison with other systems of discourse, which involve distinctive views of the world, enables the reader more clearly to perceive the particular profile of the Johannine *logos*. Its personal focus, the claim that it inaugurates a new relationship with God, and its contrast with the law of Moses, make it stand apart from the Targumic conception of the 'Memra'. Again, the association of the *logos* with a particular human being makes it seem uncongenial to a Stoic or Gnostic conception; it is too particular to be construed as a principle of reason, too material to be interpreted as a flash of light from an alien God.

Reading the New Testament within the context of its constituent worlds need not, and should not, involve reducing its message to generalities of thought in the ancient world. On the contrary, the individuality of any document, biblical or not, can only be perceived when one observes its interface with the systems of discourse that impinge upon it. Whether or not those who contributed to the New Testament were aware of the fact, the milieu in which they were nurtured gave them the vocabulary and conventions to express their faith, and an understanding of their cultural language is necessary to appreciate what they had to say. Their use of actual, literary sources, Jewish or Hellenistic (or both), can be an index of the forms of thought they applied, but the world they lived in was larger than the documents they happened to cite. Their world included a range of assumptions and expectations about God and humanity, and a language with which to speak about such issues. Consciously or unconsciously, every speaker and writer in any age brings such influences to light in what she or he says. Moreover, once a statement is made, orally or in writing, the speaker loses control of it. The statement enters the world it addresses, and is interpreted by hearers or readers within the horizon of their own world. For that reason, the meaning of the New Testament can only be appreciated with reference to the world of those who contributed to it, but also with reference to the world of those who were expected to hear or read it. As an ancient document, the New Testament is an act of communication in the past; no historical act of communication can be appreciated unless we know what was intended, and what was understood, by the words that were said. For precisely that reason, the worlds of the New Testament are the subject of increased study and vigorous research today.

FOR FURTHER READING

S. Freyne, *The World of the New Testament*: New Testament Message 2 (Wilmington: Michael Glazier, 1980) is a suitable introduction to the concept and study of 'world'. More specific discussion is available in C. Osiek, *What Are They Saying About the Social Setting of the New Testament?* (New York: Paulist Press, 1984). Further information is available, but in a somewhat dated format, in F. F. Bruce, *New Testament History* (London: Pickering and Inglis, 1982; Garden City: Doubleday, 1972).

An excellent primer in Judaism is J. Neusner, *Judaism in the Beginning of Christianity* (London: SPCK, 1984; Philadelphia: Fortress Press, 1984); a more traditionally historical treatment is A. R. C. Leaney, *The Jewish and Christian World 200 BC to AD 200*: Cambridge Commentaries on Writings of the Jewish and Christian World (Cambridge and New York: Cambridge University Press, 1984). The question of Jesus' relationship to early Judaism (and particularly to figures such as Ḥanina ben Dosa) is addressed by Vermes, whose work is noted in chapter three, and – with special reference to the Isaiah Targum – in B. D. Chilton, *A Galilean Rabbi and His Bible. Jesus' Use of the Interpreted Scripture of His Time*: Good News Studies 8 (Wilmington: Michael Glazier, 1984; London: SPCK, 1984, with the subtitle, *Jesus' own interpretation of Isaiah*). The last work also discusses how references to rabbinic literature may be located.

The development of the New Testament in its Hellenistic phase, together with an analysis of how we might approach the issues referred to under the designation, 'social world', is treated in A. J. Malherbe, *Social Aspects of Early Christianity* (Philadelphia: Fortress Press, 1983). A more substantial, but also more demanding, treatment is H. C. Kee, *Miracle in the Early Christian World. A Study in Sociohistorical Method* (New Haven and London: Yale University Press, 1983). A still more technical work, which touches on the many aspects involved in a social approach, is W. A. Meeks, *The First Urban Christians. The Social World of the Apostle Paul* (New Haven and London: Yale University Press, 1983). Philostratus' *Life of Apollonius of Tyana* was translated and abridged for a Penguin edition by C. P. Jones (Harmondsworth: Penguin, 1970).

6

The New Testament and Our World
The Task of Interpretation

Whenever two people communicate, there is interpretation. In instances of conversation every day, the listener interprets what the speaker says, without special effort. The two partners in dialogue share a common language and probably have the same (or similar) views of the world. And, if the two people belong to a single community, they can also refer to the mutual acquaintances, friends, antagonists, ideas, standard jokes and other features which characterize the life of their group. Unless the conversation is boring, the speaker does not merely repeat the conventions of social life. She or he offers a fresh bit of gossip, a new idea, a variant of humour, and the listener understands by putting the statement into context. If that proves difficult, the speaker can be questioned or challenged by the listener. In any good conversation, the listener can also seize the initiative, and become the speaker.

When two people become acquainted for the first time, conversation is normally difficult. There may be bouts of apparently aimless chatter, and long, embarrassed silences. But if they move within the same social group, they will learn to converse, if only minimally. The types of conversation we have go hand in hand with our social roles: a chat with a friend is different from an interview with an employer, a tutorial with a teacher, or a session of counselling with a pastor. Much of our talk can seem routine, even ritual, but what we say, and what we understand of what is said, are at least an index of our place in a given social group, and sometimes they can change our standing. A successful interview, a well-written essay, or a timely word with a friend can all influence both how we are treated, and how we perceive ourselves. We are judged, not only by our statements, but by our appreciation of the people we speak to in their various situations.

Our speech and action largely depend on our grasp of the people with whom and the communities within which we live. In that sense, interpretative skill is a major component of our lives in human society.

The reading of any document demands refinements of interpretative skill. A reader is not usually in a position to put direct questions to an author. Indeed, the reader may know very little of the author, except as the one who wrote the document to hand. But a published work nonetheless comes to us within a social setting. When we pick up a newspaper, we know in advance the sort of thing we will find in it, and we intend to get something out of it, be it information, entertainment, or mere diversion. Once we have looked at a newspaper, even one with which we are unfamiliar, we can fairly easily distinguish between reports of current events, editorials, feature articles, sporting news, public announcements, advertisements and listings of performances. Which section we turn to usually depends on the purpose we have in reading at that moment. Newspapers, of course, have a more fixed form (and format) than most other documents, but how we approach them does help us to see that ordinary reading is not a purely passive activity. We may seem to be silent partners in a conversation with the author, but in fact we constantly relate what is written to our own needs and concerns at the time, often without being particularly aware of the personality of the author. In the case of an article which has moved us profoundly, we might remember and reflect on something we have read years earlier, perhaps without recalling where exactly we saw it.

Our reading helps to shape our understanding of and our attitude towards the world and those around us, and therefore is a means by which we define ourselves in relation to others. The most dramatic proof of this is that people who do not read frequently feel out of touch with, and even inferior to, their neighbours. The newspapers we choose to read, or not to read, provide a useful index of the relationship we have with our society, and how we might act within it. In principle, the same is true of the books we select to educate or entertain ourselves. Someone reading a textbook on physics might appear to be doing the same thing as someone reading a romantic novel, but the two people involved are entering different intellectual worlds, addressing different needs, and they will probably look at life in different ways as a result of their reading. But no matter what document we encounter, reading involves relating its concerns to ours; anything less will result in boredom and a lack of comprehension.

As compared to contemporary documents, documents from the past require even more patience and sympathy on the part of the reader in order to be understood. By definition, they emerge from and address different worlds from our own. The information they give us is not up to date, and they frequently speak of attitudes and ideas which seem foreign to us. For all that, the western world as we know it has largely defined itself by means of the use it has made of its historical inheritance. Our philosophical heritage, as some of the discussion in chapter five may suggest, is rooted in ancient Greece; the desire for a unified government, in which effective military and political powers are combined, has come to us from Rome. The attempt to relate government to the ideals of Christianity was a dominant preoccupation of the Middle Ages (and still occasionally features in American presidential elections), while the Renaissance saw a new interest in pagan culture and the arts which is still with us. The Enlightenment gave us a scientific orientation which has transformed modern civilization, and contemporary social trends and problems can to some extent be explained with reference to the modern history of nations. Of course, no set of generalizations can sum up how our world has been influenced by what has gone on before. The point is that an awareness of history is a necessary part of understanding ourselves. The past has shaped how we think, feel, and act. History involves seeing what once happened, how it happened and why; as we consider the past, we may well see reflected in it the signs of the movements which shape our own age.

History can also be illuminating in its strangeness. The human events of the past, what was said, done, thought and believed, sometimes strike a chord with today's world, but often they seem alien to modern readers. At such times, readers are reminded that there are possibilities of human thought and action beyond the horizons of modern behaviour. The plays of Aeschylus and Shakespeare, for example, convey a vivid impression of humanity precisely because they unfold in social contexts very different from our own. History is fundamental to an understanding of what it is to be human, as distinct from what it is to be a member of a particular society. The study of the past enables us to move beyond the routine conventions of the present. Within the area of subjects known as 'the humanities', history has always been considered basic. People can certainly be looked at philosophically, sociologically, psychologically, and in a variety of other ways, but history looks at specific human events in their own contexts. For that reason, it is indispensable to humanistic learning.

'Humanism' is sometimes viewed with contempt, because it has been falsely portrayed as an alternative to faith. But a humanistic way of looking at the world does not involve excluding all considerations of God. Its focus is rather on the understanding of people, of humanity, and of what influences them to be as they are. The study of people may, and often does, entail observing their religious convictions. Obviously, however, the observation that people in the past believed – for example – in divination by means of birds' entrails does not mean the system worked. Any belief held in the past becomes a possible subject for reflection in the present, but it cannot claim any assent from the reader prior to such reflection. History, the study of human events, certainly includes how people once believed, and therefore provides possibilities for belief in the present. But, by itself, historical study cannot determine which beliefs should be preferred, although it can say which proved enduring. Historians may or may not be Christian believers; their profession does not make the choice for them.

The human past has, curiously, been growing during the period in which the modern West has taken shape. As European nations colonized more and more of the earth, they encountered other civilizations, with histories of their own. Colonial, commercial, and cultural influences certainly imposed western ways on other peoples, but there were also influences in the other direction. Today, schoolchildren in Britain must learn about India, Pakistan, and the West Indies, much as American schoolchildren have in recent years been introduced more and more to indigenous (so-called 'Indian') and Spanish culture. The technology of war has brought distant countries into intense conflict, so that those in the West can no longer restrict their attention to their own history. The histories of many different peoples are now crucially relevant to the future of humanity in general: if we do not tend to those who live in other social worlds knowledgeably, contact with them may be catastrophically violent. The prospects of our planet will, to an important extent, be a function of our ability to reconcile varying cultures, each with a history which defines it.

While the ultimate task of historical inquiry reaches global proportions, the actual business of history is meticulous. Human events are not abstract ideas which can be conveyed with generalizations; each event has particular causes, is mixed with various conditioning factors, and results in a peculiar fact of history. No two people, no two wars, no two leaders, no two countries, are exactly alike. Every occurrence needs to be observed closely and fully before it can be understood. Even then, historical events are practically never explicable on a purely theoretical basis: they are traced in sources as facts in themselves, rather than as symptoms of general trends. Economic factors, for example, can influence any course of events deeply, but they do not in themselves determine the particular actions undertaken. History is frequently tied up with great leaders, an Alexander or a Jesus, but even they do not alone fully explain the course of events. Leaders require followers, people who respond to them in such a way that history seems altered. The qualities which make for leadership in one period may not amount to a significantly historical contribution in another period. The temperament of followers, as well as the prevailing social, economic, climatic, and ideological conditions in which they live, has a determinative role to play in the rise of historical movements. In addition, the impact of human events on subsequent developments belongs within the assessment of their historical significance. Once one has assessed as many of the causes, conditions, and effects as are evidenced, one can claim an understanding of what was happening. The aim of historical consideration is to observe and comprehend, not to explain away.

Miracles

The reference of the New Testament to events which are miraculous poses a problem for interpretation. As was discussed in chapter five, miraculous abilities were associated with Jewish and Hellenistic religious figures in antiquity. Both Ḥanina ben Dosa and Apollonius of Tyana, for example, were reputed as exorcists. The stories of their exorcisms feature some proof of demonic possession, the exorcist's word of command that the demon should depart, and a tangible indication marking the departure itself. (In the Talmud, see Pesaḥim 112b; the *Life of Apollonius of Tyana* presents a relevant story at 4.25.) Implicitly, or explicitly, some note of the exorcist's fame as a result of his success usually appears also. Such a pattern appears in the story of Jesus' first public action in the Gospel according to Mark (1.21–8). There, too, there is proof of possession (in that the demon speaks, v. 24), an authoritative command to depart (v. 25), a violently tangible manifestation of the demon's departure (v. 26), a note of the open amazement of those in the synagogue where the exorcism took place (v. 27), and reference to Jesus' consequent reputation (v. 28). Clearly, the New Testament at this point speaks within the conventions of its world, and is in some tension with our usually non-demoniacal understanding of reality.

Especially in this case, however, there is no question of Jewish or Hellenistic conventions of story-telling being merely appropriated within the New Testament. The literary presentation within Mark's Gospel gives the story of Jesus' first exorcism its own peculiar significance. Before the exorcism is even reported, the congregation in the synagogue is said to be astounded at the authority of Jesus' teaching (1.22), and their amazed statement after it is over is, 'What is this? A new teaching with authority!' (1.27). When Jesus is presented as teaching within Mark, the emphasis usually falls more on the identity of the one who teaches than on what he says; here also, there is no specification of Jesus' message. The Marcan point is that the story conveys a supreme, new authority.

Jesus' authority is developed along three levels in Mark, and all three are reflected in the present story. The first level is the display of authority to Jesus' contemporaries: the narrative is placed precisely in a Jewish town, on the sabbath, and in a synagogue (1.21). The congregation immediately recognizes that Jesus does not teach as the scribes, the leaders of their own community (v. 22), and the exorcism confirms that his teaching is 'new' (v. 27). At the moment, Jesus' contemporaries are merely amazed, and spread Jesus' fame (vv. 27, 28). But as the story of the entire Gospel unfolds, their reaction will be seen more and more clearly as being so partial that it leads to resistance. Jesus' next healing in a synagogue provokes deadly opposition (3.1–6), and his fame as a teacher and healer leads on his own home ground to lack of faith, not recognition (6.1–6a). The scribes with whose teaching Jesus' message is compared in 1.22 will figure prominently in his crucifixion (see 11.18; 14.1, 43, 53; 15.1, 31). The reported amazement is therefore double-edged: it signals some awareness of the true identity of Jesus, but it also foreshadows the hardening of astonishment into mortal enmity.

Within the Marcan presentation, the story also discloses the authority of Jesus at another level, directly to the reader. As compared to Jesus' immediate contemporaries, readers are in a position of privilege. They know what those in the congregation cannot, that the Gospel concerns 'Jesus Christ, God's son' (1.1), and that Jesus was designated as God's son at his baptism (1.11). When the demon identifies Jesus as 'the holy one of God' (1.24), anyone would know that Jesus' divine origin is at issue, but only the reader can know that Jesus' *sonship* is the basis of his authority. By the end of the Gospel, the reader will also know the sense in which Jesus can be understood as God's son. Only at 15.39, when the centurion confesses, 'Truly, this man was God's son,' does any human being within Mark come to the awareness the reader is expected to have all along; that truth dawns on the centurion just as Jesus' obedient suffering and death on the cross is completed. Although readers are in a position to know more than Jesus' contemporaries, for them as well, divine sonship is gradually disclosed. Even at the close of the Gospel, the women at the tomb are said to be amazed at what they see (16.5); the Greek verb used is an even more intensive form of the term used of the congregation in 1.27. Familiarity with the ministry of Jesus among sympathetic followers does not, therefore, bring an instant or full comprehension of his sonship. Astonishment is still the natural response to the mystery of who he is, although the name of that mystery ('God's son') is known. Readers and disciples know a great deal more than some, but they do not yet know everything.

The partial recognition of Jesus' identity might bring a disastrous result, as in the case of the astonished opposition of some of his contemporaries, or a creative one, as in the case of the amazed faith of his followers. There is no doubt but that Mark shapes the reader's appreciation of Jesus towards the latter outcome, but the disclosure of Jesus' identity remains incomplete. The fundamental reason for that partiality is that Mark is composed from an eschatological perspective, as was discussed in chapter three. The reader knows, especially on the basis of the thirteenth chapter, that even the resurrection of Jesus, which is the final note of the Gospel, is not the last word that can be said about him. His story as a whole, including the resurrection, points forward to his glorious parousia as the son of man who comes in glory to judge by means of angels (see 13.24–7). From the point of view of the Marcan text, only that moment constitutes a full disclosure of the identity which the story of Jesus' exorcism intimates.

Within the story itself, there are hints of the eschatological perspective which governs the Gospel as a whole. The demon in 1.23 is identified as a single entity; it says, 'I know who you are' within v. 24, and is commanded with a singular construction in the Greek of v. 25. But in v. 24a, it says, 'What do you want with *us*': it seems to speak as a representative of the collective of evil forces which Jesus, as the son of man, will one day subdue entirely (along with every power of nature, see Mark 13.24, 25). Indeed, the demon fears Jesus has 'come to *destroy us*'. In the ancient world, demons were normally thought of as being banished by exorcists, not as being destroyed by them. The demon here intimates a fearful awareness that this particular exorcist is more than an immediate antagonist: his exorcisms signal the beginning of the end of Satan's entire régime. Jesus' contemporaries are not portrayed as perceiving the eschatological significance of the exorcism, but readers know that Jesus has already been put to the test by Satan himself (1.12, 13), and they will be told that Jesus' exorcisms indicate that Satan has been bound, so that his entire household can successfully be plundered

(3.23–7). Jesus' identity is an eschatological force, which will be fully recognized only when the new world he ushers in is realized.

The three levels of Jesus' authority, for his contemporaries, for Mark's readers, and at the end, are in no way rigidly separated from one another in the story. On the contrary, each is indicated or intimated as the single narrative of the exorcism unfolds. When the text is approached as literature, whether its literary features are considered traditional or redactional (see chapter one), its sense as a presentation of Jesus' authority and identity emerges. Although the question remains of how its reference to a miracle should be understood in our world, the story nonetheless conveys a clear meaning which can be described and appreciated. The literary sense of the narrative reminds us that its meaning is not locked up irretrievably in categories of thought and perception different from our own. However alien it may seem in some respects, it can be translated, read, and understood. By perceiving an ancient document according to the literary conventions it develops, one permits it at least partially to convey its meaning within our own world.

The development of a literary consideration, however, is no short cut through historical difficulties. Indeed, one feature of understanding an ancient text involves deciding whether it is designed to speak, and succeeds in speaking, in historical terms. The story in Mark seems to make a categorical statement about the past. Jesus' authority is said to be instanced in an event, and is not presented simply as a literary motif. Accordingly, our reading of the passage will be influenced by the decision whether a historical event is actually spoken of. If the exorcism did not take place, the claims of the text will appear purely theoretical; if we decide it did, the text will seem to offer a more substantial statement of Jesus' authority.

Jesus' parable of the strong man, in which he claims that his exorcisms demonstrate that Satan himself is bound (Mark 3.23–7), also appears in Matthew (12.25–9) and Luke (11.17–22). In another saying within the presentations of Matthew and Luke (see 12.28 and 11.20, respectively), he insists that his exorcisms signal the proximity of God's kingdom. These sayings are widely agreed to be authentic; they reflect a self-consciousness of exorcistic ability, which agrees with Jesus' reputation in the New

Testament, as well as in Jewish and Hellenistic sources outside the New Testament. There is scarcely any doubt that Jesus was thought, and considered himself, a successful exorcist. But our relative certainty in that regard does not indicate that the first story of an exorcism in Mark is historical. It is perfectly possible that, because Jesus was widely reputed as an exorcist, stories about particular exorcisms were generated among those who respected him. Nonetheless, the Marcan story is told as a plausible narrative, and the Gospel would not likely commence with a tale which was known to be dubious, especially since it was held to manifest Jesus' authority. Whatever we might decide about the historicity of the passage, it seems to have been related as an actual occurrence.

From the point of view of deciding whether the passage relates a specifically historical event, two features of the text are striking. First, the demon is reported to say to Jesus, 'I know who you are, the holy one of God' (1.24). In the Jewish and Hellenistic sources which mention exorcism, the technique of naming normally appears as a means by which an exorcist gains control over a demon. Here, that convention is reversed, because the demon is portrayed as naming Jesus, in order to ward him away. Jesus then employs an effective counter measure (v. 25), but the demon departs with violence, convulsing its victim and screaming (v. 26). Such violence, together with the demonic attempt to gain control over Jesus, does not belong to the stock and trade of narratives of exorcism, where the supreme ability of exorcists tends instead to be stressed. The demon's violent resistance is also at odds with the Marcan stress on Jesus' magisterial authority. In that regard, Matthew notably does not present the story, and Luke merely has the demon throw the man down, adding the specific assurance that it did him no harm (4.35); quite evidently, the demon's extreme violence was not thought an appropriate part of a story told principally to Jesus' credit. The demonic struggle against Jesus is therefore not a conventional feature of the story in Mark, but is in some tension with the desire to highlight the exorcist's power.

Within the Marcan presentation of the story, the demon's violent resistance is roughly consonant with the emphasis on the ultimate rejection of Jesus by his contemporaries, and on the eschatological significance of his ministry. But that feature does not fit easily with the supreme focus of Mark on Jesus' authority. The unconventional features of the passage seem rather to belong to the perception and expression of the exorcism as a specific, historical event. The best explanation of these odd elements is that the event was believed to have happened as it is narrated. That is to say, the text makes a particularly historical claim. At the very heart of the narrative, we discover an exorcism which was perceived to have occurred, and which was remembered, and handed on, as a significant story with unusual features.

Nothing about this passage suggests we are in the realm of symbol, as distinct from fact. There seems no way of denying that the claim of an actual occurrence is being made; that perceived occurrence obviously shaped the appreciation of Jesus among his followers. Moreover, there is insufficient evidence to permit of suggesting that the possessed man was suffering from an illness which modern medics could diagnose. What we are left with is the substantial claim in the New Testament, within the conventions of its world, that a specific exorcism took place. But we have also had, from the very beginning, a doubt at the back of our minds: within the conventions of our world, exorcisms are not events which are reliably reported. It is true that a questioning of scientific assumptions has recently become fashionable, and the issue of exorcism has been subjected to studies of cases. But the existence of demons is not now established as a matter of agreement, and the majority of exorcistic stories available in the media are quite fictional. We are in no position to say that all exorcisms are impossible, but we are far from accepting exorcistic stories, from the ancient or the modern world, as a matter of course.

Consideration of the text brings us, therefore, to the point where we might distinguish between historical facts and facts of our own experience. A historical fact is a human event from the past, an occurrence once perceived which influenced what happened thereafter. The story of Jesus' first exorcism in Mark belongs to that category, but its terms of reference do not belong to the common experience and perception of the present. Within a world which acknowledged the existence of demons and the general possibility of exorcism (see, for example, 9.38–41), Jesus was perceived to free a man from possession. From a more scientific perspective, one can appreciate the sense of liberation and wonderment which the event provoked, without accepting that demons exist. Taken on its own terms, the story does not, after all, attempt to prove the existence of demons. Along with such stories in Philostratus and the Talmud, it merely takes their existence for granted.

By attending to the literary sense of such passages within the world of the time, it is possible to appreciate their impact, even within the context of our own world. That process might stretch our estimate of what is possible in human experience, but it by no means requires that our own understanding of reality should be dropped. Our perceptions, as the perceptions of those who contributed to the New Testament, operate within the prevailing social world. No world is inherently superior to another, different though any two may be: just as narratives of miracles in the New Testament cannot be written off as uncritical fantasy, so the rational reserve of our age cannot be wished away as extreme scepticism. A social world is not merely an idea which can be disproved. Rather, it is the range of conventions according to which it is possible for a group of human beings to perceive, act, and speak with one another. Whether or not those conventions admit of demons, they require to be recognized as the framework of human events, past and present.

Manifestly, that framework has altered since the first century. The task of interpretation is not to gloss over that change: it is obviously important to bear in mind where and how social worlds are different. A clear appreciation of variations between worlds enables us to acknowledge the historicity of human events in the past, and yet to resist the assumption that the terms of past experience apply directly to our own. And that assumption must be resisted, since otherwise we would deny the reality of our own world, which is the only field in which we can perceive, act, and communicate. Historical interpretation involves relating the worlds of the past and the present, without confusing the two.

The parousia

The eschatological dimension of the New Testament, which was discussed in chapter three, is one of its most surprising features for modern readers. The reading of a historical document naturally orientates us to think in terms of the past. When a figure such as Apollonius is said to foresee the future (see chapter five), the predicted time is, even for the initial reader of Philostratus, in the past. The *Life of Apollonius of Tyana* does not make claims about the immediate or distant future of its intended audience. The New Testament, on the other hand, makes the absolute claim that the future belongs to God. In doing so, the documents align themselves with Jewish prophetic and apocalyptic writing. The eschatological orientation of the New Testament is unusual from the point of view of modern thinking, but it is far from unique.

'The kingdom of God', which was central to Jesus' preaching (see chapter one), is a phrase which also appears in the Aramaic Targums. For example, in the Isaiah Targum, prophets are told to announce, 'The kingdom of your God is revealed', and what follows is a description of God's eschatological judgement (40.9, 10). In Jesus' preaching, however, God's future intervention is portrayed as so near as to impinge on the present; those who heard the message of the kingdom were urgently called to repent in the face of a pressing reality (see Matthew 4.17; Mark 1.15). The feeling that the future requires urgent attention is, as it happens, not foreign to our own world. Technological change has recently occurred at such a rate, and seemingly ultimate power has become so concentrated in the hands of a few, that the options which face our species seem reduced to two stark alternatives: virtual extinction or unprecedented ease. Time may in fact bring a more muddled future than many fear or hope, but political discussion in the West since nuclear weapons were devised has tended to revolve around the twin issues of total war and eagerly sought prosperity.

Anxious scenarios and optimistic scenarios, of nearly apocalyptic detail, find their way into popular discussion, and in both cases the future is the focus of our attention. Expectations of what will come influence our attitudes, the plans we lay, and the activities we undertake in the present. And we are only too aware that the future might overrule what we do. The New Testament's preaching of a determinative future, which provides the final assessment of all human behaviour, is therefore not as foreign to today's readers as it was to those even fifty years ago. But Jesus' announcement of the kingdom was no general assertion that the future is important. He proclaimed that the divine activity which would be consummated was already operative in the present, and that it demanded recognition and response. The kingdom, as he preached it, was not the blind tyranny of time and chance, but the intervention and rule of God himself. That Jesus taught people about God seems a predictable statement, but his intimate portrayal of God's rule, especially in parables, is a feature of his teaching which made him stand out from his contemporaries. The kingdom was the hallmark of his message and also, as we have seen, of his exorcistic ministry (Matthew 12.28; Luke 11.20).

In the book of Acts, Peter makes a speech which is widely regarded as a summary of early Christian preaching, and which coheres with the portrait of Jesus' ministry in the Gospels. Notably, Peter delivers his sermon in the house of Cornelius, a Roman officer (10.1, 2, 22); the speech is particularly instructive of how preachers approached the task of explaining their faith to potential Gentile converts. Peter gives a brief account of Jesus' message and healing ministry (10.36–8). He emphasizes that he and his colleagues are witnesses of what happened, and then speaks of Jesus' crucifixion and resurrection (10.39–41). The repeated emphasis at the end of v. 41 on Jesus' fellowship with his followers, even after his death, underscores what the New Testament elsewhere attests (especially in the Gospels), that the resurrection was a historical event. Whatever we might make of the actuality of the experience, the perception of Jesus as risen from the dead transformed his followers' estimate of him. Of course, their immediate inference was that Jesus was vindicated over his enemies: the integrity of his message was confirmed by God (see Peter's statements in Acts 2.22–4, 36; 3.14, 15; 4.10). But the risen Jesus is more than an emblem of substantiated teaching. In Acts 10.42, Peter goes on to insist that Jesus commanded his followers 'to preach to the people and bear witness that he himself is appointed by God to be judge of the living and the dead'.

The shift in early Christian preaching, from an expectation of the kingdom to the proclamation that Jesus is the judge of the last time, is a signal development. But it is a development, and not an altogether fresh departure. By the end of his career, Jesus was opposed by the full weight of religious and secular institutions. If he was right in what he said about God's kingdom, then both the Jewish leaders, who condemned him, and the Roman officials, who had him executed, were disastrously wrong. One reason why Jesus' authority was so insistently stressed in the New Testament, especially in Mark, is that it came into violent conflict with other forms of authority. The resurrection designated Jesus, in his disciples' understanding, as the sole representative of God's eschatological rule. When God came to judge the earth, as they hoped he soon would, he would apply the very standards of the kingdom which Jesus alone set out. Jesus as a person, his actions as well as his words, was the pattern of God's ultimate intervention.

Chapter three outlined the principal terms, parousia and 'the son of man', in which early Christians expressed their distinctive, eschatological hope. That expectation is clearly spelled out by Paul in 1 Corinthians: Christ as raised is a 'first fruit', the beginning of a final harvest (15.20). This beginning is to be followed by those who are of Christ 'in his parousia' (15.23). But Christ is not merely a passive sign of the end; it is he who will actively 'hand over the dominion to the God and father, when he abolishes every rule, and every authority and power' (15.24). All his enemies, including death, are to be abolished under Christ (15.25–7a). At this apparently climactic point in the eschatological drama, however, Paul offers an important qualification. The submission of all things to Christ obviously does not include God (v. 27b, c), because the son will finally himself be submitted, 'that God might be all in all' (v. 28). Paul's qualification is an eloquent reminder that faith in the parousia developed within an eschatological expectation which was focused directly on God himself. Jesus was the standard and agent of divine judgement, not its replacement.

Later in the same chapter, and while addressing the same subject, Paul solemnly asserts that 'flesh and blood cannot inherit the kingdom of God' (15.50); those who believe in Christ are to be changed at their resurrection, as he was at his (15.51–7). To Paul's mind, the parousia (of which he had already spoken) was the particular means by which the inheritance of the kingdom would be won. Jesus' resurrection was the seal that he would come again, and – at the same time – the pattern of believers' eschatological transformation. Within the book of Acts, the kingdom is also portrayed as a concept which is collateral with that of the parousia. By the end of the document, Paul is clearly established as the primary spokesman of the early preaching which Peter also represented, and his sermons are consistently Christ-centred and eschatological (see chapter three). But in Acts 28.31, the last sentence of the work, Paul is portrayed as 'preaching the kingdom and teaching concerning the Lord Jesus Christ'. The point of this statement is not that Paul suddenly reverted to offering the account of the kingdom given by Jesus prior to the resurrection; rather, the kingdom and the parousia are presented as a continuous, eschatological expectation.

The Gospels also reflect the emergence of faith in the parousia as a consequence of the resurrection. The reference to the parousia in Matthew 24.3 was cited in chapter three as one instance, among others, of the way in which material ascribed to Jesus himself was shaped to address the eschatological concerns of the early Church. The degree to which the tradents and redactors of Jesus' sayings found in them a direct relevance to the parousia attests the close association in their minds between what he preached and what they themselves had come to believe. As in the letters of Paul, and Acts, the parousia in the Gospels appears as the particularly Christian form of the more generally Jewish eschatology taught by Jesus.

The New Testament's eschatology is extraordinarily specific, not in its apocalyptic expectations or a scenario of later events, but in its insistence that the standard and agent of God's judgement is a person. It leaves practically no room for an interpretation which refers only to the determinative impact of the future on the present. The future it proclaims belongs exclusively to God, and exclusively to God as made known – and soon to rule – in Christ. Whatever our anxieties and wishes for the time to come, the New Testament insists on a single hope, grounded in the resurrection and Jesus' preaching, that the only future which matters is a person. Our future is determined by how we stand in relation to him, not merely by our own decisions and the plans we might lay. No interpretation of the New Testament can be commended which fails to express, difficult though it is to understand, the irreducibly personal and final claims of Christian eschatology.

Women in the New Testament

Among the many movements of reform which emerged in the West in the 1960s, perhaps none has proved as influential as 'women's liberation'. The consciousness has steadily grown since then, while other movements have come and gone, that women are treated as inferior citizens in our societies, and that such treatment is wrong. People are people, and should not be discriminated against sexually, any more than they should be discriminated against racially or ethnically. There are striking exceptions in our history to the rule that women occupied an inferior place: learned Jewish leaders included women, Christian abbesses wielded almost episcopal power during the Middle Ages, and the scientific innovators who helped shape the modern world were not only men. But the very fact that powerful women seem notable attests the assumption, generally unexpressed, that men normally prevail.

Arguably, the worlds of the Bible were not significantly more patriarchal than our own was until recently. Indeed, although the bland preference in ancient times for the rule of aged men may seem absurd by contemporary standards, today's vogue for feminism has scarcely resulted in sexual equality. In Britain and America, women are not well represented in the most influential jobs, they themselves generally vote for male rather than female politicians, and their progress in the labour market has been most successful in what are called 'service occupations', such as secretarial and teaching positions. The more positive side of sexual discrimination includes the facts that women are not required to perform military duties as much as men are, that they frequently are not forced by circumstances to be the 'bread winners' of their families, and that they commonly enjoy preferential rates of vehicle and life insurance (because on average they drive more safely, and live longer, than men). The social realities of our time are perhaps better evidence of the place of women than the success of women's movements in getting intellectuals to say 'person', rather than 'man', and in reforming western policies on the control of pregnancy. No doubt, the reform of habits of speech, and of law, are important indicators of how societies might continue to develop. But we are less tolerant sexually than many of us could wish.

Those who contributed to the New Testament employed language, and invoked customs, which are more patriarchal than today's fashion would dictate. Jesus' élite circle of twelve disciples consisted exclusively of men, and no document in the New Testament is ascribed to the authorship of a woman. Given the dangers of travel, and the customary practice of education, these features of the texts are not surprising. Had Jesus sent out women to travel in pairs, or partnered with men in pairs, to proclaim the kingdom while tempting the heartless violence of criminals along highways, he would have confronted even more amazed opposition than he did. Within his world, to have dispatched women to be outnumbered by men would have seemed an invitation to sexual exploitation. Again, while a teacher such as Paul might accept the hospitality of a Lydia (see Acts 16.14, 15), the conventions of the time told against the possibility that women might be in a position to publish writings, or have them widely read. To charge the New Testament, or any historical document, with 'sexism' on the grounds that it conformed generally to its own world is not sensible. Those who contributed to it were in no position to be fully aware of, or to act against, sexual discrimination, any more than they could appreciate modern understandings of racism, or the development of science. Any writer or figure from the past is likely to appear 'sexist', since the recent fashion was not in force earlier. But, relative to the situation at the time, a document might have exercised a sexually liberating influence, without conforming to the language of modern feminism.

In some respects, the New Testament exerted just such an influence. The Gospel according to Luke uniquely relates the story of Martha and Mary (10.38–42): Jesus accepts Martha's

166

hospitality, but then insists that she should let her sister join those listening to him, rather than urge Mary to help with the increased housework caused by his visit. That Jesus should have permitted a woman to join the ranks of those learning from him is itself unusual, when judged by the standard of rabbinic attitudes. A certain rabbi, named Eliezer ben Hyrcanus, taught a very different rule shortly after the time of Jesus: 'Whoever teaches his daughter law, it is as if he taught her lewdness' (Mishnah Soṭah 3.4). Eliezer's statement is quite extreme in comparison to the stated views of other rabbis, and may even reflect his own marital problems, since his wife was noted for her expertise in the rabbinic discussion of law. But the rabbis generally did not include women among their students; the sexes were distinguished according to which laws they should keep, and women did not play the full role men did in synagogues. Whatever 'word' Jesus was speaking when Mary listened to him (10.39), it is related in the Lucan presentation to Torah, the guidance of God for Israel. The passage which immediately precedes (10.25–37) relates the parable of the kind Samaritan, which illustrates the commandment in Leviticus 19.18 to love one's neighbour. In Luke, Mary's place of attentive discipleship within the discussion of law is 'the good part, which shall not be taken from her' (10.42), whatever the conventions of the day might dictate.

Luke manifests a particular interest in the place of women within the ministry of Jesus. He describes some as supporting him and his twelve disciples during tours of preaching (8.1–3), much as Lydia will later support Paul (see Acts 16.15). Although supportive contributions are vital to preaching, they are also clearly subsidiary to it. But all of the Gospels agree that the witnesses of the empty tomb, which signals the resurrection of Jesus within the narratives, were women, although there is some variation in the names which are given and in the course of events described (Matthew 28.1–10; Mark 16.1–8; Luke 24.1–11; John 20.1, 2, 11–18). The story of the empty tomb occupies a crucial place in the portrayal of Jesus' resurrection, and the primacy of feminine witnesses within it is notable in two respects. First, given the convention within Judaism that women could not offer legally binding testimony, the story does not give the impression of being a made-up tale. Second, women are assigned a vital role within the very fabric of the Gospels at one of the most significant moments. The story of the empty tomb may have been included in a narrative of Jesus' passion compiled before the Gospels were written (see chapter one); in that case, the place of the female witnesses would have been secured at a very early stage. Even if the story developed later, the social inferiority of women in the ancient world makes the suggestion that the sex of the witnesses was a detail which was invented (for example, to please rich female patrons) seem improbable. Women rather belong to the structural centre of the Gospels' preaching.

The place of women in Paul's writings is, to say the least, ambiguous, and has been the subject of considerable controversy. A full discussion of 1 Corinthians 14.34, for instance, would require greater length than can be afforded here. (One reason for the ambiguity of the passage in its context is discussed in the next chapter.) In any case, the clearest argument against the leadership of women in the Church appears, not in the genuinely Pauline letters, but in 1 Timothy 2.11–15. There, the author states plainly in Paul's name that women are neither to teach, nor to wield authority over men. Eve was formed after Adam, and then was deceived in Eden. She, and women generally, will be saved by bearing children, if they behave properly. The author's teaching, of course, is based on Genesis 2.18–3.16, and conveniently excludes reference to the punishment assigned to Adam in Genesis 3.17–19. More importantly, the author applies the story in Genesis in a new way. As it stands in the Hebrew Bible, Genesis 3.16 explains why women suffer in childbirth and obey their husbands; the author of 1 Timothy takes such suffering and obedience as the only role women should fulfil. At this point, the New Testament so resists the emerging authority of women that it seems extreme, even by the prevailing Jewish and Hellenistic standards.

What is the interpreter to do in the face of contradictory assertions within the New Testament? When we read a document, whether it is by a single author or the composite product of many contributors, our normal assumption is that it will express a coherent perspective. But authors can and do contradict themselves, and people who share a claim to the same faith often disagree. Sometimes disagreements within the New Testament can be explained with reference to the differing conditions in which the followers of Jesus lived. If women were commonly agreed to be the first people to attest Jesus' resurrection, then there was little choice for his disciples, whatever the status of women at the time, but to admit the fact. And if overbearing women posed a problem for the community of 1 Timothy, the author's appeal for conventional order seems less trenchantly anti-feminist. On the other hand, the two stances remain at variance; the conditions of the statements do not explain why they move in opposite directions from one another.

The task of historical interpretation is to appreciate such contradictions, not to iron them out. To describe what the texts say, how they mean what they say, and what we might make of that meaning, is sufficiently demanding, without then trying to set one text in judgement on another. The stance of Jesus and those who framed the story of the empty tomb seems different from that of the author of 1 Timothy, but neither is historically superior to the other. One was sooner, the other later, within the development of the New Testament. But both belong within the text as a whole. The first cannot be made normative because it makes a more original, and earlier, statement, nor can the second be made the rule to judge the first because it is a more mature expression of the Christian faith at a later period. Each has its integrity within its own literary context, its social setting, and within the way it strikes the conventions of our world.

One can no more convincingly say the New Testament teaches the liberation of women, and not their submission, than one can say it proclaims the kingdom, but not the parousia. Even when texts are not at variance with one another, they may throw up interpretative questions: the historical aspect of Jesus' first exorcism in Mark indicates that demons were once perceived as significant, but it does not settle the question whether demons actually exist, or are insubstantial figments of human imagination. In respect of exorcism, eschatology, and the role of women, the New Testament – when read critically – discloses a range of options to the reader. It does not present a single answer to the issues raised within the texts, although a central focus on the revelation of God through Christ is maintained throughout.

In the absence of a completely harmonious perspective within the New Testament, readers sometimes impose their own harmony upon it. By using the hoary technique of selecting the texts one most agrees with, and interpreting them out of context, one can make the New Testament seem to support positions which are alien to it. Stories about miracles can be plundered for notices of the subjective reactions of bystanders, while any historical aspects are ignored; the result is to make miracles seem purely symbolic, although they are not portrayed as such. References to the kingdom and the parousia can be conflated to produce precisely the sort of apocalyptic scenario which the New Testament never presents. And women can be liberated or oppressed, if the appropriate texts are taken as an infallible rule.

A more honest approach would admit: 'I wish to see miracles as purely symbolic, or set out an apocalyptic scenario, or liberate/oppress women, and the New Testament in some respects accords partially with what I prefer.' In other words, at this point an interpretation of texts is not being offered at all; what is on offer is a personal opinion, and texts are cited in order to give the false impression that the New Testament as a whole supports the position. The majority of those who engage in this sort of 'interpretation' probably do so unconsciously, by confusing the sense of texts with the value they attach to their own opinions. However the mistake arises, confusion is its origin, and its result. When personal views are mixed up with the meaning of ancient texts, understanding is made impossible; at any given moment, it may be the document, or the 'interpreter', whose standpoint is represented.

Critical interpreters require sufficient self-awareness to know the difference between what they read and the opinion they prefer. That awareness will sometimes lead the interpreter to see shades of opinion, some perhaps contradictory, in the document to hand. But as interpretation proceeds, most readers will find perspectives that ring true to their own experience, and others that seem remote. The interpretation of a statement, the assessment of what it means, naturally leads the reader to reflect on the value of the statement. If one statement seems more valuable than another, that in itself does not make it any more central to the New Testament, but it says a great deal about the reader. Judgements of value are subjective, and derive from readers who encounter documents. But it is possible for those who reflect on what they read to discuss their views, and so to confirm, revise, or adjust their perceptions. At that stage, however, the document is no longer the object of inquiry; the reader is at the centre of the stage. And when readers who reflect on the New Testament discuss which aspects of its assertions about God they find more or less valuable, they have entered the field of discourse known as theology.

FOR FURTHER READING

Interpretative issues which arise from critical reading are addressed by P. Stuhlmacher, *Historical Criticism and Theological Interpretation of Scripture. Towards a Hermeneutics of Consent* (London: SPCK, 1979; Philadelphia: Fortress Press, 1978), and D. Nineham, *The Use and Abuse of the Bible. A Study of the Bible in an Age of Rapid Cultural Change* (London: Macmillan, 1976; New York: Barnes and Noble, 1976).

Some of the basic difficulties posed by narratives of miraculous events are discussed in A. Richardson, *The Bible in the Age of Science* (London: SCM Press, 1961; Philadelphia: Westminster, 1961); B. N. Kaye, *The Supernatural in the New Testament*: Interpreting the Bible (Guildford: Lutterworth, 1977; in the series entitled Miracles and Mysteries in the Bible, Philadelphia: Westminster, 1978).

The challenge of interpreting eschatology is foremost in W. Pannenberg, *Theology and the Kingdom of God* (Philadelphia: Westminster, 1969) and J. Moltmann, *Theology of Hope. On the Ground and the Implications of a Christian Eschatology* (London: SCM Press, 1967; New York: Harper and Row, 1967).

Two recent publications which deal with the place of women in the New Testament are E. and F. Stagg, *Women in the World of Jesus* (Philadelphia: Westminster, 1978) and, far more comprehensively, E. S. Fiorenza, *In Memory of Her. A Feminist Theological Reconstruction of Christian Origins* (New York: Crossroad, 1983).

7

Paths of Faith
The New Testament and Theology

Theology consists of the attempt to give an account of God, particularly as he relates to people. The bases on which theology may proceed vary enormously. The Bible features prominently in the Christian tradition as the ground upon which theological statements are made, but it is not the exclusive basis. Theologians may also offer descriptions of, and assess, the work of writers who contributed to the history of the Church, such as Augustine, Thomas Aquinas and Martin Luther. Then again, they may attempt to express theological judgements in relation to the major philosophical systems of western thought. Alongside biblical theology, therefore, there is also historical theology and systematic theology. And there is the question, how might theological insights be acted upon in the setting of our own time? That question is at the forefront of ethical theology and pastoral theology.

The branches of theological discourse have become so specialized that individual investigators normally concentrate on one of them. Practically speaking, communication among the branches is often difficult, but it is vital for the health of theology as a whole. At its end, as well as in its origin, the entire enterprise is designed to define and explain God, and to offer its conclusions for human belief and action. The nature of theological discourse is such that no convincing statement can be made about God which is limited to biblical, historical, or philosphical inquiry. Before a claim about God in the New Testament, for example, can be taken as an essential aspect of Christian faith, it must be shown to have been historically influential on the Church, and to be philosophically understandable. Theological statements must be viable in all three fields of inquiry, and they must make ethical and pastoral sense. If they are restricted to one branch of

172

theology, and do not address the concerns of our day, they will appear theoretical, rather than believable.

During the Middle Ages, theology was known as 'the queen of the sciences'. That designation reflected an awareness that theological thought is not a simple discipline, or way of looking at things, but a synthesis of what the various fields of knowledge together suggest about God. Traditionally, and quite correctly, theological training has been conducted on the assumption that students are already equipped with capability in humanistic learning. Theology is a demanding monarch, a subject which requires familiarity with exegesis, interpretation, and historical investigation, as well as philosophical and pastoral acuity. If any of these aspects is missing, theological discourse appears one-sided, and irrelevant to the issues of the contemporary world.

In addition to the complexity traditionally involved in theological discourse, the cultural ferment of our world has contributed a new complication. Although distinctive Christian denominations have arisen, each claiming to speak on behalf of the Church, none of them can conduct theology on its own. The denominations, willingly or not, find themselves in dialogue with one another. Consequently, they must increasingly justify their positions, not on the basis of what their own favourite teachers have said, but as reasoned and lucid accounts of God's revelation in Christ. Books by Baptists are read and reviewed by Catholics, and vice versa; neither lay people nor priests can be kept from theological influences which are outside the normal run of thought in any denomination. Quite apart from official discussions between different denominational churches, theology has become an ecumenical subject.

The contemporary situation places considerable pressure on theologians. No matter which branches of the subject they primarily work in, developing the particular sorts of expertise which are necessary, they must also be cognizant of what is happening in other branches. And although they have been schooled within particular Christian communities, they are responsible to the global community of theological scholarship in the statements they make. Conflicts of loyalty are inevitable. Denominations hire academic staff for employment in colleges and seminaries on the expectation that doctrines held by the community will be maintained, but a theologian may find it necessary to question or doubt some doctrines on academic grounds. Year by year, there are instances of theologians who are rebuked, and even lose their employment, because they find it necessary to question teaching which they themselves cherish. The denominational leaders involved may feel it necessary to protect their communities from assaults of doubt on central doctrines, but they cannot indefinitely resist the force of discussion and debate. Theology is an international and interdenominational subject. Churches will either learn to address themselves, directly and with integrity, to the theological issues of the day, or they will be rightly perceived as more interested in their own particular traditions than in God's claims on the world. The anxiety felt by many theologians in view of their divided loyalty is often painful to them personally, but their distress is part of the birth pangs of a new era in theology.

Christian faith has no monopoly on discussion about God. Education in universities has recently taken more account of other great religions, including Judaism, Islam, Hinduism, Buddhism, Taoism, and Confucianism. While scholars who work in denominational institutions have their own pressures to bear, their colleagues in universities face yet another challenge. Those involved in the comparative study of religions typically introduce their students to several theological systems and their customs, but it is not possible to deal with even the major religions of the world in any depth. And once selected areas have been studied, what – if anything – can be said about God? Investigating a few forms of religious expression, however sympathetically, can seem more a literary, sociological, or historical exercise than an occasion for theological discourse. The comparative study of religions is a necessary feature of higher education today, but comparative religionists still have to struggle for their identity as theologians. The purely descriptive consideration of the faith reflected in a document, be it the Koran or the New Testament, may be interesting in itself, but theology demands that the study of documents be related to an account of God.

The New Testament's account of God

Study of the New Testament is irrevocably a part of theological discussion. In broad outline, its distinctive message is that the LORD, a single and unique god, created all things, chose his people Israel, and sent his only son, Jesus Christ, to call his people to himself; Jesus is the only standard of human life acceptable to God, and by the standard and agency of his son, God will soon judge the world. Within this account, creation and eschatology, God's activity at the beginning and in the end, stand out clearly as the framework within which everything else unfolds. God makes and judges; to acknowledge the LORD involves admitting one's dependence upon, and responsibility towards, a god who is beyond the terms of ordinary existence. In the understanding reflected in the New Testament, the source and goal of human life are defined by a single god (hence, 'God'); the fulfilment of humanity resides only in that nameable, personal God (the LORD of the Old Testament). God in this account is transcendent, beyond the terms of life as we know it, because he must be outside the world he creates and judges. But this God is also described within human terms when he is conceived of as a person. In Exodus 3.13–15, God's name is given to Moses as 'Yahweh', which is normally replaced by 'LORD' or 'Lord', because Jewish teachers wished to avoid cheapening the holy name by too frequent repetition or less than fully devout invocation. But the conviction that God could be named attests the strength of the belief that he is personal. As the very image in which people are made (see Genesis 1.26, 27), the God who is transcendent is also available to humanity. Divine availability occurs by revelation; God reveals himself as Yahweh outside the usual run of events, and he also chooses Israel in a personal, but transcendent, act (see Genesis 15.7–21, discussed in chapter five).

The choice of a people as one's own is a personal act; the sending of one's son to them is even more so. In Jesus' parable of the vineyard (Matthew 21.33–46; Mark 12.1–12; Luke 20.9–19), the owner sends his son in a last attempt to acquire his due from rebellious tenants. The son is dispatched to restore a relationship which should have been running smoothly, but in the event he is killed. As it stands, the passage is composite: Jesus told a parable against those in control of the Temple which was interpreted by his followers in the light of his crucifixion at the connivance of just those authorities. The association of imagery of a vineyard with the Temple in the Isaiah Targum (5.2) was probably the point of departure of Jesus' parable, while the description of the son's being cast outside the vineyard (Mark 12.8) is probably a reminiscence of how Jesus actually died. From the point of view of understanding the faith conveyed in the New Testament, the composite nature of the passage is a great advantage. It permits us to see how the motif of God's personal intervention, centred on Jesus, became all the more intense as the New Testament was composed.

The crucifixion was the seal of God's love for his people, and also of the rejection of God by many. But precisely because Jesus was God's son, the crucifixion was the last word neither for him nor for those who rejected him. In Acts, Peter's accusation to the 'men of Israel', that they killed 'the author of life' (3.12–16, see chapter six), is not presented as an irreversible condemnation, but as an appeal for repentance (3.17, 19–21). The resurrection vindicated Jesus himself and the eschatology he preached; it was the sign that he would be the agent of God's judgement. God in Christ had revealed himself personally in the past, but in the preaching of the New Testament what mattered was one's attitude towards him in the present.

The resurrection put the divine seal on Jesus' sonship. In an earlier speech in Acts, Peter claims that the risen Jesus is exalted to God's right hand, where he sends forth the holy spirit as a sure pledge of his coming judgement (see 2.32, 33). God's spirit was thought within rabbinic Judaism to have been withdrawn from people since the age of prophecy ended. Christians claimed that God in Christ was pouring out his spirit as part of his new, eschatological activity. Those who followed Jesus, empowered by the spirit he released, could speak again on God's behalf. Peter's speech in Acts 2 is part of the scene at Pentecost, a Jewish feast of harvest, when the twelve (brought up to strength by the appointment of Matthias) were said to have been endowed with the holy spirit (2.1–4). The result is that those visiting in Jerusalem from every point of the compass hear God's praises spoken in their own languages (2.5–11). This scene epitomizes the programme of

Acts, which centres on the spread of Christian preaching from Jerusalem throughout the Mediterranean basin.

The theology of the New Testament typically portrays the resurrection of Jesus, the release of the spirit, and the mission to all nations as very closely related. Matthew's Gospel makes a clear distinction in Jesus' policy towards Gentiles before and after the resurrection. Beforehand, he has occasional contacts with them, but refers to Gentiles in disparaging terms; particularly, he insists that both he (see 15.24) and the twelve (see 10.6) are sent only 'to the lost sheep of the house of Israel'. But the risen Jesus commands the eleven to 'make disciples of all nations, baptizing them in the name of the father, and of the son, and of the holy spirit' (28.19). The conviction that God's raising of Jesus has implications for all peoples is not just a motif which is developed by mere coincidence in Acts or Matthew alone; their agreement suggests it was deeply rooted in the early Christian understanding of the resurrection.

As was discussed in chapter two, the Pauline writings are particularly engaged with the question of how God's choice of Israel can be reconciled with his promise to all people in Christ. Paul's own answer is that the covenant with Abraham – which always promised the blessing of all nations – is fulfilled by believers' identification with Christ. The polemical tone of much of what Paul says, however, makes it clear that all Christians did not fully agree with his explanation. Matthew's Jesus explicitly maintains he did not come to annul the law or the prophets (5.17), and he commends the teaching (although not the actions) of Jewish teachers (23.2, 3). And the letter of James calls its readers to complete the 'royal law' by positive attention to individual commandments (see 2.8–13), rather than by the incorporation into Christ which Paul speaks of.

Clearly, the relationship of God's choice of Israel to the sending of his son for all peoples was a matter for discussion and debate among Christians during the period of the New Testament. In this as in other matters, the theological diversity of the documents, and even of sections within individual documents, cannot reasonably be denied. Indeed, any attempt at denial would rob the texts of that individuality of message and setting which it is the business of critical reading to discover. But diversity within the New Testament is no proof that it lacks coherence. In the present case, the agreement that the God of Israel acts on behalf of all people in the resurrection is no less remarkable than the variety of ways in which Israel and believers are held to be related to one another. The coherence of the New Testament's theology is as striking as its diversity, and that coherence is among the literary and historical features which are discovered by critical reading. Moreover, a theological assessment of the New Testament naturally begins with its commonly agreed features.

Appropriating the New Testament's theology

The simple description of belief, be it biblical, historical, or philosophical, is the initial moment in theological reflection. We must know what a belief is before we can seriously decide whether or not we assent to it. The underlying coherence of the New Testament's theology is patient of description, although its rich diversity must always be allowed. The documents certainly do not, individually or collectively, present an account of God in the precise terms we have just considered. But together they reflect a common pattern of faith, and convey an internally consistent view of God. Once that view of God has been described, even if – as here – only generally and provisionally, the more properly theological question can be posed: is what is conveyed convincing?

When a statement is made with conviction, it can win our assent: we may be convinced by it, and act accordingly. The statement involved might be political, moral, philosophical or religious, but in no case can conviction be forced from us, or faked by us. To be convinced is, by definition, to be won over sincerely to a way of looking at things. There is little doubt but that the theology of the New Testament emerged from genuine conviction and became so influential that it is even of interest from a purely historical point of view. But many religious convictions have been sincerely held, and became influential: theologies are not more or less true in view of the number of adherents they can claim, or more or less compelling in view of the period of time during which they hold sway. The extent to which an argument convinces can only be judged by the person to whom it is directed. There is no external standard of success; the person either is or is not convinced.

Most readers of this volume will have decided already whether or not they find Christianity convincing. But the set of beliefs called 'Christianity' takes many forms, some of them seemingly remote from what is taught in the New Testament. The documents reflect their faith as their central concern, and deserve a hearing quite apart from the claims of institutional Christianity. Indeed, the New Testament takes its stand on the transcendent God who made all things: there is no question of a merely local divinity, limited to the conceptions of a particular group. Assertions about such a God are either convincing in respect of people generally, or they are not convincing at all.

How can people believe in God to begin with, when there is no direct evidence of his existence? That is a sensible question, if the term 'God' is used as a way of referring to a being within the world of human perception, experience, and thought. It is perfectly true that people have claimed to see God, know God and think about God, but that is different from seeing, knowing or thinking about a person or an object. People and objects 'exist': that is, they are palpably there in our world. Things can exist which we have never heard of before, such as microscopic entities which cause newly diagnosed diseases. Things can also cease to be commonly recognized as real, such as demons. But the term 'God' refers, not to one of many things which exist, or have by common consent existed, but to the single source and purpose of existence itself. God, according to the New Testament, is where the world came from, and where it is going to.

The conditions of our world cannot be imposed on the divine; God is the meaning the world can have, not an object within it. Once God's transcendence is appreciated, it follows that time is no constraint on divine being. God is both the beginning and the end of all things, because existence depends upon God for its meaning, whenever existence occurs. The idea of God's transcendence, so fundamental to the New Testament, is shared by other major faiths. It may be said to be basic to discourse about God: either we are speaking of what determines existence in all times, or theological discussion is not worthwhile. The means by which

God may be said to determine life are variously described among and within different religious systems. But that such transcendental determination is operative, whether in nature, miracle, human action, or whatever, is an importantly common element within human religious sensibility. There is no way to prove that God 'exists'; but the word 'God' is there for anyone to use in reference to what gives meaning to things.

Why should the transcendent power of meaning be addressed as 'father'? Why should the term 'God', which seems to refer to a force abstracted from the world, be thought of in personal terms? Just as God cannot be proved to be an entity within the terms of existence, there is no objective demonstration of divine personality. The Bible simply has God speak, as if a person; the conceptual 'it' is revealed as a personal 'he', and does such crucial things as choosing Israel and sending his own son. The Old and New Testaments can seem crudely anthropomorphic, especially as compared to the sublimely nuanced portraits of God in the literature of Hinduism and Buddhism. But if 'God' is the word we use to speak of the meaning of our world, what sort of meaning is at issue? At just this point, people's judgements are likely to vary very widely. Some may prefer to speak of intellectual meaning, others of artistic, philosophical or moral meaning. The meaning spoken of in the New Testament is personal. The purposes of God were best seen in the life of Israel, and then in the story of Jesus.

The genius of the New Testament lies in its insistence that, in Jesus Christ, transcendental divinity and historical humanity have intersected. This intersection is described most strikingly as the relationship between God and Jesus, which is as intimate as that of father and son, 'No one knows the son except the father, neither does anyone know the father except the son, and the person to whom the son wishes to reveal him' (Matthew 11.27, and see Luke 10.22). This claim does not in the first instance have implications about the manner of Jesus' birth, but presents Jesus as uniquely and consistently related to God. That relationship is such that fellowship with Jesus can bring a revelation of the father. Jesus' sonship is not for himself alone; it can mediate God to believers. As Paul put the matter in a discussion of baptism, God sent his son that we also might become sons (Galatians 4.4,

5). The New Testament's theology so insists on the personally human dimension of transcendental meaning that human life itself is portrayed as the normal field of God's activity.

The seriousness of the conviction that the divine and the human have intersected in the case of Jesus is reflected in two particular aspects within the theology of the New Testament. The first aspect is the persistent claim that the spirit of God is available through Jesus to those who believe in him. The lives of believers are said to be transformed by a fresh and transforming influence of God. The second aspect, which is connected with the first, is the eschatological certainty expressed in the New Testament. God was seen as actively commencing, or about to commence, a final judgement by means of Jesus as the son of man. Human life was therefore to be conducted in the expectation that divinely sanctioned behaviour would be vindicated, and divinely prohibited behaviour punished, in a judgement which was soon to come. The future belonged unavoidably to God in Christ.

Eschatology is not an incidental feature in the New Testament's theological stance, nor does it function merely to insist on the general importance of the future. God by definition is not bounded by time; his activity is directed towards a full disclosure of himself, because in his transcendence the present conditions of the world are no constraint. The end of time as a conditioning factor is therefore guaranteed by God's transcendence. But the end is not only transcendent, as determined by God; it is also ultimate in relation to people. In Christ people have been provided the means by which their personal lives intersect with the divine purpose which underlies existence. In Christ, God's purpose and human living are identified, so that those who follow Jesus experience the richness of the spirit in the present, and the assurance of their vindication in the future. In other words, the New Testament's claims about the spirit and the end of time are grounded in its assertion that humanity has discovered, or can discover, its divine purpose in Jesus.

The personal, the spiritual, and the eschatological are therefore part of the entire package of the New Testament's theology. The Old Testament's portrayal of God as personal is fundamental to the New Testament, but the conviction that God is revealed in a particular human being is a fresh departure. And that new element is rich with the implications that God's spirit is active again, and that God's ultimate judgement is near. If one person enjoys the spirit, and is transformed in a resurrected body, then humanity has the potential for a new sort of existence, a life fulfilled with divinely transcendent purpose.

Those who contributed to the New Testament were obviously convinced by the faith they conveyed, but does such faith carry conviction for us? The answer to that question depends on whether one is able to assent to the radically personal theology of the New Testament. The teachings of Jesus, the stories about him, the reflections on his significance within the early Church, all constitute occasions for assessing the faith he gave rise to. In that assessment, the crucial issue is whether one's own sense of God and transcendent purpose is, or can be, as personal as the New Testament's. The documents, individually and as a whole, give us the opportunity of confirming, adjusting, and reforming the intuition of God we start with. The process goes on within and outside the Church, wherever reflection on critical reading takes place.

Theological diversity in the New Testament

The theological coherence of the New Testament should not be mistaken for complete uniformity. Development, change, and disagreement are represented within the documents, and differences of interpretation are possible. In chapter six, three particular areas of variety were mentioned: the miraculous claims which may be made about Jesus, eschatological expectations, and the position of women. Each offers an occasion for theological consideration.

An exegesis of the first story of exorcism in Mark (1.21–8) brought us to distinguish between historical events and events within our experience. The former have to do with what was once perceived, the latter with actual occurrence. But how closely related are these two sorts of events? If the transcendent God really was active in the person called Jesus, then the possibility arises that unique occurrences were associated with him. Perhaps, in conflict with him, evil took on a personal aspect, and staged a last, desperate effort of resistance. On the other hand, it may also be argued that the story works with superstitions about demons which have been superseded. Largely as a result of Christian insistence that people are responsible solely to God, and that any other supposed divinity is powerless, demons are no longer commonly recognized as a real part of the conventional world. Within this argument, the story reflects a way of looking at things which is now defunct; the text leaves us with the impression made by Jesus, and without knowledge of what actually happened.

Within the context of Christian theology, both of these evaluations are viable. They begin with a critical reading of the text, and proceed to speak on that basis of how God is revealed in Christ. The first sees that revelation in a unique occurrence, the second sees it in the way people responded to Jesus within the conventions of their time. Both of them speak the language of history, in that an event of the past is spoken of. But each has its own distinctive implications for how God might be perceived in the present. If God once acted in a unique way in the case of Jesus, he might do so again in the case of Jesus' followers. Christians who accept that theological stance might well anticipate miraculous events in the present, as part of the divine disclosure which began with Jesus, and continues in the Church. But if the demonic element in the story was not actual, but conventional, then successive ages of Christians will be understood to find God's disclosure within the terms of reference of their own worlds, and not in the specific sorts of events the New Testament relates. The theological assessment of the story goes hand in hand with one's anticipation of divine revelation in the present and future.

Christians commonly dispute, in this and similar cases, about which line of assessment is the more adequate, and arguments can be mounted on both sides. An emphasis on literal actuality is generally associated with conservative Evangelicalism, an emphasis on conventional perception with liberal rationalism. The polemics of debate sometimes press disputants to claim that theirs is the only Christian viewpoint. In theology, however, any viewpoint is seen to be Christian which relates the New Testament, as critically understood, to the revelation of God in Christ.

Once that is achieved, the viewpoint demands attention and respect, if not agreement. Complete theological uniformity in the Church can only be bought at the price of stagnation or persecution; diversity is a mark of lively, increasingly articulate faith.

A completely undisciplined diversity, however, is neither sensible nor useful within theological discourse. The story in Mark must be read critically to be reflected on effectively. An assessment which merely assumed, for example, that everything in the Gospels reflects literal reporting would be as unconvincing as one which assumed, without discussion, that every report of a miracle is a matter of fantasy. Theology demands careful observation and reflection; the mere propagation of a bias is not its business. Critical reading, therefore, is one control on the theological claims one might make. Another controlling factor is theologians' willingness to reflect on texts within the context which the New Testament as a whole establishes. If reflection is not open to the relationship between texts and Jesus' revelation of God, then it parts company from Christian theology. Of course, a theologian might assert that she or he is speaking in terms of another sort of theology, but in that case the alternative context of discourse requires plainly to be spelled out. Unless assertions are couched within coherent accounts of God, they have no reasonable claim to being theologically meaningful.

Christians commonly hold to diverse sorts of eschatology, and claim the New Testament as the source of their teaching. Some current eschatologies may be related exegetically to what the texts convey, and some may not be. There is a clear range of such teaching within the documents, from the God-centred preaching of the kingdom, to the Christ-centred anticipation of the parousia. An emphasis one way or another is inevitable, as one attempts to express one's sense of ultimate destiny as a follower of Jesus. By focusing on the kingdom, one might stress the dawning presence of God in the teaching and ministry of Jesus; by focusing on the coming of the son of man at the absolute end of time, one might look for a fulfilment which is more radically in the future, beyond the present. But when one term of reference is assessed so as to exclude the other, the assessment is no longer within the context of the eschatology of the New Testament as a whole.

Prayers and sermons are still heard in churches, in which people are said to 'build the kingdom of God'. Jesus never used such language, because for him the kingdom was the powerful disclosure of God himself, not a human project of social or moral regeneration. The kingdom as 'built' lacks the transcendent aspect which is central to Jesus' teaching, and to the emergence of faith in the parousia. There is, on the other hand, a curious vogue among some people in America and Britain for constructing elaborate scenarios of Christ's second coming (see chapter three). Nuclear holocaust is predicted, sometimes as the result of a war involving modern Israel, and the beasts of Daniel are identified with various global powers. The predictions usually take the form of a collage of biblical elements, with bits and pieces taken from different books, which speak from and address distinctive circumstances. The result corresponds to no single scheme in the New Testament, and is at odds with its general reticence towards apocalyptic speculation. Moreover, the unique focus on an esoterically predicted future is not consonant with Jesus' conception of the kingdom, where God is so near to acting definitively that he can already be known.

The field of the New Testament's eschatology is diverse, but it presents a continuum between the kingdom and the parousia as the central expectations. Theological discourse must be selective in its use of texts; if it is to maintain an exegetical focus, only particular passages can be discussed at any given moment. But the range of the hope expressed in the documents as a whole is the appropriate context of discourse. No single kind of expectation may be said to be the exclusive eschatology of the New Testament, and an eye must be kept on its diversity as theological assessment proceeds. By this means, discussion can occur within the spectrum of stances represented in the documents, and extreme positions can be uncovered as less rooted in texts than they are in the proclivities of theologians.

Women in the New Testament are assigned such varying roles that the positions seem contradictory, not merely diverse. Within the ministry of Jesus, and its attestation by means of the Gospels, a relative liberation appears to be at work. But the more conventional strictures of 1 Timothy 2.9–15 are surprisingly vociferous. Paul appears to be caught in the contradiction of such stances, because, within a single document, he can demand the silence of women (1 Corinthians 14.34), and yet assume that women will pray and prophesy in the context of worship (1 Corinthians 11.5). For this reason, among others, it has been doubted whether Paul actually wrote the demand for the silence of women in 1 Corinthians 14.34. Whether or not he did, the fact remains there is a certain tension between positions taken in a single document ascribed to him. Having encouraged prophecy in chapters eleven and fourteen (vv. 1–5), the letter urges prophets to be silent when another speaks (14.29–33), and women to be silent generally (14.34). The later statement about prophets is part of the appeal for good order, but the statement about women seems more absolute. It may well be directed to a particular group of women, but if so the phrasing is imprecise. Moreover, supposedly the same Paul who commands the submission of women on the strength of 'the law' (1 Corinthians 14.34) can argue in another letter that, in Christ, the distinctions of the law have been overcome to the point that 'there is neither Jew nor Greek, slave nor free, male nor female' (Galatians 3.28). A spectrum of opinion is evident, as in the case of eschatology, but it does not appear to be a continuum, and the disjunction is evident within groups of documents, not only among them.

Within the account of God presented in the New Testament, then, what place is occupied by sexual distinctions? To speak purely in descriptive terms, there appears not to be a coherent answer to that question. Neither a liberated nor a conventional stance may be claimed unequivocally as the position of the New Testament as a whole. But theology is not merely a matter of description: theologians are charged by their profession to explicate the God spoken of in the texts, not only to exegete those texts.

One might perceive the God of the New Testament as one who so thoroughly revealed himself in Christ that convention, or 'law', no longer stands as the primary standard of divinely acceptable behaviour. Sexual convention would then be no more binding than conventions of slavery and religious difference; in such a perception, there is indeed neither Jew nor Greek, slave nor free, male nor female (see Galatians 3.28). The diversity of the New Testament in the case of Jewish and Gentile fellowship, however, clearly indicates that a perception of God along these lines was not uniform within the early Church (see chapter two). Even domestic servitude is an institution actually supported within the New Testament to the extent that servants are charged to be submissive to good and evil masters alike (see 1 Peter 2.18–25, and the similar charge to women within 3.1–6). Long after the New Testament was canonized, Christians came to oppose most forms of slavery and economic oppression on theological grounds, but not on purely scriptural grounds. Their conviction rested on what they knew of the God who comes to expression within texts, not on the explicit statements of those texts.

In much the same way, a feminist theology rests on a perception of God as revealed in a person, rather than in law. Anti-feminist statements within the New Testament cannot responsibly be discounted; they remain a part of what is to be explained. But they can fairly be taken as statements addressed to particular conditions, and which are out of step with the normal tendency of proclaiming Christ's liberation of believers. The diversity of the New Testament is such that one must on occasion prefer one strand of its theology over another. In a preferential assessment, however, the exclusion of a strand, in this case a conventional tendency, cannot be tolerated if continuity with the New Testament is to be maintained. Liberation from slavery and racism have indeed been realized, if only partially, in the long history of the Church. But such victories have been achieved in the crucible of diversity and conflict; the dialectic between liberation and law which the New Testament reflects is a part of Christian experience through the ages. A feminist theology grounded in the texts is both prepared to argue its account of God, and to address the reality of sincere resistance.

Those who resist feminist theology, in their turn, must be aware of the relative liberation of women, as baptized participants in communal life and worship, which the New Testament unequivocally affords. But they might reasonably insist that the hierarchical authority of women is not a part of the New Testament's programme, and take the promise to Mary and the importance of female witnesses in the Gospels as of an exceptional nature. In order for them to do so, however, it would be necessary to show how the convention of feminine subservience is connected with the New Testament's account of God. They could fairly observe that the preaching of Christ's redemption is at no point within the texts a licence to break with all regulative custom. If there is an apostle of liberation within the New Testament, that apostle is Paul, who is much concerned with the discipline which the revelation of Christ's love necessarily implies. But Paul makes his famous statement about women keeping silence in the context of a general appeal to the Corinthians to maintain order in their worship (1 Corinthians 14.26–40). Unless feminist theology is portrayed as a necessarily anarchistic challenge to good order, Paul's command would no longer obtain within the life of the Church today.

The argument in 1 Timothy seems far more fundamental: the subservience of women may here be taken as part of the very order of creation. But, as we have seen, the example of Eve results from a partial and innovative reading of Genesis 3; even more to the point, the earlier statement that God created male and female at a single moment (Genesis 1.27) is not cited. The author of 1 Timothy therefore has a scriptural example at the ready to illustrate a policy he approves of, but he does not develop a full theology of creation from Genesis. He can invoke the punishment of Eve as the warrant of women's subservience, but only on the assumption that child-bearing is accepted as their normal role (1 Timothy 2.15). The text from Genesis illustrates that role, if it is granted, but it does not establish child-bearing as the only function allotted to women. In other words, his argument turns on the reader's prior acceptance of the convention at issue, not on something which the citation from Genesis demonstrates. Any such acceptance by readers today requires that God's revelation in Christ be seen to conform to, or at least to be compatible with, that convention.

The author of 1 Timothy, reflectively or not, obviously held that the convention was a commendable aspect of Christian life. But an anti-feminist theology would have to argue that God as represented in the New Testament also commends it. That involves developing a full theology of creation, with divinely appointed orders for the sexes, which is consistent with the relative liberation of women within the New Testament. Whether such a theology would also assign distinctive roles within the Church to different ethnic and economic groups, would depend on how consistently it was applied. Clearly, however, anti-feminist theology must justify its claims against the observation that it ascribes greater importance to conventions about women than to any others. And if the orders of creation are taken as set and unchanging, the exact place of liberating salvation within the Church needs to be explained.

Because theology is the account of how God relates to the world, it is dynamic. However constant God may be, the world is an inconstant and developing thing. The diversity of the New Testament indicates that the forces of theological change were operative from the beginning of the emergence of Christian faith; those forces occasioned various expressions of a coherent viewpoint about God in Christ. Critical reading of the texts provides several options for understanding miracles, eschatology, and sexual distinctions, and suggests a framework for theological assessment. The critical recognition of diversity calls for continuing discussion and debate, with tolerant regard for that variety which is already present in the earliest documents of the faith.

Epilogue

Theological reflection and assessment are natural results of reading the New Testament, because the documents urge a view – or views – of God upon the reader. Much contemporary scholarship is concerned primarily with a critical description of what the texts say, to the exclusion of assessment. That can be frustrating to general readers, who may expect that scholars should be engaged immediately with the theological value of the texts they study. But any critical reading of the texts is of potential use to theology; the language, formation, setting, and cultural world of the documents all play a part in the meanings they convey.

The potential value of critical reading for theology is, however, no substitute for an actual contribution. The necessary specialization in theological work, brought on by new discoveries and freshly developing techniques in many fields, has resulted in a certain fragmentation. Modern inquiry has resulted in the much lamented gulf which seems to separate theologically trained preachers from their congregations, but that is only one symptom of fragmentation. Unbridgeable, or unbridged gaps have also opened up among scholars of the Old Testament, scholars of the New Testament, historians of the Church, systematic theologians, those expert in pastoral ministry, and comparative religionists. Mutual recognition of this problem (sometimes in the form of mutual accusation) is growing, but the hope that the branches of theology might share a common language seems distant.

Those who are commencing theological study, whether that involves the New Testament or another subject, will need to learn the particular techniques and acquire the working knowledge which are required for their field of inquiry. While they are doing so, however, they can relate what they read to the central claim that is being made by Christian sources: that God in Christ was displaying and setting in motion the ultimate, human value of things. There has never been a way, nor is there one now, of demanding acceptance of that claim. It belongs to the realm of faith, not demonstration. But assessing the kind of faith reflected in the New Testament from whatever perspective, including that of atheism, follows naturally from reading its documents. To avoid such assessment is to resist the typically human curiosity which asks: is what I am reading true?

During a period in which theology is fragmented, it is vital for students and scholars to bear that question in mind. Fresh challenges for analysing meaning present themselves constantly, to beginner and expert alike, and it is all too easy to permit the acquisition of new techniques of exegesis and interpretation to crowd out any reflection upon meaning. But unless one reflects from time to time on why the document at hand should be read and studied, the business of reading becomes an arid exercise. Only if a document relates in some way to what we value does it merit our time and attention. During a more settled theological era, one could have deflected the question of whether the New Testament was, in this sense, valuable; the agreed theology might have answered that question in advance. But in the present environment, students and scholars must themselves explore and express the theological dimensions of their encounter with the text.

Theological assessment, without a prior commitment to the result that should be obtained, is the goal towards which a critical reading of the New Testament tends. Texts about God encourage reflection upon God. Such reflection, and consequent discussion, might itself direct us back to the New Testament, to pose a fresh question, or just look at the text from a new angle. Moving back and forth from text to experience becomes the ordinary means of a larger task: discovering and defining those values which give us purpose and meaning. No one can dictate the names we should give those values in advance, or decree that they should only be discovered within the New Testament. But the documents speak of a supreme value, in the light of which all other values stand or fall; they invite the test of critical reading and considered reflection.

Whatever the pressures on one's time as a student or teacher, the extra effort of theological assessment is worthwhile. By itself, it may not gain many marks, or enhance one's career, but it does bring a vibrant reality to study, which heightens the urgency and precision of the quest for meaning in the texts. Moreover, a greater commitment to the evaluation of the truth of documents might help in the long run to develop a common language for the various branches of theology. In the most fundamental sense, however, theological assessment is its own reward. To decide upon the values which give purpose and meaning to our lives is a process which shapes our commitments in the present, and so enables us to influence the shape of our lives in the future. Any study, including the study of the New Testament, which permits us to do that better requires no incentive, apart from its success in its own terms. Reading and assessment belong to our rights, and perhaps to our duties, as human beings.

FOR FURTHER READING

The particular issues of interpretation dealt with in this chapter are discussed in the books mentioned at the close of chapter six.

Recent developments which influence the place of the Bible in theological discourse are traced by D. Nineham, *Explorations in Theology 1* (London: SCM Press, 1977); J. Barr, *The Scope and Authority of the*

Bible: Explorations in Theology 7 (London: SCM Press, 1980; Philadelphia: Westminster, 1981); P. Stuhlmacher (see the work cited in chapter six).

The relationship between the New Testament and theology is discussed in J. L. Houlden, *Patterns of Faith. A study in the relationship between the New Testament and Christian doctrine* (London: SCM Press, 1977); J. D. Smart, *The Past, Present and Future of Biblical Theology* (Philadelphia: Westminster, 1979).

Barr has also dealt with the problems caused by a literalistic understanding of biblical inerrancy in *Fundamentalism* (London: SCM Press, 1977; Philadelphia: Westminster, 1978) and *Beyond Fundamentalism. Biblical Foundations for Evangelical Christianity* (Philadelphia: Westminster, 1984; London: SCM Press, 1984, with the title, *Escaping from Fundamentalism*).

A consistent attempt to delineate the particular theologies of books in the New Testament with reference to its overall message is B. Childs, *An Introduction to the New Testament as Canon* (London: SCM Press, 1984; Philadelphia: Westminster, 1984, with the title, *The New Testament as Canon. An Introduction*).

Considerably advanced students, who wish to gain an understanding of possible interrelations among the branches of theology, might consult B. J. F. Lonergan, *Method in Theology* (New York: Herder, 1973; London: Darton, Longman and Todd, 1972). A less demanding work is B. Hebblethwaite, *The Problems of Theology* (Cambridge and New York: Cambridge University Press, 1980).

Index of Subjects

Abraham 54, 64–5, 72–3, 107, 122, 177
Acts xii, 51–5, 89–92, 133–4, 140–2, 162, 164, 166–7, 176–7
Alexander xi, 128–9
American Standard Version 103, 108
anti-Semitism 72–3
apocalyptic 76–82, 84–93, 161, 164, 170, 185; *see also* eschatology and 'little apocalypse'
Apocrypha 13, 17–18
Apollonius 139–42, 154, 161
apostles 14, 24–5, 60, 64; *see also* disciples
Aquinas, Thomas xiii, 4
Aratus 133
Aristotle xi, 128–9
Athanasius xiii, 16
Authorized Version 1, 95–6, 101–5, 109, 111–13
authorship of the Gospels 23–6

Babylon xi, 81
baptism 68–70, 73, 107, 109, 177, 180–1
body of Christ 67–70, 73, 131

canon 12–18

Christology 6–7, 48, 57, 65–6, 155–6, 163, 175–8, 180–2
circumcision 61–4, 67, 122, 132
commissioning of disciples 29–31
Corinthian correspondence xii, 58–61, 66–9, 90, 133, 163–4, 168, 186, 188
Counter-reformation xiii, 4
covenant 61–5, 68–9, 71–2, 76, 106–7, 122–4, 134, 145, 177
creeds xiii, 16, 121
critical reading 1–12, 18–23, 95–6, 99–100, 111, 121, 177–8, 182, 184, 191
crucifixion 176; *see also* passion narrative
Cynicism and Diogenes xi, 132–3

Daniel xi, 76–87, 89, 93, 185
dates of the Gospels 44–5
Dead Sea Scrolls xii, 5
Diaspora 128
disciples 26–33, 166; *see also* apostles and commissioning of disciples
divorce 59, 126–7; *see also* marriage
Dostoyevsky, Fyodor 2

dynamic transference 98–101,
104, 106, 108–9, 111–12

Ecclesiasticus xi, 12–13
Eliezer ben Hyrcanus 167
1 Enoch xi, 13, 78
Epicurus and Epicureanism xi,
133
Erasmus xiii, 8
eschatology 60–1, 75–6, 83–6,
94, 161, 164–5, 169, 175–6,
181, 184–5; *see also*
apocalyptic
Eusebius xiii, 17, 33
exegesis 9–10; *see also* critical
reading
exorcism 154–60, 162, 169,
182–4
Ezra xi, 125, 136
4 Ezra xii, 79–80, 87, 89, 91

Felix and Festus xii, 90
form criticism 31–2
formal correspondence 97–8,
101, 103–6, 109–13
formation of the Gospels 26–33

Galatians xii, 53, 55–8, 61–8, 70,
73, 110, 180–1, 186
Gallio xi, 55
Gnosticism 5, 14–15, 143–6
God 179–82
'Godspell' 2
Good News for Modern Man 106
Gospel according to
Thomas xiii, 17–18

haggadah 28, 47, 52, 54, 127
halakhah 26–8, 127

Ḥanina ben Dosa 136–8, 154
Hebrews 16–17
Hellenism 127–35, 140
Herod xi, 79
Hillel 28
history 151–3, 157–60

idiom 98–101
inspiration 11–12
interpretation 149–53, 160,
168–71; *see also* theological
interpretation
Isaiah xi, 75–6

Jerome xiii, 13
Jerusalem Bible 108–12
John xii, 42–3, 45, 137–9; *see
also* prologue of John
Josephus xii, 128
Judaism 122–7, 134–5, 138–9,
176–7

Kazantzakis, Nikos 2
King James Version *see*
Authorized Version
kingdom of God 37–9, 41, 60,
83–4, 91–2, 127, 157, 161–4,
166, 169–70, 184–5

last supper 58–9
literary sense 157, 160
'little apocalypse' 83–4, 87, 91–3
Living Bible 99–100, 108–9, 111
logos 97, 143–6
Lord's Prayer 27, 31, 34–6, 66
love 70–1, 101–11, 123, 167
Luke xii, 44–5, 90, 166–7, 180
Luther, Martin xiii, 4

Marcion xii, 14–15, 66
Marcus Aurelius xiii, 131
Mark xii, 44, 104, 115–17,
    154–60, 163, 182–3
marriage 59–60, 126–7; *see also*
    divorce
Matthew xii, 44–5, 82–3, 164,
    177, 180
'Memra' 144–6
Midrash 126–7
miracles 135–42, 154–60, 170
Mishnah xiii, 125–6, 167
money and evil 1
Moses 54, 123
Muratorian list xiii, 15–16
myth 21–2

Nag Hammadi library xiii, 5, 15
Nero xii, 131
New English Bible 98–100,
    104–8, 111–12
New International
    Version 109–10, 112

Origen xiii, 17

Papias xii, 33, 36
parable of the sower 36–9, 83,
    85
parable of the vineyard 175–6
paraphrase 99–101, 108–11
parousia 82–7, 93, 156, 161–5,
    169–70, 184–5
passion narrative 32–3, 46–7, 57,
    168
Pastoral Epistles xii, 71–3, 75,
    80, 88, 132, 168–9, 185, 188
1 Peter xii, 16, 87–92, 187
Pharisees 56–7, 59–60

Philo xi, 128
Philostratus xiii, 139–42, 160–1
Plato 129, 131
Pompey xi, 124
presupposition 10
prologue of John 143–7
Pseudepigrapha 13, 17–18
pseudepigraphy 80
pseudonymity 72, 77–80, 87
Pythagoras 139–40

Reader's Digest Bible 111
Received Text 103–4
redaction criticism 33–7, 39, 42,
    48–9, 52–3, 154–7
Reformation xiii, 4, 13
resurrection 11–12, 58, 60, 73,
    78–9, 89, 115, 117, 156,
    162–5, 167–9, 176
Revelation xii, 16, 80–4, 87–9,
    91–3
Revised Standard Version 98–9,
    103–5, 109, 112–13
Revised Version 103
Roman Empire 129–30
Romans xii, 69–71, 73, 101–11

second Jewish revolt xii, 79–81
Seleucid xi, 76–7, 79
Seneca xii, 131, 135
Septuagint xi, 13, 30, 128
'Sermon on the Mount' 34–5,
    84
Shammai 27–8
Shepherd of Hermas xii, 16–17
Socrates 129
'son of man' 7, 77, 79, 82–7,
    156, 163, 181, 184

Stoicism and Zeno xi, 130–1,
133–4, 140, 143, 145–6
Strauss, David Friedrich 21–2
Synoptic problem 40–2

Tacitus xii, 132
Talmud xiii, 26–8, 85, 136–8,
142, 154, 160
Targums 5–6, 126–7, 144–6,
161, 176
textual criticism 107–8, 113–18
theological interpretation 7–12,
170–91
Titus xii, 79, 81, 87, 125
Today's English
Version 98–100, 106–8,
110–12

Torah 12, 14–15, 27–8, 55–7,
59, 61–2, 64–6, 71–3, 102,
105–11, 123–6, 134–5, 145,
167, 177
tradition 29–33, 36–9, 41–2,
47–9, 56, 58–60, 158–9
translation 95–101, 111, 113–15,
117–18

Valentinus xiii, 15

'widow's mite' 1
Wisdom 13, 16, 143
women 165–70, 185–9
world 120–2, 143, 146–7, 151,
154, 159–60, 166, 169, 173,
179, 183